# ON MONEY, METHOD AND KEYNES

# On Money, Method and Keynes

## Selected Essays

Victoria Chick
*Reader in Economics*
*University College London*

Edited by
Philip Arestis
*Professor of Applied Economics*
*The Polytechnic of East London*

and

Sheila C. Dow
*Reader in Economics*
*University of Stirling*

M

St. Martin's Press

First published in Great Britain 1992 by
THE MACMILLAN PRESS LTD
Houndmills, Basingstoke, Hampshire RG21 2XS
and London
Companies and representatives
throughout the world

A catalogue record for this book is available
from the British Library

ISBN 0–333–53634–7

Printed in Great Britain by
Billing and Sons Ltd, Worcester

---

First published in the United States of America 1992 by
Scholarly and Reference Division,
ST. MARTIN'S PRESS, INC.,
175 Fifth Avenue,
New York, N.Y. 10010

ISBN 0–312–06815–8

Library of Congress Cataloging-in-Publication Data
Chick, Victoria.
On money, method and Keynes: selected essays/Victoria Chick;
edited by Philip Arestis and Sheila C. Dow.
p. cm.
Includes bibliographical references and index.
ISBN 0–312–06815–8
1. Keynes, John Maynard, 1883–1946. 2. Keynesian economics.
I. Arestis, Philip, 1941– . II. Dow, Sheila C. III. Title.
HB 103.K47C46 1992
330.15'6—dc20 91–25838
CIP

# Contents

# Editors' Acknowledgements

The editors and publishers would like to thank the following for their kind permission to include copyright articles and materials previously published (chapter number in brackets):

(1) *South African Journal of Economics*: 'A Question of Relevance: The *General Theory* in Keynes's Time and Ours' (vol. 51, no. 3, 1983).

(2) *British Review of Economic Issues*: 'Keynes's Theory, Keynesian Policy and the Postwar Inflation' (vol. 1, no. 3, 1978). Published in this volume under the title 'Inflation from a Longer-Run Perspective'.

(3) *Australian Economic Papers*: 'The Nature of the Keynesian Revolution: A Reassessment' (June, 1978).

(4) *Weltwirtschaftliches Archiv*: 'Financial Counterparts of Saving and Investment and Inconsistency in Some Simple Macro Models' (Band 109, Heft 4, 1973). Published in this volume, abridged, under the title 'Financial Counterparts of Saving and Investment and Inconsistency in a Simple Macro Model'.

(5) *Journal of Post Keynesian Economics*: 'Comment on "*IS–LM* – An Explanation"' (vol. 4, no. 3, Spring, 1982).

(6) *Thames Papers in Political Economy*: 'Keynesians, Monetarists and Keynes: The End of the Debate – or a Beginning?' (Spring, 1978). Reprinted in Arestis and Skouras (1985).

(7) Croom Helm: 'On the Structure of the Theory of Monetary Policy', in D. Currie, R. Nobay and D. Peel (eds) *Macroeconomic Analysis: Essays in Macroeconomics and Econometrics* (London: Croom Helm for the Association of University Teachers in Economics, 1981). Published in this volume under the title 'On the Structure of the Theory of Monetary Policy – Part I: Money Circulating *v.* Money Held'.

(8) Phylis Deane and Jessica Kuper: 'Money', in P. Deane and J. Kuper (eds), *A Lexicon of Economics* (London: Routledge, 1988).

(9) *De Economist*: 'Unresolved Questions in Monetary Theory: A Critical Review' (126, NR. 1, 1978).

(10) Macmillan: 'Monetary Increases and Their Consequences: Streams, Backwaters and Floods', in A. Ingham and A. M. Ulph (eds), *Demand, Equilibrium and Trade: Essays in Honour of Ivor F. Pearce* (London: Macmillan, 1984).

(11) Edward Elgar: 'Some Methodological Issues in the Theory of Speculation', in D. E. Moggridge (ed.), *Perspectives on the History of Economic Thought*, vol. 4: *Keynes, Macroeconomics and Method* (Aldershot: Edward Elgar for the History of Economics Society, 1990).
(12) *Économies et Sociétés*: 'The Evolution of the Banking System and the Theory of Saving, Investment and Interest' (Série MP, no. 3, 1986).

# Introduction

Keynes talked of *The General Theory of Employment, Interest and Money* as part of his 'long struggle to escape from habitual modes of thought and expression'. But these modes of thought and expression continued to prevail, requiring subsequent like-minded economists to engage in their own struggle to escape. Victoria Chick is one of the leading economists to engage in such a struggle, and to assist others in the process.

We are two economists whom Victoria Chick has assisted. We first came across her work, respectively, as editor of *Thames Papers in Political Economy*, and as a graduate student in Winnipeg. We have prepared this volume bearing in mind the many economists, dispersed all over the world, who have assiduously sought out Victoria Chick's scattered writings to provide illumination and inspiration, and who accordingly owe her a great debt of gratitude. It is therefore with great pleasure that we have gathered a selection of these writings in one volume.

Victoria Chick was born in 1936, in Berkeley, California. She studied at the University of California at Berkeley where she took her Bachelor's and Master's degrees. Berkeley's Department of Economics was particularly strong and eclectic at that time. Thus, very high quality and tremendous concentration of calibre were two characteristics of the environment in which Victoria Chick developed as an economist. The important ingredient of that environment was the disparity of views that were flowing in the corridors and seminar rooms of the Department. The independent character and personality of Victoria Chick were stimulated by the diversity of theoretical views there, but she did not take sides on ideology or methodology. That came later. However, a continuity in her relationship with Berkeley has been maintained through her friendship with Hyman Minsky.

At Berkeley she specialised in international trade theory and wrote a thesis on Canada's 1950s experience with flexible exchange rates. Then, in 1960 she moved to the London School of Economics (LSE) to continue postgraduate studies, where the impetus of Berkeley was maintained, indeed enhanced. That was the heyday of 'Methodology, Measurement and Testing' at the LSE. Just as at Berkeley previously, both staff and students at the LSE were of enormously high calibre; Victoria Chick took full advantage of these opportunities. The Staff and Graduate Student Seminar chaired by Lionel Robbins, Wednesday evenings in the Three Tuns, and the London–Oxford–Cambridge graduate students' seminars provided the platform for fertile ideas to be disseminated and indeed to become firmly embedded in the economics discipline. Victoria Chick was once more in the middle of different views as to how the economy worked, but still her ideas were in their gestation period.

In 1963 she took an Assistant Lectureship at University College London (UCL), and the next year she was promoted to Lecturer. She was then moving away from international economics to monetary theory and macroeconomics. Her book, *The Theory of Monetary Policy*, grew out of her teaching, a clear indication that she takes seriously the ideal of blending teaching with research; she continues an old tradition of publishing new material as 'lectures'. The book was a conscious attempt to impose an order on monetary theory, an order which by comparison to international economics was sadly lacking at that time. That she did extremely well.

The approach of that book was simultaneously sympathetic to and critical of Keynesians and monetarists alike. Ultimately, though, she rejected both schools of thought as theoretically inadequate. Inevitably, the *IS–LM* apparatus, the accepted framework of monetary debate, had to go as well. The article printed here as Chapter 4 shows why: she had uncovered a logical inconsistency in the model which was connected with its static method. The paper was not well-received either by the Anglo–American journals or by her own colleagues. But she persisted until it was published, some five years after its drafting.

As these ideas were falling into place, she attended the 1971 meeting of the American Economic Association in New Orleans, where Joan Robinson gave her famous Ely Lecture, 'The Second Crisis in Economics'. At that gathering Joan Robinson and Paul Davidson called a meeting of like-minded people, which gave Victoria Chick great courage in discovering that she was not alone and thus provided her a tremendous impetus to carry on.

Publishing *The Theory of Monetary Policy* had created a vacuum: mainstream macroeconomics had been shown to be inadequate. Perhaps as a belated response to Hyman Minsky's earlier attempt, at Berkeley, to teach her Keynes's *General Theory* (see her *Macroeconomics after Keynes*, p. viii), she returned to that book and began teaching it to her undergraduate students and developing her views in the process. When she felt that she had a coherent and systematic story to tell she published *Macroeconomics after Keynes*. With this book Victoria Chick made a major contribution to post–Keynesian thinking. As will become clear from the rest of this introduction and the papers that follow it, she had already made her distinctive mark on post–Keynesian thought. *Macroeconomics after Keynes* consolidated her position as one of the more important and regular contributors to the attempt to complete and elucidate the post–Keynesian paradigm. She was promoted to Reader in 1984.

During the time Victoria Chick has spent at UCL she has also taught at a number of universities throughout the world. These include McGill University in Canada, University of California at Berkeley and at Santa Cruz in the USA, Aarhus University in Denmark and the Catholic University of Louvain in Belgium. As well as visiting universities, she spent a summer at the Federal Reserve Bank of New York and eighteen months at the Reserve Bank of Australia in Sydney.

Victoria Chick has been an active member of two British Study Groups, funded by the ESRC: she served on the Committee of the influential *Money Study Group* for many years; and she and Philip Arestis recently initiated and now jointly chair an active and successful Post–Keynesian Economics Study Group. She is a member of the editorial board of two journals: the *Review of Political Economy* and the *European Journal of Political Economy*.

The opportunity offered here to sample a selection of Victoria Chick's writings is important for three reasons. First, we see the work of a particularly innovative economist who takes nothing for granted. Even the most well-established theories are called into question. Second, we observe a concern here, rare in economics, both to understand theory, and to mould it, with reference to stylised facts. Third, although these essays cover a period of fifteen years (more than twenty if we consider drafts), there is a strong continuity and evolution of thought amongst them. We may also suggest that it is notable how many ideas were first aired in the papers that follow: the weakness of *IS–LM* analysis, the similarity of the monetarist and Keynesian models, endogeneity of credit creation, the macroeconomic significance of innovation in banking systems, and the importance of Keynes's (for a long time unpublished) work explicitly on monetary production economies.

Many of the issues raised in these papers still remain unresolved, particularly those in monetary theory. Victoria Chick has an outstanding capacity to analyse critically the logical foundations of theoretical structures and to uncover hidden assumptions. Her analysis goes beyond the level of theory to that of method, where many of the apparent differences between theories have their source. She analyses theories on their own terms, yet she does not hesitate to point out where she regards these terms as unduly limiting with respect to real-world issues and to suggest more fruitful lines of enquiry. Nor does she hesitate to criticise Keynes's framework, with which she is most strongly identified.

Although Victoria Chick's own methodological approach has much in common with that of Keynes, she has an emphasis which he left largely implicit: the historical particularity of theories, i.e., the fact that different types of abstraction may be better suited to some historical periods than others. This approach encourages the fair-mindedness with which Victoria

Chick explores different theoretical approaches for useful theories to deal with particular problems. She is not afraid to state her views on each theory, and on how it is used: views which are founded on a high standard of scholarship. The value of this aspect of Victoria Chick's work cannot really be repeated enough.

Chapter 1, 'A Question of Relevance: The *General Theory* in Keynes's Time and Ours', constitutes in part a statement about the methodological approach implicit in the rest of the volume. Here Victoria Chick examines the role of the stylised facts of Keynes's time in shaping the *General Theory* and assesses his assumptions for their modern relevance. The clear implication is that macroeconomics itself emerges from its context and should be expected to change with changing economic conditions: different assumptions, unlike axioms, may suggest different theoretical structures. It is clearly implied that the areas of the *General Theory* most in need of revision concern the treatment of inflation, the endogeneity of the money stock and the macroeconomic role of government.

However, theoretical structures have a habit of solidifying in practice. Victoria Chick demonstrates in the second chapter, 'Inflation from a Longer–Run Perspective', the unfortunate inflationary consequences of misapplications of Keynesian policy. The analysis is drawn forward to consider some uncomfortable notions about the inevitability of stagnation after a long period of capital accumulation.

The *General Theory*, with its explanation for an unemployment equilibrium, is interpreted from a neoclassical perspective as a theory of disequilibrium or as a theory of equilibrium conditioned by market imperfections. In the third chapter, 'The Nature of the Keynesian Revolution: A Reassessment', Victoria Chick challenges these interpretations, as put forward in Clower's famous article. Rather, the unemployment equilibrium result is shown to derive from the fact that production takes time, a factor disallowed in neoclassical analysis. The significance of historical time for economic process is a thread running through the volume, particularly in contrast to the analytical convenience of static analysis.

The neoclassical framework for macroeconomic analysis is, of course, *IS–LM*. In 'Financial Counterparts of Saving and Investment and Inconsistency in a Simple Macro Model', Victoria Chick provides one of the earliest critiques of the internal logic of *IS–LM* analysis by asking two elementary questions: into which assets do savings flow? and how is investment financed? In attempting to answer these questions she demonstrates that the *IS–LM* apparatus has only a stationary-state equilibrium and that, also, it displays very peculiar behaviour in the (normally excluded) bond market. She argues that in answering the elementary questions posed above, the problem cannot be avoided by appealing to the short run. Although she now sees this paper as combining loanable-funds considerations with Keynesian concerns, its emphasis on stock–flow interaction, though mentioned by Laidler (1969), did not emerge again until the work of Godley and Cripps (1983).

Beyond the question of internal consistency there is the question of the capacity of *IS–LM* to capture the essence of the *General Theory*. In her 'Comment on Hicks's "*IS–LM*: An Explanation"' (Chapter 5), she argues that the core of the problem lies in the incompatibility of Hicks's 'maintained method' (which is Walrasian) with the method of Keynes. In particular, Victoria Chick argues that the *IS–LM* model requires the assumption of perfect foresight to generate an equilibrium value for money income. Since the analysis lacks a supply dimension, the fixprice assumption is necessary to generate a solution for output and employment.

Chapter 6, 'Keynesians, Monetarists and Keynes: The End of the Debate – or a Beginning?', concentrates on issues of method in the debate on monetary policy in the 1970s. It is argued that for a discussion of monetary policy, comparative static analysis is very limited; there must be an analysis of process. Within a process framework it becomes clear that the debate is three–sided. Victoria Chick criticises Keynes for not devoting enough attention to the process by which money enters the economic system. Open-market operations being, in Keynes's time, the most common vehicle for monetary policy, it was natural for him to argue that the effect of monetary policy will be transmitted initially through a change in interest rates.

In the chapter 'On the Structure of the Theory of Monetary Policy', Victoria Chick probes deep into the logical structures of different demand-for-money theories: the quantity theory, Keynes, *IS–LM*, Tobin–Brainard, Radcliffe and Friedman. She notes particularly the logical problems entailed in the transactions demand for money within models of asset demand; historical time again is the key. In the course of the chapter the loanable-funds and liquidity-preference theories are discussed. The latter is seen as suffering from being expressed as a critique of loanable-funds theory. The author's methodology is evident here in her advocacy of the search for some hybrid of existing theories to fit with current institutional arrangements and theoretical requirements.

Victoria Chick turns to the definition of 'Money' in the encyclopaedia entry which is the eighth chapter. Here we have a succinct definition of money in terms of its general acceptability, a product both of the state and of private sector consensus. (Acceptability is measured by the degree to which actual holdings stray from the demand curve.) As a corollary, general acceptability is context-specific and so must be the definition of money.

Chapter 9, 'Unresolved Questions in Monetary Theory: A Critical Review', stays with the definition of money. The issues of the definition of money are explored in depth in this chapter, with particular attention to the role of financial innovations and the significance of confidence. It is an interesting comment on the state of economics at the time (late 1970s) that in order to publish this piece she had to prune sharply a section dealing with the connection between money and power.

Victoria Chick, in 'Monetary Increases and their Consequences', Chapter 10, anticipates the 1980s discussion on the finance motive and her own concern with speculation. She emphasises the role of bank credit in investment finance, rather than idle balances as such. But whether the end result is inflationary depends on a wide range of factors. She suggests that it is unwise to neglect changes in the money supply when its rate of change becomes rapid.

In the next chapter, 'Some Methodological Issues in the Theory of Speculation', Victoria Chick demonstrates again her skill in digging deep into theoretical structures; she explores the treatment of speculation by rational expectations theory, the Friedman–Baumol–Telser approach, and Keynes (particularly as interpreted by Shackle). She draws an analogy with methodological developments in physics and argues that Keynes's approach corresponds most closely to modern developments in physics.

Finally, in 'The Evolution of the Banking System and the Theory of Saving, Investment and Interest', Victoria Chick returns to the question of the importance to theory of history and institutional structure, which is made most explicit. She demonstrates the change in relevant monetary theory as banking systems evolve in historical time. The primacy of investment over saving is shown to be established at the stage in banking development when bank deposits gain general acceptability as money. The credit creation capacity of banks is then independent of saving. Recent developments are shown, however, to shift the initiative for credit creation from borrowers to the banks themselves. At the same time, liability management encourages a true asset demand for money, further increasing the credit creation power of banks irrespective of real economic conditions. Meanwhile, the speculative demand for money is focused increasingly on foreign exchange markets.

Most of the selection consists of analytical critiques of different aspects of neoclassical economics. But running through the critiques are signposts to the alternative approach to theorising which we now classify, and indeed referred to above, as post-Keynesian economics. The spelling out of the alternative becomes more apparent in her recent writings, of which a few are included. Of these, probably the most important is the evolutionary theory of banking, with its implications for macroeconomic theory.

Finally, we would very much like to thank Victoria Chick for her help in preparing this volume, and particularly this Foreword, where she was prepared to discuss in detail the intellectual links between the chapters.

PHILIP ARESTIS
SHEILA C. DOW

# Author's Acknowledgements

My warmest thanks to Philip Arestis and Sheila Dow for editing this volume. It is a special pleasure that two such good friends and close colleagues have willingly undertaken a task which brings them very little professional reward, and done it with such care and lively interest.

My thanks too to Tim Farmiloe, who first proposed such a volume during the Eighth Keynes Conference at Kent. I thank him for his original interest and for shepherding the volume through the process of publication.

I have taken the opportunity offered by reprinting to make minor alterations and amendments. I have also added an Author's Note, in small type, at the top of most of the chapters, explaining the context of the piece and pointing to related work. As Philip and Sheila say in their Introduction, much of my early work was done in almost complete isolation. But the later pieces in this volume were often sparked off by particular conversations or events. Acknowledgements of these personal factors, out of place in professional journals, seem appropriate to this volume. I have included them in the Author's Notes. The general point can be made here, however, that much of my later work is a response to the interest shown by my fellow economists. I am deeply grateful for their encouragement and support.

The banner of Cowell College, University of California at Santa Cruz, bears a motto I should like to adopt as my own:

'The Pursuit of Truth in the Company of Friends.'

VICTORIA CHICK

# 1 A Question of Relevance: The *General Theory* in Keynes's Time and Ours*

**Author's Note**

This piece began in conversation with Mario Seccareccia, who popped in to my office at McGill one day in 1981 to invite me to contribute to a conference on Keynes and Sraffa, forthcoming at his university, Ottawa.

*Macroeconomics After Keynes* was by that time well under way, and *Inflation From a Long-Term Perspective* (Chapter 2, this volume) was behind me, but it was during the conversation with Mario that the list of what I considered to be the main stylised facts lying implicit behind the *General Theory* began to take shape. That was a lovely afternoon, and the conference too was a great success. Its proceedings can be found, in French, in *L'Actualité Économique*, January–June 1982.

I was very happy to have this piece ready for revision when the *South African Journal of Economics* asked me to contribute to their Keynes Centenary number.

## INTRODUCTION

Nothing could stand as a better monument to Keynes, whose centenary this issue of *The South African Journal of Economics* is celebrating, than the fact that people are still arguing about his work: arguing not only for the sake of setting the record straight but also to understand what his work has to tell us about our present-day world. The *General Theory* (Keynes, 1936) is the focus of most of this discussion, and for good reason: despite the enormous volume of work which has been done since under the name of 'macroeconomics', the *General Theory* still stands as the major work in which macroeconomic questions – the theory of output-as-a-whole and of aggregate employment – have all been dealt with in a coherent manner. It is a theory whose parts fit together. Later 'macro-theorists' have tinkered with the parts and never put the pieces back together again to create something new. So we find, somewhat surprisingly, that after half a century the *General Theory* is still the best macroeconomics we have.

---

* I am grateful to Mario Seccareccia for his invitation and for his enthusiasm and also to participants in the conference on Keynes and Sraffa for their comments and suggestions.

It is, therefore, worth asking if Keynes's theory is still relevant, and if not, in what areas is it most in need of revision? That is the purpose of the present chapter. As a by-product, the exercise suggests an empirical basis for some of the misunderstandings and criticisms of the *General Theory* which have led to 'Keynesian' reformulations of an unhelpful nature.

There is a basic belief underlying this exercise: a belief that economic theories are seldom true or false in any absolute sense except that of logical consistency. A theory one describes as 'true' captures important features of reality as one perceives it. A theory which is 'true' in that sense can become 'false' through the mere passage of time, not because it is, or ever was, 'wrong', but because the world has changed.

The chapter proceeds to set out the assumptions which the author believes to be central to the structure of the *General Theory* and to evaluate their relevance to interwar Britain. Then their robustness through time is evaluated, indicating where modification or even radical reconstruction seems to be necessary, to take account of major changes.

## ASSUMPTIONS OF THE *GENERAL THEORY*

In this author's view there are eight key assumptions – although they are at very different levels – on which the *General Theory* depends. They are the following:

1. unemployment is the norm;
2. there is broad price stability;
3. the money supply is quite inelastic;
4. the capital stock and techniques are given;
5. the population is not growing substantially;
6. the capital stock is 'inadequate';
7. the economy is 'closed';
8. the government is but a minor economic agent.

Not all these assumptions are heralded as such in the *General Theory*, and not all of them are sustained throughout: for example, there are remarks on the balance-of-payments repercussions of wage changes, and Chapter 17 is devoted to the longer-run consequences of capital accumulation. Nevertheless these assumptions were decisive in determining the overall shape of the argument in the *General Theory*.

## UNEMPLOYMENT

Keynes based his claim for 'generality' on the fact that his theory encompassed both full employment and unemployment states. The theory against which he was setting himself, neoclassical theory, argued for the existence of forces which would continually restore full employment. His theory concludes that there is no case to suggest the existence of such forces. On the face of it that would seem to suggest either that full employment and unemployment were equally likely or that, since for any level of wages there was one position of full employment but many positions of unemployment, unemployment was the more likely.

Whether from the latter reasoning or from empirical observation, Keynes for his analytical work *assumed* that unemployment was the norm. He gave reasons for supposing unemployment to be the *long-term* outcome, but gave none for the dominant, short-run context.

Table 1.1 illustrates the realism of the assumption in relation to the British economy in the 1920s and 1930s. The American experience, it will be noted, was very different: there was no long-drawn-out depression from the 1920s but a sharp decline in the 1930s. This different experience may partly account for the resistance to the notion of unemployment equilibrium by the American Keynesians, since there was no such phenomenon requiring explanation.

Analytically, the assumption of unemployment as the norm suggests beginning any analysis of labour market phenomena from an unemployment position, whereas a neoclassicist would automatically begin from a position of full employment. The assumption that one begins from positions of unemployment gives Keynes an enormous technical advantage in presenting the static version of his theory, for it is then possible to talk about variations in the demand for labour without changes in money wages (in *either* direction). This is important if one wants to discuss variations in levels of aggregate demand independently of changes in aggregate supply, for the aggregate supply function (in money terms) is determined for a *given* wage; a change in wages shifts the curve. Once the aggregate supply curve is fixed in position it is possible to demonstrate that there is a stop to expansion determined by demand, and that such a stop may operate before full employment is reached. If wages do not change as demand increases it is further possible to argue that a rise in demand will unambiguously improve employment, whereas if wages rose, the advantage given by the increase in demand might be diminished by rising costs. Indeed what happens when wages change is entirely unclear, since both aggregate demand and aggregate supply will shift.

*Table* 1.1 Unemployment and wages: United Kingdom and United States, 1922–39

| | United Kingdom | | United States | |
|---|---|---|---|---|
| | *Unemployment as % of insured* workers* | *Average Weekly wage rate*† (1931 = 100) | *Unemployment*‡ *(millions)* | *Hourly Earnings*§ *(1931 = 100)* |
| 1922 | 14.3 | 114 | — | — |
| 1923 | 11.7 | 102 | — | — |
| 1924 | 10.3 | 103 | — | — |
| 1925 | 11.3 | 105 | — | — |
| 1926 | 12.5 | 105 | — | — |
| 1927 | 9.7 | 103 | — | 102 |
| 1928 | 10.8 | 102 | — | 103 |
| 1929 | 10.4 | 102 | 1.4 | 105 |
| 1930 | 16.1 | 101 | 4.2 | 104 |
| 1931 | 21.3 | 100 | 7.9 | 100 |
| 1932 | 22.1 | 98 | 11.9 | 87 |
| 1933 | 19.9 | 97 | 12.6 | 87 |
| 1934 | 16.7 | 97 | 11.0 | 104 |
| 1935 | 15.5 | 98 | 10.2 | 107 |
| 1936 | 13.1 | 100 | 8.6 | 108 |
| 1937 | 10.8 | 104 | 7.3 | — |
| 1938 | 13.5 | 107 | 9.9 | — |
| 1939 | — | — | 8.8 | — |

*Notes and Sources*:

* Feinstein (1972), Table 58.

† Ibid., Table 65. Wages are those of males in manufacturing. Index converted from 1913 = 100.

‡ ILO. *Yearbook of Statistics*, 1945/6, Table 7.

§ ILO. *Yearbook of Statistics*, 1937, Table 8. The data are for unskilled males, in industry, but the pattern is similar if skilled males are included.

The conventional wisdom is that the *General Theory* is based throughout on the assumption of fixed wages. This is, of course, nonsense, as the very title of Chapter 19 would illustrate to anyone who reads the Table of Contents. What Keynes did was to assume they were fixed for analytical convenience until Chapter 19 and to provide reasons why in practice they could be expected to be *sticky*: in part, wage-stickiness is a corollary of the existence of unemployment, but in the upward, not the downward, direction. The foundations of sticky wages can be discussed with the aid of a supply-and-demand-for-labour apparatus, with labour-hours and money wages on the two axes (Figure 1.1).

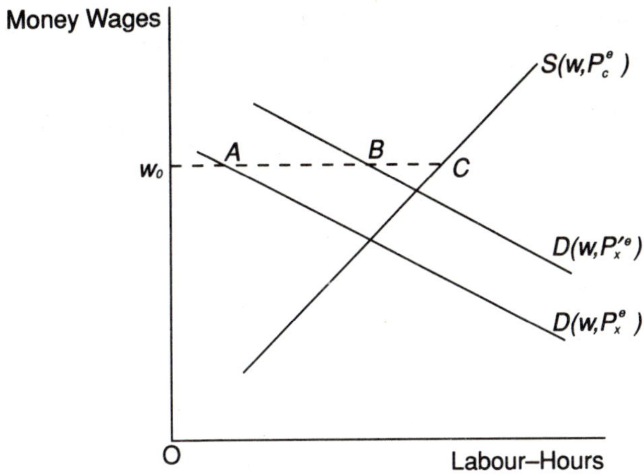


*Figure* 1.1

The supply curve of labour is a function of the real wage, here represented by the money wages, *w*, and a particular expectation of consumer prices, . The demand for labour depends on the wage and expected product prices, . If one begins with unemployment, say at A, and expected product demand rises, so that rises to , the demand for labour will shift, but there is no necessity – and certainly no incentive – for firms to raise the wage, and since by definition there are people willing to work at the going wage $w_o$, it will remain there, until demand rises to an intersection with supply beyond point C.

In the downward direction it matters not whether one begins at full or less-than-full employment, so long as there exist 'sticky wages' – wages which are in principle perfectly able to fall but because of the absence of effective downward pressure from either firms or the unemployed (the employed are hardly likely to exert such pressure!), fail to do so. In the downward direction the stickiness of wages does not depend on the assertion of initial unemployment, but on the absence of downward forces.

Stickiness is thus seen as entirely different from fixity: it is the propensity not to move of a variable which *analytically* is assumed to be flexible, i.e. able to move. Stickiness – upward or downward, if there is unemployment to start with – is a prediction of Keynes's analysis. Fixity is an assumption.

It may have been difficult to perceive the distinction between sticky and fixed because one observed, in the British economy after the disruptions of 1920–1, wages which were so sticky as to *seem* fixed. (See Table 1.1.) Again the British experience was markedly different from the American one, where the 1930s brought a sharp fall in wages. Had the *General Theory* been written against the American background, sticky wages would have seemed a purely analytical device – and analytical assumptions tend toward the extremes: hence fixed, instead of sticky. In any case the distinction made at the end of the previous paragraph is not an easy one to make, but it would be particularly difficult for the American Keynesians in the light of their observations.

## PRICE STABILITY

### Prices and Labour Supply

An assumption underlying Figure 1.1 which I would say was part of Keynes's mental equipment, concerns an asymmetry of expectations. The demand curve shifts because expected demand for output changes. These changes are represented by the expected price of output. The supply curve of labour, in contrast, is drawn for a *given* expectation of the price by which the money wage rate is deflated to arrive at the 'real' wage which ought to determine their optimal offers of labour. (The relevant price also differs from that entering the demand function, but that will not detain us here.) This asymmetry is connected to the underlying view of the behaviour of prices, the second of our listed assumptions.

In Keynes's time, despite periods of growth and violent cyclical changes, the underlying vision was of a stable economic system with fluctuations. When England was largely agricultural, this view quite reasonably applied to both prices and output, and it seems to have been carried over into the neoclassical view of output despite the Industrial Revolution. The key concept was the stationary state: the economy which is 'just ticking over', on average, though there might be substantial ups and downs. Certainly the view was that prices were broadly stable over long (but not too long) periods: cyclical fluctuations could be quite dramatic and even longer waves could be observed, but there was no expectation, such as that which we have today, that prices might be on an ever-upward *trend* with cycles around that trend.

It is an open question what sort of time horizon is relevant to workers' expectations of prices. Table 1.2 presents data compiled by Lewis (1949) to highlight cyclical variation; it illustrates well the proposition that prices, within the range of memory of three generations of workers in 1930, had been observed to fall about as often as they rose. A longer time horizon would suggest a secular rising trend as the norm; the view put here is that workers would tend to be less impressed with the fact that the Tudor inflations were not reversed than with the observation that the inflations following the Napoleonic Wars and the 1914–18 War *were* reversed. There is no suggestion of an ever-upward trend against which workers ought continually to fight to protect themselves, as now.

*Table* 1.2 Price and wage indexes: United Kingdom (1913 = 100)

| | *Wholesale prices** *(cycle averages)* | *Retail prices*† *(cycle averages)* | | *Retail prices*‡ | *Real wages*§ |
|---|---|---|---|---|---|
| 1811–18 | 176 | — | 1921 | 222 | 115 |
| 1819–25 | 129 | — | 1922 | 179 | 111 |
| 1826–36 | 111 | — | 1923 | 171 | 103 |
| 1837–46 | 109 | — | 1924 | 172 | 103 |
| 1847–53 | 96 | — | 1925 | 173 | 107 |
| 1854–60¶ | 116 | 110 | 1926 | 169 | 105 |
| 1861–65 | 119 | 112 | 1927 | 164 | 109 |
| 1866–74 | 108 | 113 | 1928 | 163 | 109 |
| 1875–83 | 103 | 103 | 1929 | 161 | 109 |
| 1884–89 | 83 | 88 | 1930 | 155 | 113 |
| 1890–99 | 77 | 84 | 1931 | 145 | 119 |
| 1900–07 | 85 | 88 | 1932 | 141 | 121 |
| 1908–13 | 93 | 95 | 1933 | 137 | 123 |
| 1914–20 | 193 | 170 | 1934 | 138 | 122 |
| 1921–29 | 154 | 175 | 1935 | 140 | 121 |
| 1930–37 | 102 | 144 | 1936 | 144 | 120 |
| | | | 1937 | 152 | 118 |

*Notes and Sources*:
* Lewis (1949), p. 202.
† Feinstein (1972), Table 65.
‡ Ibid.
§ Ibid. Average weekly wage rate index ÷ retail price index.
¶ 1855–60 in second column.

One might ask, if there exists this expectation of underlying price stability, why Figure 1.1 portrays firms as changing their price expectations while labour does not change theirs. It has been said that Keynes postulated money illusion for workers but not for firms. This charge is too shallow. The asymmetry in their responses is explicable precisely in the context outlined – cycles around a basic stability – given the nature of the decisions facing firms and households. As producers, firms *must* anticipate changes in demand and making pricing and output decisions (or at least output decisions based on anticipated prices if they really *are* 'price takers') sufficiently often to capture adequate profits. The firm in the *General Theory* is a small firm and is a profit maximiser, but one does not have to assume continuous adjustment, i.e. extremely short-run profit-maximisation, to assert that these firms will adjust their demand for labour to perceived or anticipated fluctuations in demand for output, which is reflected in prices. The Marshallian concept of normal price, the idea that prices are not adjusted to *every* variation in demand, is quite consistent with this: cyclical variations are strong enough to require adjustment of output and labour demands to changes in output demand which, by the nature of their activities, firms must forecast. The very fact that cycles in employment, output, and prices are observed corroborates this.

It is clearly implicit in the stable demand curve of Figure 1.1 that labour is not assumed to make forecasts of prices over a similar time horizon. Keynes justifies this on the grounds that price changes affect all kinds of labour equally and wage bargaining is typically orientated towards the maintenance of stable relativities between money wages for different sorts of labour. Therefore, he argued, labour was likely to be insensitive to *small* changes in the prices of wage goods.

But there is a further argument one might make. Labour is in a fundamentally different position from that of firms. Firms must anticipate changes in demand and set prices. Labour has a more passive role: it does not set prices; it only adjusts to them or to anticipations of them. In an environment in which it is perceived that, on the whole, prices go down about as often as they go up, it might not be worthwhile for labour, either individually or collectively, to renegotiate wage rates during cyclical upswings to keep real wages constant, but rather to anticipate that prices will fall subsequently and reckon on averaging out fluctuations in real wages. Firms of course would resist rises in (money) wages in any event but especially in view of the institutional difficulty of cutting them later, and workers must be aware of this. The net result is a plausible explanation for a certain insensitivity of the labour-supply curve to anticipated price changes arising both from the stickiness of the anticipations themselves and sluggishness in acting upon them. $P_c^e$ in Figure 1.1 could stand for a *range* of prices. There is the additional point, often made much of, that the prices relevant to workers and firms are different; there is, therefore, no reason to expect their anticipations to be the same.

The asymmetry between firms and the suppliers of labour is lessened when the expectation of stable prices with cyclical variation gives way to experience of a rising price trend which persistently undermines the validity of the money wage as a proxy for the real wage. It is, of course, only against *rising* prices that workers have to protect themselves, and only shifts to the left in the labour-supply curve which would, if carried far enough, force wages to move.

The experience of the 1920s and 1930s would not suggest that any harm was done by assuming a stable labour-supply curve. In Britain prices were falling from 1922 to 1934 (Table 1.2) and falling while money wages were relatively stable. Thus if anything the labour-supply curve should have been shifting rightwards, becoming less and less relevant to the determination of employment.There was no particular case for taking real wages into account instead of money wages.

The experience of a steadily *rising* price level, after the Second World War, however, renders the assumption of absence of feedback from firms' price decisions to optimum labour supply less satisfactory than it was in Keynes's time. Milton Friedman and others have already made much of this point, though they have confused the issue by speaking as if it were a matter of principle (Keynes's formulation implies money illusion) rather than addressing the real question of whether such an assumption is still reasonable in today's world.

The more rapidly and completely labour adjusts to the possibility of inflation, the less likely is the stability of the money wage on which the demand-orientation of conventional Keynesianism depends. When wages are changing, the point of effective demand becomes as much determined by shifts in aggregate supply as by shifts in aggregate demand.

It is regrettable that an incomplete recognition of one of the assumptions of Keynes's model had to be pointed out by monetarists. They, however, no less than Keynesians -- be they neo-Keynesians, post-Keynesians, bastard Keynesians or what you will – have not integrated changing wages into a full macroeconomic model, and that is not surprising, for the point of Chapter 19 is that when wages change, *both* curves will shift and the net effect on aggregate demand is not altogether predictable.

## Causes of Price Stability and its Breakdown

I have been concentrating on price stability in order to draw inferences about the appropriate modelling of labour supply and the implications for aggregate supply and demand. But it is worth commenting on the change that has taken place since the Second World War in the whole vision of the economy. The prewar assumption was that the economy exhibited fluctuations around some stable level associated with the 'long run'. Now, and probably, since the mid-1950s, our vision of the economy is one in which something – exactly what will be elaborated in a moment – is going up. (One could perhaps also argue that the expected amplitude of fluctuations around the upward trend has decreased.)

In the 1970s and since, it is mainly prices which have gone up. In the years 1945 to 1965, the upward-sloping trend that is the basis of the new world-view had to do not so much with prices but rather with output – reflecting the expectation of balanced growth which we were encouraged by our own theories to believe could go on for ever.

Let us look at the post-1965 period more closely. It has become quite a commonplace to suggest that the stable supply curve of labour is no longer applicable (this seems reasonable) and that to take price expectations into account more generally is absolutely essential. The time span over which prices have been observed to rise steadily to an extent which makes the incorporation of price expectations into *all* areas of theorising imperative is, however, quite short. The period cannot be dated precisely, but one can say that it is only in the 1970s that the upward trend changed its character definitely from a description of real (i.e. output) growth to one of inflation.

Table 1.3 presents data on inflation, to remind us how low those rates were in the 1960s. The data are percentage rates of change of implicit price deflators for the United States and Britain. They may give a better general impression than more respectable indexes would do. Wholesale price indexes for both countries and the CPI for the United States behave similarly. Peak and trough rates are summarised in Table 1.4. From this table one discerns the tendency, since the Korean War, for cycles to begin from progressively higher rates at the trough and to reach successively higher peaks.

What those data suggest is that the upward-sloping trend which in the first two decades since the Second World War we thought of as a trend in output was transformed into an upward trend in prices. This fact almost reinforces the suggestion that the time horizon is short: the postwar period has seen money income rising steadily, but does it not rather matter whether the rise is in output or prices? Can we view the whole period as a unit, or are we seeing two separate phenomena? In any case, is not forty years a rather short time in which to change a world view? Could it not be that we are merely observing part of a long wave, rather like the long waves displayed in the cyclical averages in Table 1.2?

If we *are* observing something transitory is it worth remodelling our theory? That depends on what one is trying to explain. In the present climate, even a theory which is not intended to cover a long period of calendar time must take inflationary expectations into account. But the question remains whether these expectations and the observations which generate them are transitory phenomena which will disappear again; for if they do disappear, the old theory may come back into its own. The question is one of the degree of myopia.

A strong case can be made that the upward trend is not a myopic perception, but that the price changes we have witnessed since 1970 might be part of a longer-run phenomenon, based on fundamental changes in the monetary system, and that the experience of 1945–65 can be seen as a part of the same phenomenon, but a luckier part, where the conjunction of

*Table* 1.3 Rates of inflation: United States and United Kingdom, 1948–79*

| | *US*† | *UK*‡ |
|---|---|---|
| 1949 | –0.6T | — |
| 1950 | 1.4 | — |
| 1951 | 6.7P | — |
| 1952 | 2.2 | — |
| 1953 | 0.9T | — |
| 1954 | 1.5 | 1.2 |
| 1955 | 1.5 | 3.9 |
| 1956 | 3.4 | 5.4P |
| 1957 | 3.7P | 3.5 |
| 1958 | 2.6 | 2.3 |
| 1959 | 1.6 | 1.1T |
| 1960 | 1.7 | 1.4 |
| 1961 | 1.3 | 2.7 |
| 1962 | 1.1T | 3.2P |
| 1963 | 1.3 | 2.2T |
| 1964 | 1.6 | 3.3 |
| 1965 | 1.8 | 4.4P |
| 1966 | 2.6 | 4.1 |
| 1967 | 3.1 | 2.9T |
| 1968 | 4.3 | 5.6 |
| 1969 | 4.8 | 5.0 |
| 1970 | 5.5P | 7.3 |
| 1971 | 5.0 | 8.0P |
| 1972 | 4.2T | 7.0T |
| 1973 | 5.8 | 10.2 |
| 1974 | 9.6 | 20.6 |
| 1975 | 9.7P | 23.8P |
| 1976 | 5.1T | 16.0 |
| 1977 | 6.0 | 14.0 |
| 1978 | 7.3 | 8.9T |
| 1979 | 8.8 | 13.0 |

Notes and Sources:

* Implicit price deflators: Percentage change from previous year (P = Peak, T = Trough).

† GNP deflator: *The National Income and Product Accounts of the US, 1929–1965* and *Survey of Current Business*, various dates.

‡ Deflator for total final expenditure: Central Statistical Office, *National Income and Expenditure* (Blue Book): 1980, Table 2.6; 1974, Table 17; 1963, Table 16.

*Table* 1.4 Summary: rates of inflation at cyclical peaks and troughs

| *US: GNP deflator* | | | | *UK: Deflator for total final expenditure* | | | |
|---|---|---|---|---|---|---|---|
| *Trough* | | *Peak* | | *Trough* | | *Peak* | |
| 1949 | –0.6 | 1951 | 6.7 | 1959 | 1.1 | 1956 | 5.4 |
| 1953 | 0.9 | 1957 | 3.7 | 1963 | 2.2 | 1962 | 3.2 |
| 1962 | 1.1 | 1970 | 5.5 | 1967 | 2.9 | 1965 | 4.4 |
| 1972 | 3.2 | 1974 | 9.7 | 1972 | 6.8 | 1971 | 8.0 |
| 1976 | 5.1 | — | — | — | — | 1975 | 24.3 |

*Source*: Table 1.3
*Note*: The data, which were compiled for another paper, have not been brought up to date where this was not necessary to support the argument.

several factors came together to turn what would have been an inflationary episode into an episode of growth.

Before discussing this major point, some remarks concerning the period 1945 (or 1950) to 1965 are pertinent. During that period, except during the Korean War, prices, particularly in the United States, were remarkably stable (Table 1.3). This was the period, and the country, in which Keynes was transmuted into Keynesianism. The idea that expansion, achieved by manipulating aggregate demand, would take the form chiefly of increases in output and not create much inflation, was substantiated by the data that surrounded those American economists who were responsible for this transformation of Keynes into the 'fixprice' or even (the quite different) fixed-price theory of the textbooks and gave rise to a growth theory which was quite divorced from 'Keynesian' macroeconomics. This is no accident: in the period 1945–65 there were features of the economic system which were extremely favourable to price stability and real growth in the United States.

The first two decades after the Second World War were years of very rapid technical change, and technical change in principle operates to keep prices down. It is most likely to do so after a period of slow growth or after a war, when the economy is undercapitalised to begin with and the real pay-off from almost any investment is likely to be high. The postwar period began with a devastated productive capacity in Europe, so that the United States had little competition in the early years. Demand was buoyant within the country and was only restricted abroad by the dollar shortage.

The shortage of international liquidity is a critical part of the story.

European countries – indeed any country which could get its hands on them – were perfectly happy to hold US dollars as international reserves at least in the early years (the 'gold rushes' began in 1958) and they typically held them in US government liabilities. This meant that it was possible to stimulate US demand by means which in other circumstances would raise the money supply and threaten to be inflationary, but insofar as the rise in demand spilled over into imports, part of the monetary increase went abroad to be held in the form of idle balances in the form of US government debt, thus both mitigating the inflationary impact of monetary increases and allowing low interest rates to be sustained.

These monetary factors, in conjunction with a rapid rate of technical change, could explain the US experience of near-stability of prices in the face of rapid expansion. The observed price stability in turn had two effects: (i) the contrast between the assumption in 'Keynesian' theory of fixed wages or (even more strongly) fixed prices and the flexible prices of Keynes's theory went unrecognised (thus helping the Bowdlerised version of Keynes to gain credence), and (ii) the short-run and monetary assumptions of Keynes's theory or even 'Keynesian' theory could be left undisturbed despite their inappropriateness to the postwar world. We shall now elaborate the second point.

## THE MONEY SUPPLY

### The Gold Standard and Inelasticity

Let us compare the monetary system at the time of the *General Theory* and the monetary system as it has developed since the Second World War. It is implicit in the *General Theory* that a tie to gold and fixed exchange rates were being taken as the norm, even though the international gold exchange standard crumbled in the 1930s after Britain had departed from it in 1931. It was the only *system* anybody knew; *ad hoc* arrangements such as existed in the 1930s were thought to be temporary only. So a return to it was expected.

The operation of the gold standard encouraged (though it did not ensure) the low elasticity of the supply of money which Keynes cites as one of the essential properties of money (Chapter 17). Money supply data for 1922–34 (Table 1.5) illustrate the reasonableness of assuming a stable money supply in interwar Britain and the extent to which such an assumption would be foolish now. (Once again the American experience in the 1930s was very different – see Friedman and Schwartz, 1963b. The money supply contracted sharply. In recent years monetary growth rates have been – as in Britain – consistently positive.)

In the present monetary system the constraints which were taken for granted by Keynes have been completely dismantled. And yet mainstream macroeconomic theory has steadfastly refused to acknowledge this fact. On a national level the dismantling was quite intentional. It was felt, and quite reasonably, that the inelasticity of the monetary system bore a great responsibility for unemployment and in one country after another the relationship between domestic currency and gold was first weakened and then abandoned in favour of a managed paper currency and credit money.

Until quite recently it was firmly believed that this management was both possible and adequate. These assumptions have now been called into question both by those who see the 'endogeneity of money' as essential to 'Keynesianism' (e.g., Kaldor 1980) and those who argue that the central bank is not *able* to control the money supply (e.g., Goodhart, 1975). There are, however, some even deeper issues: the rise of the importance of commercial banks in the international monetary system (and the lesser position of central banks) (Aronson, 1977; Cohen, 1981), the relationship between the internationalisation of banking and of enterprise (Chick, 1979), and the demise of a coherent international monetary system. An international banking system has grown up, destroying national monetary boundaries as the transnational corporations have done on the 'real' side. These banks now enjoy some assurance of lender-of-last-resort facilities from the major central banks, with few concomitant checks on their expansion. The international money supply under present arrangements can expand very rapidly indeed, when such expansion is profitable for the banks, and it is difficult for the advanced western countries to 'sterilise' the resulting monetary impact on what are quaintly called their 'domestic' economies, as if one could, any longer, shut the door on the outside world.

There is inevitably some relationship between the speed with which the money supply increases and the distribution of the expansion of money demand between prices and output. One needs no quantity theory, old or new, no theory of any kind, to understand that the more rapidly money increases the more likely it is that the effect will fall chiefly on prices, simply because it takes *time* to expand output. When the money supply rises as rapidly as it did in the 1960s and 1970s, the emergence of rather high rates of inflation is surely not surprising.

It is common sense that tells us this, or good financial journalism, not formal economic theory. The implications of a monetary system which has a substantial inflationary bias, which does *not* have the 'essential property' of low elasticity of supply, simply has not been incorporated into macroeconomic theory.

*Table* 1.5 Indexes of money supply:* United Kingdom, 1922–37 and 1960–75

| *(1922 = 100)* | | *(1960 = 100)* | |
|---|---|---|---|
| 1922 | 100 | 1960 | 100 |
| 1923 | 96 | 1961 | 102 |
| 1924 | 95 | 1962 | 104 |
| 1925 | 93 | 1963 | 109 |
| 1926 | 94 | 1964 | 114 |
| 1927 | 95 | 1965 | 121 |
| 1928 | 97 | 1966 | 126 |
| 1929 | 98 | 1967 | 131 |
| 1930 | 99 | 1968 | 141 |
| 1931 | 97 | 1969 | 148 |
| 1932 | 100 | 1970 | 157 |
| 1933 | 105 | 1971 | 175 |
| 1934 | 105 | 1972 | 210 |
| 1935 | 109 | 1973 | 262 |
| 1936 | 116 | 1974 | 316 |
| 1937 | 121 | 1975 | 348 |

*Notes and Source*:

* Gross deposits at London clearing banks and other domestic deposit banks (and the National Giro since 1968), less interbank and transit items plus private deposits at the Bank of England and currency held by the public. Friedman and Schwartz (1982), Table 4.9.

## Money in the Short Run

Money in the *General Theory* has both short-run and long-run roles to play. Its short-run role is to determine the rate of interest, through variations in supply engineered by open-market operations against a demand determined by liquidity preference. The new feature of liquidity preference, introduced in the *General Theory*, was of course the speculative motive. One can view the speculative demand for money from a narrow perspective or a broad one. If one views speculative demand from a narrow perspective, as some people seem absolutely determined to do, it can be described in terms of a choice between money and long-term debt. The meaning of these categories has been further narrowed to non-interest-bearing money and perpetuities ('Consols'). Understandably, the choice between these categories was seen as unduly restrictive, even slightly absurd: who would hold non-interest-bearing money when interest-bearing deposits or Treasury bills are available!

It is Keynes's interpreters who have been too narrow, not Keynes himself, but it is worth pointing out that if Keynes *had* been thinking in terms of these assets, in his time it would not have been too unreasonable. Consols are a curiosum these days, but Consols were widely held in the 1930s, and it was a consistent policy to fund the debt. Private-sector holdings of these securities increased steadily in importance in the 1920s to reach by 1932 some 60 per cent of private-sector holdings of government debt with more than five years to run (Howson, 1975, p. 162) – so it was not a trivial sort of security to discuss.

Not only were Consols of some practical importance; they are also analytically convenient, for the inverse relationship between market interest rates and capital value of these securities is not interrupted by a maturity date. Thus they are the ideal instrument when using changes in the rate of interest to represent capital gains and losses, expectations of which are the motive for speculation.

On the money side, the non-interest-bearing quality of deposits is irrelevant (Kaldor, 1980) shows himself to be un-Keynesian on this point): it is the absence of capital-loss risk which is important. Deposit accounts or Treasury bills are the appropriate safe haven for bear speculators. However, with short rates less than one per cent (rates on Treasury bills in the 1930s were between $\frac{1}{2}$ to $\frac{3}{4}$ of one per cent), and rates on deposit accounts similarly low, the return was hardly worth chasing. It is just possible that the money withdrawn from securities would remain in current accounts.

Although one can justify the framing of speculative demand in terms of these two assets in terms of their relevance in Keynes's time, one would be hard pressed to take such a narrow view now. There is, however, no need to do so; Keynes himself made no such identification, as the following shows:

> We can draw the line between 'money' and 'debts' at whatever point is most convenient for handling a particular problem. . . . It is often convenient in practice to include in *money* time-deposits with banks and even such instruments as (*e.g.*) Treasury bills. (Keynes, 1936, p. 167, n. 1.)

Thus as a general rule one would expect that if a bear speculator's time horizon is three months he will hold a treasury bill, not money; in this context the Treasury bill counts as 'money'. This is not an easy idea to accept if your primary concern in theory-building is logical consistency, for the speculative demand has to be fitted in with transactions demand and the definitions of money are not the same for both.

Although it is interesting and instructive to be aware of the features of the economy of Keynes's day that may have shaped his formulation of speculative demand, speculative demand does not stand or fall on the assets included. And to stop at the choice-theoretic stage is to take a narrow view of what the speculative demand is all about. What we should be concerned with are the implications for macroeconomic theory as a whole.

The point about the speculative demand for money is that there are times when funds could in principle be lent out or placed in securities in such a way as to bring the rate of interest down, but instead, because potential buyers of securities fear capital losses, funds are held off securities markets and the rate remains unduly high.

In an inflationary time, the first thing one might query is why one should hold speculative balances in monetary assets (whether money/Treasury bills or long bonds) at all. Indeed it is a good question, a question to which the experience in Britain in 1972 is particularly relevant. That year saw heavy speculation in land or, more generally, property. Keynes himself mentions land as an 'infinite sink of purchasing power' every bit as important at some times in history as he believed idle balances to be in his own.

It may well be that the speculative margin has moved from that between 'money' and 'bonds' to something else – that point will be taken up in a moment. The central point to grasp is the broader significance of speculative demand, irrespective of any shift in the form that speculation takes. Speculative demand broke the link between saving and investment which followed from the identification of saving with lending. Keynes observed that savings can be held in idle balances, too. But he could have said more – that even when saving takes the form of purchases of securities, there is no guarantee of a flow of funds to firms for investment: that depends on the timing of new issues. If new issues lag behind saving, the funds are tied up in unrealised capital gains until, in aggregate, there is a desire to realise those gains. This just isn't a story told in macroeconomic theory.

It is hardly surprising that inflation has brought about a rethinking of speculative demand. It would be a mistake, however, to suggest that the phenomenon of speculation had lost significance just because Consols seem irrelevant in today's world or the appropriate definition of money is obscure.

There will always be scope for speculation in financial assets, for even when the rate of inflation is very high, short of a hyperinflation in which the currency is repudiated, speculation in real assets is limited by the indivisibilities and high transactions cost involved. Equities, often treated (misleadingly) as a proxy for real assets, were a suitable hedge, and even a speculation, against inflation when the inflation was chiefly demand-induced, but equities have not served that role well in recent years. The most obvious speculative margin under the present arrangement of flexible exchange rates is foreign exchange, where one may speculate on relative rates of inflation, relative interest rates, and the differing styles of national policies.

Speculation in equities or foreign exchange is not subject to the same impediments as property speculation, yet it produces the same results – the siphoning-off of purchasing power into unrealised capital gains rather than the transfer of that purchasing power to those who might use it to finance productive activity. Speculation in foreign exchange is difficult to handle analytically at the pedagogic level because it involves buying foreign exchange and interest-bearing assets at the same time, but that does not mean we should not at least try to make the point that the exchange rate, when pushed too high by speculative activity, will have the same depressing effect on aggregate demand as a too-high rate of interest did in the *General Theory*.

As pointed out earlier, money has both short-term and long-term implications in the *General Theory*. The role of money in the long term for Keynes is discussed in the infamous Chapter 17, where the significance of money derives from its being the most liquid asset, the standard of liquidity against which all other things, being less liquid, are measured. Given the liquidity premium on money, or liquidity yield, the next most liquid asset, which is presumably a financial asset, requires a positive rate of interest in order for anyone to be interested in holding it. So the *existence* of money serves as a stop to the fall of interest rates. In the long-term perspective of Chapter 17, where previously-made investment in capital stock is allowed to have its effect on supply, Keynes asserts the tendency of the marginal efficiency of further additions to capital to be falling as capital accumulates.[1] Thus if investment is not to grind to a halt, the rate of interest must fall gradually. This it may do for a time, but the liquidity premium on money provides a floor.

When an inflationary climate becomes established, what happens to the analysis of Chapter 17? Keynes took the inelasticity of supply of money for granted as a basic property and with it the underlying stability of prices. The result is a positive floor to the rate of interest in real as well as money terms. The striking attribute of inflation in this context is the possibility of negative real rates of interest,[2] which emerged systematically in the US Treasury bill rate in the 1950s. They appeared sporadically in Britain in the postwar years. Experience of negative real rates was commonplace in the 1970s (see Table 1.6).[3] Positive real rates have since been re-established.

The data presented as illustration in Table 1.6 are not ideal, but they are adequate. The rate of change in the GNP deflator is again used as a measure of inflation, and Treasury bills have little to do with corporate financing. Nevertheless, they illustrate the main point, that a positive floor to the

*Table* 1.6 Real rates of interest (range over year)

| | *UK: 3-month Treasury bill rate less rate of inflation* | | *US: 3-month Treasury bill rate less rate of inflation* | |
|---|---|---|---|---|
| | *low* | *high* | *low* | *high* |
| 1968 | 0.8 | 1.9 | 0.5 | 1.4 |
| 1969 | 1.8 | 3.0 | 1.2 | 2.9 |
| 1970 | –0.4 | 1.4 | –0.4 | 2.6 |
| 1971 | –3.6 | –2.1 | –1.6 | 0.4 |
| 1972 | –2.4 | 1.2 | –0.9 | 0.7 |
| 1973 | –2.0 | 5.0 | 0.0 | 3.3 |
| 1974 | –9.5 | –8.3 | –2.6 | 0.2 |
| 1975 | –14.3 | –12.0 | –4.8 | –3.1 |
| 1976 | –7.4 | 1.1 | –0.6 | 0.5 |
| 1977 | –9.6 | 2.5 | –1.5 | 0.5 |
| 1978 | –3.0 | 3.4 | –0.9 | 2.0 |
| 1979 | 0.8 | 3.9 | 0.8 | 5.7 |

*Sources*: Interest rates from Bank of England *Quarterly Bulletin*, December issues. Rates of inflation from Table 1.3.

*Note*: The rate of inflation is the annual rate of change of the GNP or TFE deflator. Hence the range of variation of real rates derives from within-year variations in the interest rates. For the years 1974–9 they are taken from data on Friday rates. The portion of the year covered in the December *Bulletin* decreases as one works backward, but the omissions did not seem to be significant until 1973, after which the range was taken from a combination of Friday and end-of-month data.

(money) rate of interest is not to be relied on for predicting the long-term outcome of employment and output[4] when the supply of money becomes more elastic.

When money becomes elastic it loses an 'essential property' and as a consequence it loses some of its liquidity premium. Its superior liquidity as a medium of exchange for frequently-bought items is unimpaired, but as a longer-term standard of value it suffers *vis-à-vis* real assets. If one's horizon is ten years or more, a house might be a more liquid asset than money, in the sense of maintaining its exchange value (though not in terms of immediacy of sale). The liquid asset is difficult to identify; different ones serve as liquid depending on one's purposes and time horizon. This means that the interest rate or yield towards which other interest rates are driven as output increases and capital accumulates is itself not easy to identify, and the concept of a floor interest rate below which other rates of return cannot fall is called into question. Thus we can no longer argue, without further justification designed to fit the facts of our present environment, that the existence of money is solely or chiefly responsible for the eventual drying-up of investment. We must look also at other non-reproducible or only-slowly-reproducible assets to determine which of them – if indeed we can focus on any one of them – is playing that role.

Those who would reformulate macroeconomic relationships using the real rate of interest instead of the nominal rate do not seem sufficiently provoked by the emergence of negative real rates of interest to explain why those negative rates did not encourage a sufficient level of investment to prevent the emergence of stagflation, characterised by substantial unemployment. One obvious answer is that the word 'inflation' does not discriminate between profit and wage inflation and that it rather matters which of these is going on.

## THE SHORT RUN

The last two sections have touched on aspects of the *General Theory* which appear to need rethinking in the light of the emergence since the Second World War of a monetary and financial system vastly different from that envisaged by Keynes. But let us go on to the fourth assumption on which the *General Theory* is based, namely the short run: a given capital stock and a given body of known techniques.

At one level, the assumption of the short run is simply dictated by the problem Keynes wants to solve, namely the determination of output-as-a-whole. All production always takes place in the short run; firms produce with the capital stock which they have. At another level, it is worth noting that the assumption of a fixed capital stock does very little violence to the actual facts of the British economy at that time in its history.

Matthews, in his very important article, 'Why has Britain had Full Employment Since the War?' (1968), calls attention to the fact that 'In the forty years preceding 1948, the stock of fixed capital in the United Kingdom is estimated to have risen at scarcely more than one per cent per annum.' That is not a high rate of capital accumulation! If there was very much technical progress, it had precious little chance of becoming embodied in actual capital except through replacement. Thus one could argue that the British economy in those years approximated in reality and in aggregate the theoretical construct of the Marshallian short run. Once again we see that the actual facts of the economy were mirrored in Keynes's assumptions.

It is a pity that, as a profession, we did not think that through. Keynes's short-run theory was applied in the 1950s and 1960s without modification, though this was a period of exceedingly rapid capital accumulation and technical change. Theory and the real world were dramatically disparate, but there was little recognition of this fact. Matthews (1968) is outstanding in looking at this feature in the British context; indeed, the answer he gives to the question he poses is that investment, relative to national income, was significantly higher from the end of the Second World War to his time of writing than it had ever been before. The scope for technical change he offers as an important reason for this. Technical change was also rapid in the USA at this time.

An appreciation of Keynes's theory which accepted the aggregate supply curve and understood the implications of the short-run assumption would have led to a recognition that with technical change the aggregate supply curve should be shifted downward, implying that prices should fall. This might have led economists either to wonder why prices did *not* fall or to conclude that investments were not as efficient, technically, as they seemed. Instead, Keynesians clung to the idea of a multiplier which describes expansion in real terms, and the observation of considerable price stability allowed this misconception of Keynes's theory to be perpetuated.

Had the dissonance between the short-run assumption in the *General Theory* and reality in the postwar decades been recognised, there might have been greater preparedness to discuss the effects of the slow-down in technical change in the latter part of the 1960s. (Though difficult to measure,[5] there seems to be a consensus that it has occurred.) This slow-down suggests that the advanced economies in the 1970s might have returned to a closer approximation to the short run (though of course it has lost its conformity to other assumptions), so that the inflationary impact of expansionary demand management began to show itself.

## STABLE POPULATION

Finally, there are two assumptions which pertain to the underlying, long-run situation, of which, again, little acknowledgement seems to have been given. One is an expectation of a virtually stable population. British data on population growth beginning in 1821–31 show a 1.54 per cent annual average increase in that decade and a persistent decline to less than of one per cent per year between 1911 and 1931. The data for the United States show a higher rate of growth: the figures range around 3 per cent per year through most of the nineteenth century and decrease to less than one per cent between 1930 and 1940.

In the postwar period the same pattern obtains: British population growth rose above one per cent per year only in the quinquennium 1950–4 and fell to virtually zero growth in 1970–4. The rates for the United States remain higher but have fallen from 1.65 per cent per year in 1945–9 to 1.06 per cent in 1970–4.

British demographic stability may have influenced Keynes in taking consumption to be a stable function of employment; no growth in consumption could be hoped for simply because there would be more mouths to feed. Thus when he discusses ways out of what he perceives as the long-run dilemma caused by the failure of the rate of interest to fall adequately, he proposes income redistribution towards wages to keep demand high, not foreseeing the upward drift in consumption which American economists were later to observe.[6] Stable population would have been coupled, in Keynes's mind, with a conception of a fairly stable social pattern of consumption which also has completely changed – not just the pattern, but the stability of the pattern.

The difference in both data and social structure between Britain in the interwar years and the United States since the Second World War might have suggested that the theory of consumption would be unlikely to 'go through' without alteration as Keynesianism developed in the postwar America from its British roots. The significance of the inapplicability of the stable-population assumption is that the difficulty of sustaining demand over a long span of years in which capital was accumulating can be offset to some extent by upward shifts in the consumption function; these rises acted, along with technical change, to delay the fall in the marginal efficiency of investment.

## INADEQUATE CAPITAL

With the background of a stable consumption function in mind we come to the assumption which may be the most basic, and certainly the most hidden: a key sentence, crucial to the entire argument of the *General Theory*, is buried away in the Notes on the Trade Cycle (Chapter 22): 'I am myself impressed with the great social advantages of increasing the stock of capital until it ceases to be scarce' (p. 325). The assumption that capital is scarce, or inadequate, informs Keynes's entire argument, based on his judgement that not in Britain nor even in the United States had the capital stock reached the point of what he called full investment – that circumstance in which a net increment to the capital stock cannot be expected to yield enough to cover replacement cost, *even* if demand is sustained at full-employment levels throughout.

In understanding this concept one must distinguish between over-investment in the sense that the yield which was expected on an investment is not fulfilled because of a cyclical downturn, which with its unemployment and decreased sales does not generate the expected rate of profit though it would have done had full employment been sustained, and full investment as defined above, when further investment is not justified even in the most favourable light.

Full investment, therefore, is a notion of capital saturation or capital adequacy which is contingent on continuous full employment (on a theoretical not a practical level). When an investment fails to provide the entrepreneur with his expected profit the project may still be judged *socially* beneficial if it *would* have fulfilled expectations had full employment been sustained.

Note that this concept is quite separate from the question of whether the capital is adequate to provide employment opportunities – a concept of adequacy rather more relevant to underdeveloped countries. (On pre-1914 Britain as an underdeveloped country see Matthews, 1968.)

To repeat, it was Keynes's judgement that the return from further investment would almost certainly be positive if a full-employment context could be sustained. At a time when (perhaps) there was less reason to question the identification of the ability of firms to make profits with the ability to satisfy wants than there has been since the emergence of the giant corporation, it is an easy step from this to the proposition that the *social* rate of return on further investment is also unlikely to be zero.[7]

In a world in which the social return from investment is almost bound to be positive, almost *any* investment is a good thing. Building pyramids and cathedrals and burying notes in bottles are almost as good as anything else: the activities and subsequent multiplier effects would provide employment at little cost in terms of inflation in Keynes's world. Keynes admits the possibility of *misdirected* investment, that is, investment which mal-allocates resources because the activity does not pay off in the sense defined, but it is clearly not a possibility which alarms him: 'It would be more sensible to build houses and the like, but . . . the above would be better than nothing' (Keynes, 1936, p. 129).

It is a property of capital, however, that it can be accumulated: unlike land there is nothing inherent in capital which should cause it to remain scarce. Therefore there is no good reason not to push the expansion of the capital stock until it does 'cease to be scarce' – i.e., until the rate of interest covers only a return to risk and entrepreneurship (even if that means saying 'bad luck' to a few rentier friends).

When capital is not scarce in Keynes's sense, might it not occur to one to ask the following question: if we choose to attempt to alleviate unemployment by stimulating aggregate demand, and that part of aggregate demand most amenable to stimulus is investment, would it not be wise to ask what *kinds* of investment should be stimulated, in order to assess whether the increased employment we buy with higher rates of investment could not be bought more cheaply by careful *direction* of that investment rather than by giving a stimulus, indiscriminately, to investment as a whole? This is a question which, long overdue, is beginning to be asked, despite the political difficulties it poses. It has become too obvious that some industries are overcapitalised, in the context of world competition: on a global basis there is too much productive capacity in, for example, steel and motor car manufacturing. In this context, the bland assumption implicit in Keynesian macroeconomic theory and policy advice, that one investment is as good as any other, is an anachronism and a costly one.

## A CLOSED ECONOMY

Harry Johnson (1975) has made much of the role of the closed-economy assumption in shaping Keynes's argument in the *General Theory*. He goes so far as to say that:

> Had the exchange value of the pound been fixed realistically in the 1920s . . . there would have been no need for mass unemployment hence no need for a revolutionary new theory to explain it. (Johnson, 1975, p. 110.)

There is little doubt that the desire to return to a prewar parity was responsible for much of the unemployment of the 1920s (see Moggridge, 1969; Pollard, 1970). Need we, however, go along with Johnson's reasons for Keynes's choice of the closed-economy assumption in the *General Theory*? He argues that Keynes accepted the return to gold in 1925 as a *fait accompli* and turned to advocating public works and even, in 1931, protection, as ways of improving employment which might gain political acceptance.

It is a slightly strange argument to make, in view of the fact that the *General Theory* did not begin to take shape until after Britain's departure from the gold standard in 1931. It has been argued above that Keynes assumed an inelastic money supply presumably on the grounds that some kind of gold exchange standard was the norm, but it *was* temporarily in abeyance.

Are there not other reasons one might adduce for ignoring international trade as a potential source of demand in much (not all) of the *General*

*Theory*? One possible interpretation is that he was just following the line of enquiry, begun in the *Treatise*, into the saving–investment nexus, and the closed-economy assumption was only a simplifying device. An additional possibility, however, is that the potential for influencing domestic demand by encouraging exports had, by the time the *General Theory* was published, been drastically curtailed by the 'Great Contraction' of the American economy and the shrinkage of world trade.[8] Surely even an 'elasticity-optimist' would not pin his hopes on export-led growth in this period.

Trade fell even more than GNP in the 1930s. The ratio of exports (including property income from abroad) to GNP, which had averaged 33 per cent from 1922 to 1929 and fluctuated little, fell to 27 per cent in 1930 and declined to 19.5 per cent in 1932 (Feinstein, 1972). The ratio of imports to GNP tells the same story. While at no time in its documented history could the British economy seriously be described as closed, perhaps it was less absurd to ignore trade then than at most other times – certainly now. Not only has international competition become a vital issue but the money and foreign exchange markets of the world are more closely linked than they have ever been before.

## THE ROLE OF GOVERNMENT

'Keynesianism' is associated, in the public mind, with 'government intervention' and 'demand management'. It is therefore startling for those who come to the *General Theory* for the first time to discover how little analysis it contains of government in this role. There is advocacy of public works programmes in a slump, to be sure, and an important caution that monetary policy should see that the financing of such programmes did not raise interest rates and 'crowd out' private investment, but there are no pages of government expenditure multipliers, taxation multipliers and the like which the readers of Keynesian textbooks have come to expect.

The focus of attention in the *General Theory* is on explanation rather than curative action. And the main forces that Keynes saw as driving the economy were generated in the relationships between households and firms, not between government and the private sector. Thus households supplied labour and firms may or may not demand sufficient of it; labour income is a cost to firms but also a major source of demand; households consume, constrained by income, and entrepreneurs invest, using money borrowed partly, but not entirely, from households. Only the cost of that borrowing is determined by forces not wholly to do with this grouping into households and firms.

Monetary policy is an accepted part of the background against which the forces of enterprise and speculation do their work; the authorities have a continuing presence in financial markets. But government in its role as provider of demand and employment appears only sporadically, in emergencies.

There is a further role *proposed* for government, a new role with wide-ranging powers: for Keynes suggests that the state should become directly involved in investment decisions. That had happened only to a limited degree. But Keynes appears not to have envisaged what *has* been such a notable feature of Western economies since the Second World War: the rise of government as a permanent employer and source of demand.

Much attention has been directed to this development, of course, and Table 1.7 presents some data for the United States as well as for Britain;

*Table* 1.7 Government expenditure as a percentage of GNP

| | *Britain* | | *United States* | |
|---|---|---|---|---|
| | | | *Expenditure** | *Wages and salaries*† |
| 1870 | 5.1 | 1929 | 8.5 | 9.5 |
| 1880 | 5.4 | 1930 | 10.5 | 10.8 |
| 1890 | 5.8 | 1933 | 14.7 | 15.5 |
| 1900 | 9.4 | 1950 | 13.4 | 7.2 |
| 1910 | 8.1 | 1960 | 20.0 | 18.1 |
| 1920 | 8.3 | 1970 | 22.2 | 21.3 |
| 1930 | 10.0 | 1980 | 20.4 | 18.9 |
| 1935 | 11.0 | | | |
| 1950 | 17.6 | | | |
| 1960 | 18.3 | | | |
| 1970 | 20.9 | | | |
| 1975 | 24.6 | | | |

*Notes and Sources*:
Britain: Public authorities' current expenditure on goods and services as a percentage of GNP at factor cost. 1870–1960: Feinstein (1972), Table 2; 1970, 1975: *CSO Annual Abstract of Statistics*, 1976, Table 344.

United States:
*Government purchases of goods and services as a percentage of GNP. *Statistical Abstract of the US*, 1981, Table 699.

†Wages and salaries paid by government and government enterprises as a percentage of all wages and salaries, excluding armed forces. 1929–33: *Statistical Abstract of the US*, 1943, Table 422; 1950–80, ibid.; 1981, Table 709.

*Table* 1.8 Flows of funds: United Kingdom, 1980 (£ billions)

| *Sectoral surpluses and deficits*[*] | | *Public sector finance*[†] | |
|---|---|---|---|
| Personal sector | 16.6 | Public sector borrowing requirement | 12.3 |
| Industrial and commercial companies | –2.8 | External finance | 0.0 |
| Public sector | –10.0 | Domestic finance | 12.3 |
| Banking and other financial institutions | 0.9 | Banks (£ borrowing) | 2.4 |
| Overseas | –2.7 | Other financial institutions | 5.5 |
| | | Industrial and commercial companies | 0.4 |
| | | Personal sector | 4.0 |

Sources:
* Bain (1981, p. 30).
† Ibid. (p. 134).

proportions of GNP accounted for by government expenditure for both countries and the data pertaining to employment tell the same, well-known story, even though these data only include current expenditures and exclude the nationalised industries.

It can be seen that it was reasonable to assign to government a minor role in the 1930s, but the situation has changed. This point is reinforced when one looks at the pattern of sectoral surpluses and deficits. This very week [the first week of March 1983], it was announced that the US federal deficit was now larger than the aggregate of personal savings! British data for 1980 (Table 1.8), which are not unrepresentative of the trend of the last decade, show that the important flow of funds is between the personal and public sectors, not between the personal and industrial sectors, and that the bulk of the flow of funds is mediated by financial institutions. The corporate sector is largely self-financing.

The policy-makers have already shifted their attention away from investment toward the public sector deficit. The fact that mainstream Keynesianism ignored the need to develop the financial side of government policy (and has never integrated a theory of the behaviour of financial institutions into its main corpus) has left the policy-makers prey to what some would feel was less than constructive advice.

## CONCLUSION

What do I conclude from this exploration? Primarily it illustrates the dangers of treating economic theory as a body of abstract logical analysis based on general principles applicable to all times and types of economic systems.

This is not to say, however, that all theorising is useless and one is bound to the confines of institutional and historical description. Nor is it legitimate to conclude that the level of generality of economic theory is limited by the historical nature of the object of study: it is also limited by our imaginative powers and the youth of our discipline. But whatever the level of generality attained, the capacity of theories to capture the salient facts must remain under constant review.

It is, I think, fair to say that macroeconomic theory has not moved adequately with the times, and that our failure to realise this has been partly responsible for our giving misleading policy advice and taking credit when little was due : Matthews (1968) argues quite strongly that the high level of employment in Britain until the late 1960s had little to do with Keynesian policy, and this chapter suggests reasons why the apparent success could even reinforce some theoretical misconceptions.

Failure to realise that the postwar world no longer conformed closely enough to Keynes's world to allow policy prescriptions to go through without alteration is bad enough: that is the well-known phenomenon of generals always fighting the previous war. But when they win the war by luck, despite and not because of their theory, they will be *two* wars out of date when the next one comes. The next one did come – stagflation – and we looked very foolish.

Despite the importance of the changes outlined here, I believe that the *General Theory* still contains much that is useful to us: the idea of aggregating expenditure according to the degree of autonomy from current income (though we may now wish to draw the line elsewhere); Keynes's restoration (from classical authors) of the periodic importance of speculation and his recognition of its displacement to the financial sphere; the integration of the consequence of asset-holding with the flows of production and investment – these ideas still hold. And the fundamental, contradictory relationship between households and producers is still the core of the problem of how capitalism functions, though now it is functioning with a degree of international integration Keynes did not foresee and with government mediation on a scale for which the theory had no place.

I believe that even in the present environment, some of the elements of Keynes's theory can, with extension or modification, be retained. Others may take the view that to find a theoretical expression of the relationships between the key elements of the economic system, the best procedure is to use the *General Theory* as an instruction manual in the art of doing economics, but otherwise to start afresh. I admire their courage and wish them good luck. In a few years I may even join them. I will not join those who have 'updated' macroeconomics by trivial extension and even twisting of

Keynes's ideas, the chief result of which has been to remove most of what was arresting, original and relevant to his time and also to ours.

**Notes**

1. For those who at this point would raise the problems associated with the Cambridge capital-theory debate, there are two points to make: (i) Keynes's proposition relates to marginal efficiency, not marginal productivity, so demand factors play a role and (ii) since marginal efficiency can only be calculated for a particular type of capital and then aggregated, it must be assumed that the composition of capital is not altering, only the scale. In that case (and in that case only) the rate of growth of the capital stock is a meaningful concept.
2. Chick (1978c; this volume, ch. 2) explored the significance of this development in the 1950s and 1960s.
3. See also Grant (1972, p. 110).
4. A serious analysis of the relationships between the rate of interest and the marginal efficiency of capital under inflationary conditions has yet to be presented; the glib substitution of the 'real' rate of interest for nominal rates in saving and investment functions seems to have satisfied most people (not the present author).
5. See Schott (1981) for a summary of the evidence and references.
6. There is no suggestion that population growth was entirely responsible for those observations; just that it may have played a role.
7. This proposition is made for aggregates, of course, and that means on average. No one is suggesting that every investment made was or would be successful in the sense defined above.
8. See Nurkse (1944) for a chronicle of trade and exchange rate experience in this period.

# 2 Inflation from a Longer-Run Perspective*

**Author's Note**

This paper has two origins. In an unpublished paper called 'The Changing Ideology of Inflation' I explored why it was that the right wing had begun, in the late 1960s, to put out articles on indexation and 'learning to live with inflation'. This was a period of demand inflation, which is good for profits. But just as I was preparing to submit the piece to journals, some time in 1972, the wage inflation began and (since wage inflation is bad for profits) the right wing changed its tune.

The second antecedent was my experience in Australia in 1975–6. Everyone seemed convinced that the recession, by this time spreading throughout the OECD countries, was just a 'blip'. Policy harmonisation was the favoured answer to the problem. I dissented, arguing that the recession would be a long one, a natural consequence of a long period of capital accumulation. I was almost treated like the messenger who brings bad news. I do not quite know how I arrived at my assessment but when I came to defend it I found all the support needed in the *General Theory*, which undoubtedly was my unconscious inspiration. Is it not ironic that those who criticise the *General Theory* for being a 'short-run' theory, are so unwilling to take a long view themselves!

I have here restored the title I first gave the paper. The paper was published in the *British Review of Economic Issues*, as a consequence of my presenting the paper to the Association of Polytechnic Teachers of Economics in 1977, under the title 'Keynes's Theory, Keynesian Policy and the Postwar Inflation'. This title may give a better indication of the paper's contents, but it has never felt quite right to me.

* The author wishes to thank A. B. Atkinson, G. C. Harcourt, P. D. Jonson, J. A. Kregel, J. C. Michaelsen, H. P. Minsky, K. Schott, J. Spraos, I. Steedman, and E. L. Wheelwright for their comments. Most of the above had some strenuous objections, and doubtless not all of these have been met to their satisfaction. The paper has also benefited from the assistance of the editors of the *British Review of Economic Issues*. The author remains solely responsible for the final product. The paper was read at the 1977 Association of Polytechnic Teachers in Economics Conference in Bristol and at the First Australian Political Economy Conference in 1976.

## INTRODUCTION

The acceleration of inflation since the late 1960s, with its explosion of wage claims and government borrowing requirements, has been dazzling. Interpretations of the current inflation have tended to focus on immediate causes – the role of irresponsible unions or lax monetary authorities (depending on the proponent's reading of the data and political inclinations) and special features such as Russian wheat purchases and the oil crisis. These factors are, of course, important, but they should not be allowed to divert attention from a disturbing underlying pattern. Looking at the pattern of inflation in the UK and USA over the period since the Korean War as a whole, a steady rise in the inflation rate at the troughs of cyclical swings is revealed. The upswing, taking off from a rising floor, has generated progressively higher peak inflation rates (in the UK the 1956 peak is an exception to this pattern). Table 2.1 gives the data. In my view the recent inflation is best understood as the culmination of a process which began at the end of the Second World War, to which the special factors mentioned above have given added impetus. My thesis is that the root cause of the current inflation is a misapplication of the policy prescription of the *General Theory*; a policy designed as a short-run remedy has been turned into a long-run stimulus to growth, without examining its long-run implications.

*Table* 2.1 Rates of inflation at cyclical peaks and troughs: US and UK implicit price deflators: percentage change from previous year

| *UK: Total final output* | | *UK: Total final Expenditure* | | *US: GNP* | |
|---|---|---|---|---|---|
| *Trough* | *Peak* | *Trough* | *Peak* | *Trough* | *Peak* |
| 1948: 2.8 | 1950:12.4 | n.a. | n.a. | 1949: –0.6 | 1951: 6.7 |
| 1952: 0.5 | 1957: 5.5 | n.a. | 1956: 5.4 | 1953: 0.9 | 1957: 3.7 |
| | | 1960: 1.4 | 1962: 3.2 | 1962: 1.1 | 1970: 5.5 |
| | | 1963: 2.2 | 1965: 4.4 | 1972: 3.2 | 1974: 10.0 |
| | | 1967: 2.9 | 1971: 8.0 | | |
| | | 1972: 6.8 | 1975:24.3 | | |

*Source*: See Appendix Table A.2.1, which gives annual data.

The simple message taken from the *General Theory* was that to raise income one must invest. Hence postwar policy has offered direct or indirect encouragement to investment. Tax concessions to retained earnings and capital gains, investment allowances and grants, and accelerated depreciation allowances have been used fairly continuously; monetary policy aimed to lower interest rates and fiscal policy designed to raise demand have been used episodically.

Keynes's policy prescription was designed for a specific illness – unemployment and excess capital capacity in a world in which there was still considerable potential gain from further capital accumulation. The prescription, furthermore, was for a limited dose, designed to shock the patient into self-sustained recovery. It was not designed to sustain him over a long period. In administering Keynesian medicine continuously (though in fitful doses) for 30 years, we failed to heed Keynes's warning:

> *Each time we secure to-day's equilibrium by increased investment we are aggravating the difficulty of securing equilibrium tomorrow.* (1936, p. 105,[1] italics added.)

If full employment is adopted as a goal the maintenance of real wage income and a positive return on capital imply that the economy must *grow*. But to sustain ever higher levels of income, investment or government expenditure must continuously expand – at least in absolute terms and in the short term also relatively to national income – to fill the ever-widening gap between income and consumption.

Keynesians, though not Keynes, have assumed that expansionary policy will have no effect on prices when there is unemployment. For this reason the use of 'stabilisation' policies was not considered actually or potentially inflationary (since actively expansionary policies were pursued mainly in times of slack capacity). This optimistic expectation of price stability might be justified in the case of short-term or 'one-shot' use of expansionary policy, not, however, on Keynesian grounds but on the grounds of the potential price-reducing effects of improved technology and the capacity of a growing economy to absorb the new money used to finance deficits or monetise the public debt.

But the long-term effect of semi-continuous expansionary policy is bound to be inflationary, for growth cannot be sustained indefinitely. Theorems of balanced growth depend on population growth and technological change; without them, the economy moves to a stationary state. Growth theory also ignores problems created by the residue of money and debt left in the wake of investment. In the real world, the marginal efficiency of investment is expected to decline as the stock of capital increases,[2] partly because there are limits to the profitability of increasingly roundabout methods of production, and partly because the incentive to implement inventions, embodying them in new equipment at a rate sufficient to fill the ever-widening gap between consumption and income implied by growth, requires the expectation of an ever-increasing demand for the output of such equipment. In the absence of a significant income redistribution, achievement of the required rate of growth of demand depends on population growth. With a stable population ever-greater stimuli are required to maintain profitability and the growth of demand, and these generate, over time, an increasing volume which must be absorbed; continuous deficits or the pursuit of permanently low interest rates carry with them changes in the money supply which may vary in their pace but not in direction.

The postwar inflation can be looked upon as a way of forestalling the inevitable consequence of an increasing capital stock. It is both the concomitant of fiscal and monetary policies designed to promote growth – indeed, to maintain the viability of corporate enterprise as we know it – and a useful instrument in its own right, for it drives down the real rate of interest and reduces the burden of corporate and public debt.

While capital was still relatively scarce and technical change was keeping profits up and prices down, Keynesian policies appeared to be successful. In the body of the paper I shall argue that their success was short-lived – that Keynesian policies sowed the seeds of today's problem, precisely as Keynes had said.

But first I give a potted history of the experience of the UK and the USA (which very likely pertains to other developed countries as well) in the postwar period, for these are the stylised facts which bear on the theoretical discussion.

## SOME STYLISED FACTS

The postwar period began with a need for massive capital accumulation for reconstruction in Europe. Britain was particularly short of both productive capital and housing, having gone through a longer interwar slump than America or Europe due to her 1925 exchange rate decision. Indeed, rates of investment had been low even before the First World War. Matthews (1968) states that 'there had not been a single real boom in domestic investment in the whole of the twentieth century up to the end of the Second World War'.[3] In the interwar period, investment as a proportion of national income had reached only 8.8 per cent in 1929 and 10.3 per cent by the comparatively healthy year of 1937.[4]

Although not suffering the direct wartime destruction of industrial capital and housing, America also entered the postwar period with a depleted stock of capital suitable to peacetime production. Redirection of production toward consumer goods provided a strong impetus for investment, while pent-up demand, reinforced by the baby boom, could be financed from the high levels of liquid assets acquired during the war.

Furthermore, war is a great spur to technological progress; new, more capital-intensive modes of production were waiting to be applied to peacetime uses, and the sheer habit of invention had become established. The 1950s saw many new products, which kept demand high, while the embodiment of considerable technological progress reduced costs and the relative prices of consumer durables and raised the standard of living generally. Rising profits and rising real wages were compatible.

At the level of casual empiricism, one could say that, particularly in the USA, cracks in the system began to appear towards the end of the 1950s: built-in obsolescence and the creation of wants by advertising were the signals that genuine new product development and technical breakthroughs were giving way to trivial changes designed to stimulate conspicuous consumption without requiring major changes in productive techniques. The emphasis of technological change shifted away from cost-reducing innovations to demand-stimulating ones – and insofar as the latter relied on product changes, these were minor. This amounts to doing more of the same rather than doing something different or doing it by a different method, which is important in assessing the likely trend of marginal efficiency (see note 2).

The above remarks concern the quality of technical change. Estimates for the UK (Schott, 1976) indicate that the overall *scale* of technical change also has slowed down, though later – in the 1960s. Private industrial expenditure on research and development, deflated by an index of direct costs (manpower, materials and rent), rose steadily from 1950 to 1962, then fell for two years, recovered in the next two, and fell again from 1967 to 1970. In the USA, the Council of Economic Advisors in its 1977 *Report* noted a fall in output per man-hour from an average of 3.3 per cent per year in 1948–66 to 2.1 per cent in 1966–73, attributed to the slowing of the growth of capital, though whether this is due to a reduction in the embodiment of technical change is not stated.

The general picture is one in which technical change has slackened off, quantitatively and qualitatively, and in such circumstances one would expect to observe a decline in the marginal efficiency of capital. This implies a fall in the incentive to invest, unless compensated by a rising propensity to consume or an ever-falling interest rate.

The propensity to consume could be expected to respond to population growth or a redistribution of income toward lower income groups. Thus the postwar baby boom provided buoyancy for a time, but the rate of growth of population has now decreased in both countries (Appendix Table A.2.2). Evidence concerning income distribution is inconclusive. Appendix Table

A.2.3 indicates an early postwar redistribution toward the middle-income ranges away from both the high and low extremes in the UK. The US distribution exhibits some gain for lower-income groups; however, their low absolute levels of income would limit the rise in demand in absolute terms. Most favourable for demand is a significant shift towards the middle-, away from the upper-, income groups, and this does not appear to be substantial.[5] Blinder's investigations (1975), using a life-cycle approach, suggest that the consumption effect of redistribution in the USA (1949–72) may even have been perverse. Overall, it seems safe to say that there has been little obvious incentive to investment coming from income redistribution.

Interest rates, on the other hand, have offered encouragement, as they have tended to lag behind inflation. Real rates (the nominal rate less the rate of inflation) have often been negative (see Appendix Table A.2.4).

An indication of the fall of profits is given in Appendix Table A.2.5. The ratio of profits to GNP has been used instead of the theoretically preferable measure of the ratio of profits to capital because of the impossibility of measuring the latter. The roundaboutness of production has increased over the period, so Table A.2.5 gives an underestimate of the downward trend of the rate of profit on capital.

The tendency of the profitability of investment to fall is, of course, intolerable to enterprise and by the end of the 1950s probably also unacceptable to consumers, who had come to expect their incomes to grow. Investment must rise to achieve this growth but the incentive to invest formerly given by technological change had declined, and the stock of capital had by this time built up substantially. Thus to sustain a given rate of growth, greater policy action was necessary.

In the mid-1960s, as declining profit rates became readily apparent, the proportion of government expenditure in GNP began to rise sharply in the UK, and it continued its steady rise in the USA (Appendix Table A.2.6): if the tax, interest and demand incentives prove insufficient to close the gap between income and consumption, government expenditure must close the gap instead. At the same time, in the UK the inflation rate accelerated sharply in 1968 to continue its dramatic climb to the 24 per cent rate of 1975. The US rate showed the elevated cyclical pattern pointed to earlier (Table 2.1).

The acceleration of inflation at this time, possibly already underway to recoup private sector losses on investment where return had not fulfilled expectations, would have been exacerbated by the low productivity or long pay-off of most government expenditure. Expenditure on health and housing does not contribute, at least immediately, to the ability of the economy to produce. Indirect cost and price reductions deriving from a healthier population are delayed and intangible. Other forms of government expenditure, while more directly industrial, are long-term projects. The income-creating expenditure comes long before output, and tends to be inflationary meanwhile.

There are obvious examples of small or long-delayed returns – in the USA, the space programme and the war in Vietnam, in the UK, Concorde and aid to declining and inefficient industries. The present inflation has its roots in a prolonged period of artificially induced and misdirected investment and wasteful government expenditure in the name of *aggregate* demand management, undertaken without careful regard to the composition of demand or of production.

## SHORT-RUN EXCESS CAPACITY AND LONG-RUN CAPITAL INADEQUACY AS A BACKGROUND FOR POLICY

The theoretical justification for this interpretation of history is best understood against the background which generated The *General Theory* and led to its subsequent bowdlerisation.

Everyone is aware that the *General Theory* was written in a period of massive unemployment. But few (judging from my casual and biased sample) are aware of a basic assumption of the book, also derived from the immediate surroundings: that the existing stock of capital was inadequate, and that it was in the social interest to expand it substantially. Buried away in the Notes on the Trade Cycle is the keystone to the entire structure of argument in the *General Theory:*

> I am myself impressed with the great social advantages of increasing the stock of capital until it ceases to be scarce. (p. 327.)

In Keynes's view (pp. 322–3) even the country with the strongest claim to capital saturation, the United States, was a long way from it in 1929. This empirical assessment adds long-run desirability to short-run expediency in advocating government provision of a stimulus not just to demand generally but to investment in particular.

### The Role of Investment

It was easy to grasp the message that stimulating investment would encourage growth and employment, and Keynesians took it up with enthusiasm.

Not only was a country whose capital was increasing obviously growing; it was seen as becoming more *efficient* as well. Following the American pattern, the efficiency of productive techniques was evaluated in terms of output per head: capital-intensive methods of production were systematically encouraged. Particularly, failure of British industry to compete was (and still is) blamed largely on the low level of labour productivity.

Keynes's reasons for concentrating on investment demand in stimulating expansion were, however, somewhat different. Investment expenditure, being heavily dependent on expectations, is *volatile*; it can be manipulated as long as expectations themselves can be changed – in the Keynesian case, changed by unexpected sales, whether generated directly by government purchases or from a general rise in incomes fostered by government expenditure.

Expenditure on investment goods has the added advantage that the wisdom of that expenditure is not subject to rapid falsification through immediate confrontation with the market demand for its product. There is a lag; not only is there a gestation period before any product at all appears, but profits are realised over a long run of production, during which fluctuations in demand would normally be expected. A single disappointing year would not be taken as a sign that the investment was a mistake. Therefore, a successful shift of expectations towards greater optimism may be expected to induce a flow of investment for a considerable period. In contrast, expansion of the production of consumer goods is all too quickly submitted to the market test and cannot be relied upon to sustain a boom unless demand itself can be relied upon to remain high.

**The Gap between Income and Consumption**

Investment was not only useful, as the most volatile component of demand, in being easily manipulated by policy to cure a cyclical downturn. It was also essential that some portion of output always be devoted to it if income is to be raised permanently to a new level.

> [If] there is no change in the propensity to consume, employment cannot increase, unless at the same time $D_2$ is increasing so as to fill the increasing gap between $Z$ and $D_1$. (p. 30.)

This must be one of the best-known propositions in macroeconomics, yet its long-run significance appears to have been lost entirely. There are profound reasons for this, which are worth exploring.

The Keynesian short-run consumption function (with a positive intercept) presents an alarming picture: for higher levels of income to be sustained, a larger proportion of output will have to be devoted to non-consumption expenditure. So much the worse if we believe that the marginal propensity to consume declines with income. The spectre of secular stagnation or the alternative of an ever-increasing proportion of government expenditure was perhaps the subconscious spur to the development of theories of long-run consumption and empirical estimates of that function,[6] a homogeneous consumption function at least implies no long-term rise in the *share* of non-consumption expenditure.

This result offers false comfort, for it is still true that the *absolute* size of investment or government expenditure or both must rise, just to sustain a higher level of income. As is well known, Hansen's (1953) equilibrium interpretation of the multiplier (which I think was not what Keynes intended) shows that for the equilibrium level of income to be permanently changed, investment or government expenditure must permanently rise to a new level. If there is to be growth, the level must *continue* to rise. This result was obtained *without* considering the declining marginal efficiency of investment, which acts to accelerate the approach to the stationary state.

The policy of going for growth by stimulating investment and measuring success in terms of output per worker became an article of faith. There seems little concern about the long-run implications of these policies.[7] In so far as the long run has been taken into account we have had the reassurances of neoclassical growth theory in which balanced growth is possible. Keynes himself was more perceptive:

> The consumption for which we can profitably provide in advance cannot be pushed indefinitely into the future. . . . The greater, moreover, the consumption for which we have provided in advance, the more difficult it is to find something further to provide for in advance, and the greater our dependence on present consumption as a source of demand. Yet the larger our incomes, the greater, unfortunately, is the margin between our incomes and our consumption. . . .
>
> Or look at the matter thus. Consumption is satisfied partly by objects produced currently and partly by objects produced previously, i.e. by disinvestment. To the extent that consumption is satisfied by the latter, there is a contraction of current demand, since to that extent a part of current expenditure fails to find its way back as a part of net income. Contrariwise whenever an object is produced within the period with a view to satisfying consumption subsequently, an expansion of current demand is set up. Now all capital-investment is destined to result, sooner

> or later, in capital-disinvestment. Thus the problem of providing that new capital-investment shall always outrun capital-disinvestment sufficiently to fill the gap between net income and consumption, presents a problem which is increasingly difficult as capital increases. (p. 104–5.)

> [There is] no answer to the riddle, except that there must be sufficient unemployment to keep us so poor that our consumption falls short of our income by no more than the equivalent of the physical provision for future consumption which it pays to produce to-day. (p. 105.)

That is, the system converges to the stationary state, not the steady-state growth which we have come to expect and which postwar theory has led us to believe we could have.

## Stable Consumption and the Declining Marginal Efficiency of Capital

The difference between Keynes and the steady-state growthmen has perhaps two (real) roots. One concerns the dependence of investment on expected growth of future consumption. The growthmen rely on population growth to provide this stimulus. Even if population growth had not declined, however, consumption cannot be expected to increase without limit, even though *wants* are not similarly constrained. And the consumption-increasing potential of income redistribution has its limits, even when the redistribution itself is not opposed politically. Furthermore, there is no reason to suppose that incremental consumption will fall on the products of those industries with great scope for increasing the roundaboutness of their production methods, and it is these which must be encouraged if investment is to be maintained.

In the early postwar period the development of new products helped to keep up demand. But while firms may exercise considerable imagination in this sphere there is no guarantee that they will develop those products with the highest potential demand. (The profit motive does not ensure optimal innovation, for a want which cannot be translated into a demand for an existing product exerts no market pressure; market research is the only guide.) Indeed, much of the trouble lies with the failure of technological innovation and incremental consumption to *match*, for when they do not, the returns expected from the investment will not be forthcoming, and firms will consider raising prices on other product lines to cover losses on the unsuccessful projects.

In any case it has been argued above that as time went on, many 'new' products were only refinements, and there appear to be limits to the growth of expenditure on essentially similar products. Keynes remarked that this point was appreciated in the context of public expenditure but in fact held more force in the realm of private sector investment:

> It is commonly urged as an objection to schemes for raising employment by investment under the auspices of public authority that it is laying up trouble for the future. 'What will you do,' it is asked, 'when you have built all the houses and roads and town halls and electric grids and water supplies and so forth which the stationary population of the future can be expected to require?' But it is not so easily understood that the same difficulty applies to private investment and to industrial expansion; particularly to the latter, since it is much easier to see an early satiation of the demand for new factories and plant which absorb individually but little money, than of the demand for dwelling-houses. (p. 106.)

It is expansion along well-worked lines that exhausts demand and lowers the marginal efficiency of further investment in those lines. And here lies the second source of difference with the growthmen. They see growth chiefly as the embodiment of technical change, which counteracts the fall in the marginal efficiency. It is highly significant that in the absence of either population growth or continuous technological change, not only Keynes, but *modern growth theory also* predicts convergence to the stationary state.[8]

The falling marginal efficiency of successive increases of capital compounds the problem begun by the ever-increasing gap between consumption and income.

> But worse still. Not only is the marginal propensity to consume weaker in a wealthy community, but, owing to its accumulation of capital being already larger, the opportunities for further investment are less attractive unless the rate of interest falls at a sufficiently rapid rate. (p. 31.)

The rate of interest must fall at an ever-increasing rate (other things being equal), until it reaches its floor, after which net investment will be zero: the stationary state.

## THE AVOIDANCE OF THE STATIONARY STATE

Firms which live and grow by finding new outlets for expansion will not easily accept the state of affairs to which the accumulation of stocks of capital inexorably leads; investment covers only replacement, and profit can be no more than is strictly necessary to keep the productive machine ticking over. The gambling instinct would keep the stock exchange going:

> Provided there was some measurable unwillingness to undertake risk, there would also be a positive net yield from the aggregate of risky assets over a period of time. (p. 221.)

Not that it could be relied upon to do the job well:

> But it is not unlikely that, in such circumstances, the eagerness to obtain a yield from doubtful investments might be such that they would show in the aggregate a *negative* net yield. (*Ibid.*)

But apart from a return from genuine risk (which may backfire) the scope for saving at zero interest was, Keynes thought, nil:

> [A] little reflection will show what enormous social changes would result from a gradual disappearance of a rate of return on accumulated wealth. A man would still be free to accumulate his earned income with a view to spending it at a later date. But his accumulation would not grow. He would simply be in the position of Pope's father, who, when he retired from business, carried a chest of guineas with him to his villa at Twickenham and met his household expenses from it as required. (*Ibid.*)

This last supposition turns out not to be correct.[9] In aggregate, the normal profits of capital can be distributed to its owners or creditors. But the real interest on saving – that is, real consumption obtainable by the non-working, dissaving portion of the population in excess of the amount they had forgone – depends, in a stable population with stable consumption, on the ratio of working to non-working years. In more general terms it depends on some arrangement between the working and non-working sectors, *not* on the return to real investment or (necessarily the savers') time preference. A positive return to saving is not to be taken for granted, even though capital's net yield is just enough to pay its owners to keep it in production.

The political and social consequences of these features of the stationary state are obviously alarming. I have not seen them debated. Nor does there seem to be much discussion of the long-run effects of the substitution of capital for labour on employment. When economists deplore the narrow view of workers protesting against automation, the assumption is that expansion of capital generates enough income to provide employment for labour displaced by capital-intensive techniques. But this can only continue so long as the economy is growing. When it ceases to grow, equilibrium employment may be lower in the more capital-intensive economy.[10] Any expansion of capital poses this potential problem; it is exacerbated by the introduction of labour-saving techniques. Once again, the *General Theory* provides a warning absent from contemporary discussion:

> Assuming correct foresight, the equilibrium stock of capital which will have a marginal efficiency of precisely zero will, of course, be a smaller stock than would correspond to full employment of the available labour; for it will be the equipment which corresponds to that proportion of unemployment which ensures zero saving.
>
> The only alternative position of equilibrium would be given by a situation in which a stock of capital sufficiently great to have a marginal efficiency of zero also represents an amount of wealth sufficiently great to satiate to the full the aggregate desire on the part of the public to make provision for the future, even with full employment, in circumstances where no bonus is obtainable in the form of interest. It would, however, be an unlikely coincidence . . . (p. 218.)

What is suggested by this forecast is that government policy designed to stimulate private investment may be helpful for a time, although it is doomed to failure in the absence of renewed population growth, technical change or income redistribution, *or* a shift in the composition of output. Nevertheless, since the long-term end of capital accumulation threatens the social structure, government policies to support investment were pursued. Each time demand management or a low interest rate policy is pursued for contracyclical purposes it helps to forestall the long run – not because of the rise in demand or low interest themselves, for these are not adequate[11] – but by the inflationary consequences of these policies. Let us examine the mechanism more closely.

## The Inflation Mechanism

When demand is raised by a tax cut or increased government expenditure, money incomes are raised in advance of output. The inflationary impact is the more pronounced the greater the proportion of the deficit financed by new money. (A careful reading of the *General Theory*, p. 200, will show that Keynes assumed that the entire deficit would be so financed). The rise in money income shifts the aggregate demand curve upwards. The result, if the money wage is unchanged, is to raise the profit-maximising output of the industry *and* permit whatever rise in price is necessary to compensate for diminishing returns. Profits and prices rise and real wages fall. Expansionary policy can also be used to permit prices to rise to cover increased wage costs.

Keynes did not count all price rises as inflation. He distinguished between price rises which were necessary to make it profitable for firms to increase output, and 'true inflation'. The latter was defined as the extreme case in which prices rose with *no attendant expansion of output whatsoever*. It can be seen that true inflation occurs when demand rises in the context of perfectly full capacity or when an expected rise in demand is matched by an equivalent expected rise in input prices.

The concept of true inflation was designed to convince policy-makers that not all inflation was bad, and thus influence their judgement of what constituted legitimate expenditure. The demonstration that the protection of employment through demand management does not give rise to *true* inflation if the threat to employment is due to slack demand was important politically. And in the Marshallian long run even a bout of 'true inflation' in some industries may not matter, as long as there is excess capacity in the capital goods industries, for demand pressure on resources (or the combination of demand and cost pressure) may lead to the installation of new capital, reducing costs and possibly (but not necessarily) reducing prices. Cases of 'true inflation' are not likely; even the validation of wage claims is unlikely to be 'perfect'.[12] In general expansionary policies will result in some increase in output, some increase in prices. The important point is that over time, larger and larger stimuli will be required to obtain the same increase in output;[13] a given stimulus will result in progressively larger price increases and progressively smaller output increases. This will be so even if labour does not attempt fully to restore its real wage.

The same remarks apply to interest rate policy through monetisation of the public debt. Over the longer term, the rate of interest must be made to fall at ever more rapid rates to achieve the same investment result. Larger and larger increases in the money supply will be necessary and this must be inflationary.

## Inflation, the Real Rate of Interest and the Debt Burden

But inflation is not just a by-product of fiscal and monetary policies – it has a beneficial effect on investment in its own right; it not only bolsters total revenue, but also reduces the real rate of interest and lowers the real value of outstanding debt. It was a despairing complaint of the *General Theory* that the rate of interest could not be pushed down indefinitely; the absolute floor was set by the existence of an acceptable non-interest-bearing asset, and for practical purposes the floor was somewhat higher, determined by belief concerning the normal rate. Inflation, in contrast, has no ceiling, short of repudiation of the monetary standard. However, *real* rates of interest can be (and are) negative and can continue to fall over time as long as inflation is not fully anticipated by savers or as long as they do not have a range of action adequate to ensure that they obtain a satisfactory rate of return. Both these factors operate, the second if for no other reason than the high transactions costs and low liquidity associated with placing saving in some markets. Hence, inflation permits borrowers, notably corporations and the government, to obtain funds cheaply.

Inflation achieves a permanent transfer of resources from surplus to deficit sectors, and a permanent destruction of some of the real value of financial wealth. The extent to which inflation has destroyed the real value of claims in the United States has been estimated by Bach and Stephenson (1974). On the assumption that one-half to two-thirds of actual rates of inflation were anticipated by creditors, $500–667 billion were destroyed between 1946 and 1972.[14] These funds were effectively transferred to debtors – that is, to government and industry, to finance investment or government expenditure. With $4.2 trillion of debt outstanding in 1973, each 1 per cent of unanticipated inflation transferred $42 billion from creditors to debtors for further capital accumulation or government expenditure.The usefulness of inflation in reducing the real rate of interest and transferring funds does however appear to have limits, through its effects on company balance sheets.

## Wasteful and Misdirected Investment

The amount of inflation a given expansionary stimulus will generate depends on how well funds are channelled into productive investment. After years of concentrating on broad Keynesian aggregates, this point has finally got through to the British Government, as these remarks by Chancellor of the Exchequer Denis Healey (1975) illustrate:

> It is no good throwing money down the drain to keep firms or industries going if they are not producing the sort of things which the world is going to buy. . . . The fact is that our manufacturing industry is badly wrong at present. We are producing far too many things that other people do not want and at prices they cannot afford.

The short-run implication is clear. If we are prepared to administer Keynesian medicine selectively, we should be able to maintain a given level of employment at a far lower cost in terms of inflation.

To look at the point from the opposite direction, the inflationary impact of wasteful expenditure can most easily be seen in the extreme case, when, in the short run at least, money incomes are generated but there is no additional output. It is a matter of arithmetic that prices will rise.

Price rises can also compensate for investment projects which, *ex post*, proved not to yield their expected return, and hence can be used to shift the burden of entrepreneurial error or government misestimate away from those directly responsible on to the public at large. The more of such expenditure there is, the more inflationary is any expansionary policy.

The point is so obvious that one wonders why such an unselective approach to policy has been taken heretofore. I suggest three reasons. The first is that it avoids any suggestion of planning or directing activity which, it is widely believed (especially in the United States), should be controlled by private enterprise. The second derives from the environment which shaped Keynes's views: in a period of large-scale unemployment it did not much matter *what* was produced as long as more jobs were offered. Furthermore, even wasteful and misdirected expenditure would have multiplier effects – and these would largely affect output, not prices, in a period of slack capacity:

> It may be that [a policy of deterring over-optimism with high interest rates] overlooks the social advantage which accrues from the increased consumption which attends even on investment which proves to have been totally misdirected, so that even such investment may be more beneficial than no investment at all. (p. 327.)

Not that he approved:

> It would, indeed, be more sensible to build houses and the like; but if there are political and practical difficulties in the way of this, the above would be better than nothing. (p. 129.)

The third possibility is that wasteful expenditure is a blessing in disguise! It may even have been encouraged consciously, to serve a real social purpose, for it postpones the day when 'the abundance of capital will interfere with the abundance of output':

> Ancient Egypt was doubly fortunate, and doubtless owed to this its fabled wealth, in that it possessed two activities, namely, pyramid-building as

> well as the search for the precious metals, the fruits of which, since they could not serve the needs of man by being consumed, did not stale with abundance. The Middle Ages built cathedrals and sang dirges. Two pyramids, two masses for the dead, are twice as good as one; but not so two railways from London to York. (p. 131.)

For a time, when inflation was beneficial in promoting investment, there was no conflict between these two ways of postponing the stationary state. And perhaps now that a recession has developed in earnest, there is no immediate need for these measures, for the recession itself will see to the writing-off of capital when less painful methods have failed. If what Western economies need is to restructure their technology to take account of radically altered fuel costs and to re-estimate future demand patterns, there may have been no real alternative to recession, given that demand management was generating an inflation which itself had become unproductive.

## AN ALTERNATIVE

There is a more humane form of postponement of the stationary state. This was Keynes's suggestion:

> The wisest course is to advance on both fronts at once. Whilst aiming at a socially controlled rate of investment with a view to a progressive decline in the marginal efficiency of capital, I should support at the same time all sorts of policies for increasing the propensity to consume. For it is unlikely that full employment can be maintained, whatever we may do about investment, with the existing propensity to consume. There is room, therefore, for both policies to operate together; – to promote investment and, at the same time, to promote consumption, not merely to the level which with the existing propensity to consume would correspond to the increased investment, but to a higher level still. (p. 325.)

Increased consumption is not a panacea. There are limits to income redistribution, although internationally the scope is vast. But growth theory tells us that for growth to be sustained, the proportion of consumption to investment must be *exactly right*, continuously, even when there is technical change and population growth to support a positive growth path. (Getting the composition of output right was the subject of Chancellor Healey's remarks cited above.) In their absence, the process converges on the stationary state as before, though private consumption would displace some of the government expenditure that currently keeps the system going.

## CONCLUSION

Without a large-scale destruction of capital by war, natural disaster or major recession or other economic upheaval, the stationary state is inevitable. Attempts to forestall it are inflationary; they can be more or less so depending on the areas to which funds are channelled, but the outcome is inescapable. It is merely a matter of time.

If we had felt the need for an estimate, Keynes provided one. From the *General Theory* we have:

> It is, indeed, very possible that the prolongation of approximately full employment over a period of years would be associated in countries so wealthy as Great Britain or the United States with a volume of new investment, assuming the existing propensity to consume, so great that it would eventually lead to a state of full investment in the sense that an aggregate gross yield in excess of replacement cost could no longer be expected on a reasonable calculation from a further increment of durable goods of any type whatever. Moreover, this situation might be reached comparatively soon – say within twenty-five years or less. (pp. 323–4.)

That brings us to 1961. And from Lord Kahn (1956; 1972, p. 108) we have the following:

> Not that the right balance between consumption and investment lends itself to dogmatic assertion. In 1943 Keynes was discussing this point with Mr Josiah Wedgwood and wrote: 'It would be in the interests of the standard of life in the long run if we increased our capital quite materially. After twenty years of large-scale investment I should expect to have to change my mind'.

And we should have expected to change our theory of economic policy.

### Notes

1. All page references are to the *General Theory*, unless otherwise specified.
2. It is not being claimed that the aggregate stock of capital can be measured. Indeed, the marginal efficiency of investment is only unambiguously defined for each type of capital equipment taken alone. Hence in aggregate it applies, strictly, only to additions to capital which are identical to the existing stock.

Clearly this formal concept cannot be applied to actual investment with any degree of precision; it is meant to convey the admittedly immeasurable notion that the net contribution to output from each increment to capital falls as the stock of capital increases. The concept is more applicable in aggregate the slower the rate of technical change.

3. (1968, p. 561.) He continues, 'In forty years preceding 1948 the domestic stock of fixed capital is estimated to have risen at a rate of scarcely more than one per cent per annum.'
4. Matthews, 1968, pp. 559 and 561. I am indebted to Joan Vipond for calling this article to my attention.
5. Atkinson (1975, p. 53) perceives some gain for the two groups just below the top 20 per cent at the expense of the extremes, similar to the UK pattern.
6. It is almost superfluous to cite the pioneering theoretical work of Duesenberry (1959), Friedman (1957) and Modigliani and Ando (1960) and the estimates of Kuznets (1946).
7. Indeed the very concept of the Marshallian long run has given way to quite another definition: the state in which everything is perfectly anticipated.
8. It is also significant that financial aspects of growth are omitted. It has been shown that even the *IS–LM* version of Keynes (which, being strictly short-run, leaves no room for downward shifts in the MEI schedule) converges to the stationary state once financing of investment is taken into account (Chick, 1973a; ch. 4, this volume).
9. I am grateful to Professor J. Michaelsen, not only for pointing this out to me but working with me until we got it (I hope) right. Later I remembered Samuelson (1958) and Robinson (1960), who explore the point.
10. The result depends on the level of income to which the system converges.
11. Recall that a *low* interest rate stimulates investment for a time, but a *falling* rate is necessary to raise it permanently to a new level. A rise in demand will stimulate investment in the short run but it must be expected to continue rising for the new level to be maintained.
12. It is worth pointing out that even if costs are exactly covered, *profit* margins in general will not be left unchanged; if profits are measured as the mark-up over marginal cost, only an isoelastic shift of demand will leave them unaffected.
13. Friedman argues this point, but on other grounds, namely, that a given rate of inflation becomes ineffective as it becomes anticipated.
14. The figure would be $1.5 trillion if inflation were wholly unanticipated.

**Appendix**

*Table* A.2.1 Implicit price deflators: US, 1946–76; UK, 1948–76: percentage change from previous year P = Peak T = Trough

| *During* | *US: GNP* | *UK: Total final expenditure* | *UK: Total final output* |
|---|---|---|---|
| 1946 | 12.2 | | |
| 1947 | 18.4 P | | |
| 1948 | 6.7 | | 2.8 T |
| 1949 | −0.6 T | | 3.4 |
| 1950 | 1.4 | | 12.4 P |
| 1951 | 6.7 P | | 5.7 |
| 1952 | 2.2 | | 0.5 T |
| 1953 | 0.9 T | | 1.4 |
| 1954 | 1.5 | 1.2 | 4.1 |
| 1955 | 1.5 | 3.9 | 5.5 |
| 1956 | 3.4 | 5.4 P | 5.5 |
| 1957 | 3.7 | 3.5 | 5.5 P |
| 1958 | 2.6 | 2.3 | 3.5 |
| 1959 | 1.6 | 1.1 | |
| 1960 | 1.7 | 1.4 T | |
| 1961 | 1.3 | 2.7 | |
| 1962 | 1.1 T | 3.2 P | |
| 1963 | 1.3 | 2.2 T | |
| 1964 | 1.6 | 3.3 | |
| 1965 | 1.8 | 4.4 P | |
| 1966 | 2.6 | 4.1 | |
| 1967 | 3.1 | 2.9 T | |
| 1968 | 4.3 | 5.6 | |
| 1969 | 4.8 | 5.0 | |
| 1970 | 5.5 P | 7.3 | |
| 1971 | 4.7 | 8.0 P | |
| 1972 | 3.2 T | 6.8 T | |
| 1973 | 5.5 | 10.2 | |
| 1974 | 10.0 P | 19.0 | |
| 1975 | 9.6 | 24.3 P | |
| 1976 | 5.3 | 16.7 | |

*Sources*:
US: *The National Income and Product Accounts of the US, 1929–1965* and *Survey of Current Business.*
UK: 1948–53, 1963 Blue Book, Table 16; 1954–73, 1974 Blue Book, Table 17; 1975–6, 1977 Blue Book, Table 2.5.

*Table* A.2.2 Population growth, US and UK, 1945–75: Percentage change over five-year periods

| | *US* | *UK* |
|---|---|---|
| 1945–50 | 8.57 | 2.85 |
| 1950–55 | 9.21 | 5.93 |
| 1955–60 | 9.04 | 2.95 |
| 1960–65 | 7.18 | 3.63 |
| 1965–70 | 5.67 | 2.21 |
| 1970–75 | 4.39 | 0.91 |

*Sources*:
US: *Statistical Abstract of the US*, 1976.
UK: *Annual Abstract of Statistics*, 1952, 1977.

*Table* A.2.3 Income distribution

(a) Official estimates of distribution of income, before and after tax, United Kingdom 1949–67: Percentage share of total income

| | *Before tax* | | | *After tax* | | |
|---|---|---|---|---|---|---|
| | *Top 10%* | *Next 60%* | *Bottom 30%* | *Top 10%* | *Next 60%* | *Bottom 30%* |
| 1949 | 33.2 | 54.1 | 12.7 | 27.1 | 58.3 | 14.6 |
| 1954 | 29.8 | 59.3 | 10.9 | 24.8 | 63.1 | 12.1 |
| 1959 | 29.4 | 60.9 | 9.7 | 25.2 | 63.5 | 11.2 |
| 1964 | 29.0 | 61.4 | 9.6 | 25.1 | 64.1 | 10.8 |
| 1967 | 28.0 | 61.6 | 10.4 | 24.3 | 63.7 | 12.0 |

(b) Official estimates of distribution of income before tax, United States 1947–72: Percentage share of total income

| | *Top 20%* | *Next 20%* | *Middle 20%* | *Fourth 20%* | *Bottom 20%* |
|---|---|---|---|---|---|
| 1947 | 45.5 | 23.8 | 16.8 | 10.5 | 3.4 |
| 1952 | 44.0 | 24.3 | 17.4 | 10.9 | 3.4 |
| 1957 | 43.4 | 25.2 | 18.1 | 10.3 | 3.0 |
| 1962 | 44.1 | 24.9 | 17.2 | 10.5 | 3.3 |
| 1967a | 43.9 | 24.7 | 17.2 | 10.5 | 3.7 |
| 1967b | 42.7 | 24.7 | 17.6 | 10.5 | 4.5 |
| 1972 | 43.9 | 24.6 | 16.8 | 10.5 | 4.2 |

*Source*: Atkinson (1975), p. 52. 1947–67a and 1967b–72 from different primary sources.

*Table* A.2.4. Real yields: UK and US, 1946-76
(per cent per year)

| Year | *UK* Dividend yield less 1 | Treasury bill rate less 2 | *US* Treasury bill rate less 3 |
|---|---|---|---|
| 1946 | n.a. | n.a. | –11.8 |
| 1947 | n.a. | n.a. | –18.0 |
| 1948 | 2.36 | –2.29 | –5.7 |
| 1949 | 2.26 | –2.88 | 1.8 |
| 1950 | –6.55 | –11.89 | –0.2 |
| 1951 | –0.09 | –5.19 | –4.8 |
| 1952 | 6.66 | 1.95 | –0.5 |
| 1953 | 5.52 | 0.97 | 1.1 |
| 1954 | 4.99 | 0.41 | –0.9 |
| 1955 | 2.27 | 0.07 | –0.1 |
| 1956 | 1.60 | –0.26 | –0.9 |
| 1957 | 3.41 | 0.35 | –0.5 |
| 1958 | 4.77 | 1.99 | –1.8 |
| 1959 | 4.17 | 2.28 | 1.7 |
| 1960 | 3.41 | 4.16 | 0.4 |
| 1961 | 2.54 | 1.77 | 1.0 |
| 1962 | { 2.50 | 0.18 | 1.8 |
| 1963 | { 2.73 | 1.46 | 1.7 |
| | 2.31 | | |
| 1964 | 1.31 | 1.11 | 1.8 |
| 1965 | 1.51 | 1.07 | 2.0 |
| 1966 | 0.98 | 1.58 | 1.8 |
| 1967 | 2.26 | 2.29 | 0.7 |
| 1968 | –1.91 | 1.69 | 1.1 |
| 1969 | –1.10 | 2.93 | 1.4 |
| 1970 | –2.78 | –0.45 | 1.0 |
| 1971 | –4.04 | –2.41 | 1.5 |
| 1972 | –3.49 | –1.16 | 0.8 |
| 1973 | –6.10 | –3.24 | 2.0 |
| 1974 | –11.00 | –7.76 | –2.3 |
| 1975 | –17.60 | –14.82 | –3.7 |
| 1976 | –10.54 | –5.44 | 0.1 |

*Notes and Sources*:
Col. 1: Industrial ordinary share dividend yield. Average over the year. 1948–66: Grant (1972), p. 110. 1967–76: *Annual Abstract of Statistics*, 1977.
from Table A.2.1. 1948–53, deflator for total final output. 1954–76, deflator for total final expenditure.
Col. 2: 3-month allotment rate, last trading day of June. Bank of England *Financial Statistics*, 1970 and *Quarterly Bulletin*. as for Col. 1.
Col. 3: 3-month rate. Source as for Col. 2. from Table A.2.1.

*Table* A.2.5 Profit shares; US and UK, 1946–76

| *Year* | *UK* *Profit as a percentage of total final output* | | *US* *Corporate profits as a percentage of national income* |
|---|---|---|---|
| | *a* | *b* | |
| 1946 | | 25.6 | n.a. |
| 1950 | | 23.4 | 12.2 |
| 1955 | | 23.6 | 13.1 |
| 1960 | | 24.4 | 12.1 |
| 1965 | | 23.5 | 13.3 |
| 1966 | 22.6 | 22.3 | 13.2 |
| 1967 | 22.8 | 22.5 | 12.1 |
| 1968 | 22.9 | 21.7 | 11.4 |
| 1969 | 22.1 | | 9.6 |
| 1970 | 21.1 | | 7.9 |
| 1971 | 21.5 | | 8.4 |
| 1972 | 22.3 | | 9.0 |
| 1973 | 21.5 | | 7.6 |
| 1974 | 18.4 | | 4.0 |
| 1975 | 18.1 | | 6.6 |
| 1976 | 18.5 | | n.a. |

*Notes and Sources*:
UK: Gross profits and other trading income, before providing for depreciation but after providing for stock appreciation. Source: Col. a, 1975 Blue Book; Col. b, 1969 and earlier Blue Books.
US: Corporate profits before tax and depreciation allowance but after inventory valuation adjustment. Source: *Statistical Abstract of the US*.

*Table* A.2.6 Share of government spending

| *Year* | *UK, 1962–76* | *US, 1947–76* |
|---|---|---|
| 1947 | | 0.109 |
| 1948 | | 0.123 |
| 1949 | | 0.148 |
| 1950 | | 0.133 |
| 1951 | | 0.180 |
| 1952 | | 0.216 |
| 1953 | | 0.224 |
| 1954 | | 0.205 |
| 1955 | | 0.186 |
| 1956 | | 0.188 |
| 1957 | | 0.195 |
| 1958 | | 0.211 |
| 1959 | | 0.201 |
| 1960 | | 0.198 |
| 1961 | | 0.207 |
| 1962 | 0.194 | 0.209 |
| 1963 | 0.193 | 0.207 |
| 1964 | 0.188 | 0.204 |
| 1965 | 0.193 | 0.200 |
| 1966 | 0.198 | 0.209 |
| 1967 | 0.208 | 0.227 |
| 1968 | 0.206 | 0.231 |
| 1969 | 0.205 | 0.226 |
| 1970 | 0.210 | 0.225 |
| 1971 | 0.207 | 0.222 |
| 1972 | 0.212 | 0.221 |
| 1973 | 0.208 | 0.213 |
| 1974 | 0.224 | 0.221 |
| 1975 | 0.244 | 0.222 |
| 1976 | 0.244 | 0.212 |

*Notes and Sources*:
UK: Public authorities' expenditure on goods and services as a share of GDP, Blue Book, 1977 and earlier.
US: Government purchases of goods and services as a share of GNP, *Survey of Current Business*, Table 1, and the *The National Income and Product Accounts of the US, 1929–65*, Table 1.

# 3 The Nature of the Keynesian Revolution: A Reassessment*

## Author's Note

Bob Clower's 1965 paper, 'The Keynesian Counter-revolution', was a great breakthrough. I can still remember thinking quickly enough, at its presentation in Durham, to anticipate, and to be knocked over by, its conclusion – for at that time the applicability to macroeconomics of the neo-Walrasian system of counting equations and unknowns was unquestioned. A calypso from an LSE students' sketch began:

Come mister tallyman, tally me equation
What de hell is Walras' Law?

I read Walras's *Elements* in 1968. I can remember, because that year Hy Minsky was visiting Cambridge and London. I was deeply engrossed one evening when I broke off and walked through the snow to the Minskys' flat in The Pryors, on Hampstead Heath, where Jim Thomas and I had been invited for 10 p.m. It seemed an odd hour; I was completely unaware that it was New Year's Eve.

I was also working my way out of *IS–LM* – the first drafts of Chapter 4 were written then – and into Myrdal and back to the *General Theory*. I began to see that although Clower had done something very important, what he had said was not, actually, quite right. I began an early draft with a paraphrase of lines from *Murder in the Cathedral:*

This last temptation is the highest treason:
To say the right thing for the wrong reason.

The problem lay as much with the gap between Walras's economics and the economics of Walras as with the applicability of the former to the *General Theory*. It would have been obvious that the economics of Walras and of Keynes were worlds apart, but the starting point, both for Clower and for the rest of us, was, rather, Walrasian and Keynesian economics.

No paper has ever cost me such expense of spirit: every inch of it has been fought over. Special thanks are due to Geoff Harcourt as editor of the *Australian Economic Papers* for his encouragement and for publishing it.

In *Australian Economic Papers*, December 1981, there is a comment by G. W. Harrison, a younger colleague of Clower's at UCLA, and my reply. Since in my

* The author wishes to thank members of staff seminars at the Universities of Oxford, Reading and Louvain, Susan Howson, Geoff Harcourt and anonymous referees for their comments and criticism of an earlier version of this paper.

view no new ground was broken by this exchange, it is not printed here. Readers might also like to look at Colin Rogers's 'Critique of Clower's Dual Decision Hypothesis', *South African Journal of Economics*, 1985.

*Note*: I have punctuated the possessive of Walras according to the conventions of speech, hence 'Walras's economics', 'Walras' Law'.

## INTRODUCTION

Two propositions, widely held, are evidence that the Keynesian Revolution remains to be made:

1. The macroeconomics of the *General Theory* (Keynes, 1936) do not rest on proper microeconomic foundations.
2. The *General Theory* is the economics of disequilibrium.

The first proposition implies that the economic malfunctioning described by Keynes is due to irrationality or some other impediment to 'correct' behaviour on the part of households and firms (utility and profit maximisation, respectively) and fosters the idea that the consumption function is based on *ad hoc* assumptions[1] rather than solid microeconomic foundations.[2] The second proposition lends modern support to the classical view that unemployment is really only transitory – largely frictional – thus paving the way for Phelps *et al.* (1970) to argue that if only labour were to be fully informed about the true situation, they would, in periods of unemployment, quickly accept a lower wage rather than continuing a fruitless search for employment at the going wage.[3] As it is, some argue, the economy (for some unspecified reason) is slow to adjust to labour market disequilibrium: Keynes's 'unemployment equilibrium' is just a disequilibrium that lasts a long time.[4] Others assert that at best, Keynes established a 'modified temporary equilibrium' (Bliss, 1975). In contrast, Keynes, by demonstrating the possibility of underemployment equilibrium, drew attention to the possibility that unemployment might persist indefinitely if left untouched by policy (Keynes, 1936, p. 30). The private sector in this state generates no force for adjustment towards full employment.[5]

Even those economists not alarmed by the implication that there could be situations in which the private sector was utterly reliant on either chance or the state to cure its ills were repelled by the idea of a system which did not tend to eliminate imbalance of supply and demand in all markets. In fact, to most economists in Keynes's time and our own, unemployment equilibrium is a sheer contradiction in terms. We have at last been told what we knew all along, that the persistent denial of the possibility of underemployment equilibrium is necessary 'If the purity of neoclassical equilibrium is [to be] preserved' (Tobin, 1975, p. 196). At the more general level, the overall assessment of the *General Theory* as an analysis of disequilibrium situations[6] leaves open the question of whether the classical theory is consistent with Keynes, as a special case valid only in equilibrium. Clower (1965) asserted that the classical theory, including Walras' Law, continues to hold in equilibrium, the Keynesian Revolution notwithstanding. Arrow (1967) is agnostic on this point.

These views, that the *General Theory* only analyses disequilibrium situations and that it has no proper microeconomic foundation, challenge both the analytical foundations and the generality of the *General Theory*, reducing it to a 'special' theory of limited applicability. The burden of the argument in this paper is that such views are erroneous and that they obscure the true nature of the Keynesian Revolution.

Important support for these false ideas came from Clower's celebrated appraisal of the Keynesian Counter-revolution (Clower, 1965). I shall argue that although his central conclusion – that Walras' Law does not hold in Keynes's system – is correct and has been a liberating force of considerable power, the analysis which leads to that conclusion is not correct; thus the same analysis is able to support the erroneous conclusions as well.

This chapter has a two-fold purpose:

1. To make the case that Keynes's Revolution lies in his choice of analytical method. Keynes applied a rudimentary process analysis to an economy characterised by a definite sequence of decisions and events through time.[7] In contrast, in the neoclassical economy, to all intents and purposes everything happens at once. As a result of this change of method, it is no longer appropriate to treat 'equilibrium' as synonymous with the absence of excess demand or supply in every market.
2. To demonstrate that Clower's analysis is, with respect to the above contrast, neoclassical in structure and thus unable to illuminate the nature of the Keynesian Revolution. It is also flawed. In particular, I shall argue, contradicting Clower,

   (i) that the general-equilibrium equations are quantity-constrained; hence quantity constraints cannot be an innovation of Keynes;
   (ii) that the dual decision hypothesis, which has been widely taken up[8] and used as the basis for further theoretical development,[9] is inconsistent with Keynes's method and is a misspecification of the behaviour of households;
   (iii) that Keynes's analysis is inconsistent with general-equilibrium

> analysis, but not with the theory of household behaviour.[10] The consumption function is firmly rooted in standard value theory.

My perspective is not historical. I shall not comment on the nature of the break Keynes made or thought he made with classical economic theory as it was understood in his time. The Keynesian Counter-revolution keeps cropping up in different guises; one can fruitfully contrast Keynes with the dominant theory – which has never ceased to be neoclassical – at any stage of the development of that theory. The question, 'What do we understand by Keynes's contribution?' is at least as important as, 'What did Keynes think he was doing?' So while I am well aware that from the standpoint of the latter question, it would not be correct to use the consumer theory of Hicks and Allen (1934) and Hicks's (1939) interpretation of Walras as the point of departure for Keynes's innovation, it is not illegitimate in terms of the former question. Indeed, it is these elements of neoclassical analysis that form the backdrop in Clower's piece; for the most part I shall adopt the same convention. I shall introduce Walras's own conceptions as well, while recognising that there is no evidence that the *Elements* (Walras, 1926) had much influence on Keynes.

## KEYNES *v.* GENERAL EQUILIBRIUM

No one doubts that Keynes's economics differs from general-equilibrium analysis in some way.[11] The point at issue is the nature of that difference. Again, no one doubts that in Keynes not all plans are realised, for perfect realisation would preclude involuntary unemployment. The important question is *why* they are not realised.

Earlier explanations in terms of rigidities imposed by assumption have given way to Clower's proposition that the introduction of quantity constraints is the distinguishing feature of Keynes's system. Keynes, Clower argues, recognised that unemployment gives rise to a dual decision, in which plans are revised according to realised incomes, thus introducing quantity constraints. This system is shown to be inconsistent with Walras' Law. Since Walras' Law always holds in general-equilibrium analysis, Clower concludes that the dual decision hypothesis constitutes Keynes's radical contribution.

### Exchange Models

In coming to his conclusion, Clower contrasts Keynes with a bastardised Walrasian model, which while appearing and purporting to be a production model, is in fact a model of exchange. The significance of this choice will be explored further below. Here, let us note the main features of Walras's (as opposed to the bastard Walrasian) exchange model:

1. Total quantities of the exchangeable items are fixed.
2. There is no borrowing.
3. Because there is no production and no borrowing there are no derived demands (for example, for labour as a productive input or for funds to finance expenditure).
4. Prices, and contracts to exchange, are fixed at a point of time.
5. Once prices are set, they apply to all exchange transactions taking place within the 'Hicksian week', as well as determining the value of the budget constraint to which all exchanges are subject.
6. Finding the equilibrium price vector is assumed to be a costless procedure; no trade takes place until it is found.
7. Everyone has perfect knowledge of prices; hence all traders will attain the optimum consistent with their constraints. (Plans will be realised.)
8. Trading is riskless and costless; hence there is no need for a medium of exchange.

In contrast, the *General Theory* presents a model of a *production* economy, using *money*, moving through *time*, subject to *uncertainty* and the possibility of *error*. Is it any wonder that Walras' Law does not hold!?

It would be foolish to try to identify *one* of these differences as the key to the Keynesian Revolution – they all occurred at once. But while much has been made of the role of money, little significance has been attached to Keynes's emphasising that he was analysing a production economy.[12] Production, unlike exchange, *necessarily takes time*. As such, it imposes an *ordered sequence of economic decisions*, necessarily overlapping continuously in time at the macroeconomic level but quite distinct at the micro level.

## Keynes's Production Theory and Time

It is now commonplace to describe the *General Theory* as a theory of an ongoing economy in which time enters in a significant way.[13] But this is more asserted than explained. The role of production is crucial. In the nature of things, production is a decision to produce now in order to offer output for sale in the future – and the future is unknown.[14] In Keynes's world, firms are not allowed to know or arrange the future but are made to act on forecasts of demand. They must commit resources to production *before* knowing for certain what the demand for the output will be.

The lapse of time during production is one source of uncertainty. Households are also uncertain. When planning how much labour to offer, they cannot be sure whether they will be able to sell it, nor do they know future consumer prices.

The time-consuming nature of production does more than introduce general uncertainty. Recognition of the ordered sequence of economic decisions which is inherent in production necessitated a change in the whole method of analysis, away from the solution of simultaneous comparative static equations towards process analysis.[15] The structure of that sequence is responsible for an asymmetry in the ability of households and firms to influence economic events, and so to reach optimum positions. This asymmetry is crucial to the existence of underemployment equilibrium.

A unit production period may be imagined to be divided into four subperiods. The sequence, which is of course going on continuously as firms make decisions at different times, is as follows:

$t = 0$: Plans are made:

In a given climate of long-run expectations,[16] firms formulate their short-run expectations of costs and demand and determine their output and supply price on this basis. In terms of Keynes's aggregate approach the point of intersection between the aggregate supply function and firms' estimate of the aggregate demand function[17] gives the point of effective demand – the profit-maximising output/price combination given the forecast level of demand. The output decision determines the demand for labour.

At the same time, households simultaneously decide how much labour to offer, on the basis of *their* expectations of prices and wages, and how their income shall be allocated between consumption and saving. This is assumed to be done in accordance with the principles of consumer choice (a full derivation is given in the following section). In addition to this plan, which conforms to the anticipated outcome, they also formulate contingency plans for other levels of income, in case their expectations of wages or employment are disappointed. Thus they have a consumption *schedule*, not just one planned consumption *level*, the point on the schedule which they most expect.

$t = 1/4$: The labour market 'opens':

Households and firms now interact, as firms make their offers of employment. There is no 'auctioneer' to ensure that these offers are adequate to employ everyone wishing to work. For simplicity, we follow Keynes in assuming that firms can get all the labour they want at the wage they expected to pay. Then all production plans can be met. Households, however, may not succeed in selling all they wish.

$t = 2/4$: Implementation of plans:

In Keynes there is no recontracting; whatever the outcome, the labour market is now *closed*. (This establishes the possibility of unemployment, but does not yet establish unemployment equilibrium.) Given the assumptions we have made, firms pursue their production targets as planned in $t = 0$.

If households' expectations are met, and their wage expectations were the same as firms', they too shall implement the planned offer of employment and *level* of consumption thought most likely at $t = 0$. Households' expectations of income may, however, be disappointed. Assume for simplicity that the wage was as expected; disappointment comes in the form of unemployment. If there is an excess supply of labour, households revise downwards their planned consumption level to suit the income they have now contracted to receive during the 'year', in accordance with the contingency plan made in $t = 0$; that is, they move to a lower point on their consumption schedules.

$t = 3/4$: The goods market 'opens':

The goods come onto the market. Once again there is no recontracting; the goods have been produced and their prices set. Firms' estimates of demand are either confirmed or falsified.

If falsified, some revision of price and output may take place, *next* period or some subsequent period. (More than one observation may be required.) Offers of employment may change when the labour market 'reopens'. If firms' expectations are confirmed, output, prices and offers of employment will not change next period. *This is a state of equilibrium*. This state is independent of whether households' expectations are realised or not and regardless of whether the outcome in the labour market represents an optimal division of time between labour and leisure.

By choosing 'to confine discussion to current values of all magnitudes', Clower (1965; 1969, p. 273, n. 7) is unable to take the sequential nature of Keynes's model into account and grasp its significance for Walras' Law and the contrast with general-equilibrium theory. We shall examine Clower's argument closely, after first supporting the assertion, made above, that the household behaviour implicit in the *General Theory* was entirely orthodox.

## Keynes and the Theory of Household Behaviour

In contradiction to Clower, I wish to argue that Keynesian economics is consistent with the neoclassical theory of household behaviour (though not with the theory of general equilibrium). The theory of household behaviour is concerned with the formulation of plans to work, consume, and save. Figure 3.1 derives the consumption and labour supply functions *according to absolutely orthodox principles of the theory of consumer choice*. Labour is assumed to be the only initial endowment and $C$ is a composite bundle of consumer goods. Real income is $WL/P$, where $W$ is the money wage, $L$ is labour-hours and $P$ is the consumer price level expected to prevail during the expenditure horizon or income period.

Quadrant I illustrates the labour–leisure choice. Beginning at the origin $O_2$, the amount of labour offered increases to the left, the distance $O_2\,O_1$ measuring the total number of labour-hours available. The choice of how much labour to offer is made with respect to all possible hypothetical money wage rates at a given level of $P$. (A similar exercise could be conducted keeping $W$ constant and allowing $P$ to vary.) $O_2\,A$ through $O_2\,E$ are representative budget lines; their intersections with the $O_1$, $WL/P$ axis give the maximum income available at each wage. The labour supply decision is made by maximising the utility derived from consumption, saving and leisure. The decision to offer labour is made simultaneously with the plan to consume, in accordance with the usual rule excluding gifts and stealing as means of acquiring goods (what Clower calls Say's Principle). The labour supply curve for given expected prices is given in Quadrant IV. It has been drawn as a monotonically increasing function of the wage, though this is in no way essential. Incomes $Y_1$, $Y_2$, $Y_3$, and $Y_4$ are optimal at the wage rate implicit in the budget lines $O_2\,A$, $O_2\,B$, $O_2\,D$ and $O_2\,E$ respectively.

Quadrant III illustrates the consumption-saving choice. The lines $Y_1\,Y_1$ to $Y_4\,Y_4$ are the income constraints corresponding to the four labour supply decisions illustrated in Quadrant I, but there exist an infinite number of them, to cover all wage rates.[18] Consider the wage $W_4$. This gives the budget line $O_2\,E$. Households choose, at point $F$, to offer $L_4^s$ labour-hours, which will result in income $Y_4$, if they succeed in selling $L_4^s$. Trace $Y_4$ through Quadrant II by means of the 45° line. Arriving in Quadrant III we see that utility maximisation (at $K$) results in a plan to consume $C_4$ and save $S_4$. Similar choices are illustrated for incomes $Y_1$ to $Y_3$; at $Y_1$ all income is consumed.

These choices can now be related to income, forming the consumption function in Quadrant II. Points $G, H, I, J$, have respectively, the coordinates

I Labour–leisure choice
II Consumption function
III Consumption–saving choice
IV Labour supply function

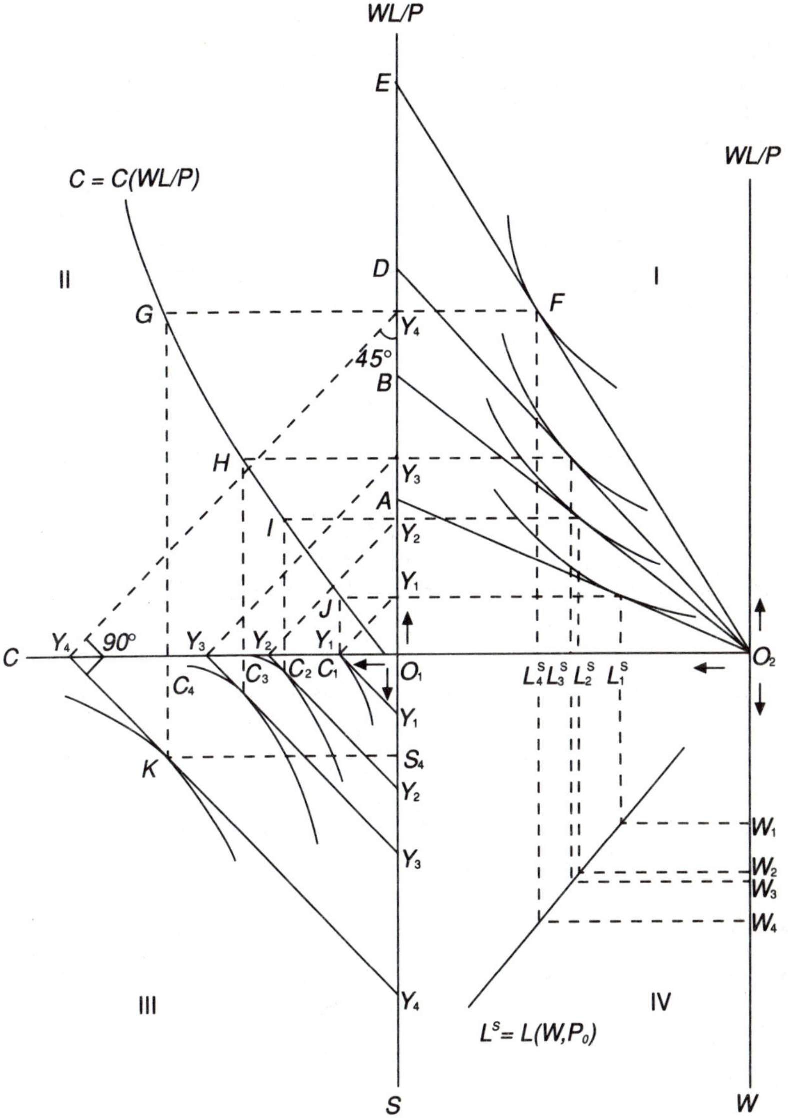


*Figure* 3.1

$C_4\ Y_4$, $C_3\ Y_3$, $C_2\ Y_2$, and $C_1\ Y_1$. It is a simple matter to aggregate over individual transactors to find the function relating aggregate hypothetical consumption plans to income, bearing in mind only that it is defined for a given income distribution and a given state of expectations concerning prices, as held by each consumer. (They need not hold the *same* expectations.)

So far, unemployment has not been mentioned; the exercise was concerned with the behaviour of one side of the market only, for its purpose was to demonstrate the consistency of Keynes's behavioural relationships with the theory of household behaviour. That theory concerns the formulation of plans, given a set of price expectations and hypothetical wages; it does not say whether expectations are met or which wage will actually prevail. To discuss these matters it is necessary to consider not just the theory of household behaviour but the interaction of households with firms; we must bring in the demand for labour. It is better to postpone this until after the discussion of Clower's model and the dual decision hypothesis in particular.

## CLOWER'S ARGUMENT

Clower's demonstration of this central proposition, that Walras' Law is inconsistent with Keynes's model, proceeds as follows. He sets up a model of the economy consisting of two groups of decision units, households and firms. Then to conform to each group he defines two mutually exclusive sets of commodities, one of which, designated by subscript $i$ ($i = 1, \ldots, m$), is supplied by firms and the other, designated by subscript $j$ ($j = m + 1, \ldots, n$) is supplied by households. On these depend households' utility

$$U\,(d_1, \ldots, d_m;\ s_{m+1}, \ldots, s_n) \tag{3.1}$$

and firms' profits

$$\mathrm{r} = \sum_i^m \mathbf{p}_i s_i - \sum_j^n \mathbf{p}_j d_j\,, \tag{3.2}$$

where $\mathbf{p}_k$ are prevailing market prices and $s_k$, $d_k$ are excess demand and supply of commodity $k$. In an orthodox world these are maximised subject to the 'budget restraint'

$$\sum_i^m \mathrm{p}_i d_i - \sum_j^n \mathrm{p}_j s_j - \mathrm{r} = 0 \tag{3.3}$$

in the case of households (where r is realised profits, treated here as a constant) and the transformation function

$$T(s_1, \ldots, s_m; d_{m+1}, \ldots, d_n) = 0 \tag{3.4}$$

in the case of firms.

By suitably dealing with the problem of profits (see the first part of the next section) and aggregating over households to get $\bar{d}_i$, $\bar{s}_i$ and over firms to get $\bar{d}_j$, $\bar{s}_j$ we arrive at Walras' Law:

$$\sum_i^m p_i[\bar{d}_i(P) - \bar{s}_i(P)] + \sum_j^n p_j[\bar{d}_j(P) - \bar{s}_j(P)] = 0; \tag{3.5}$$

the sum of excess demands and supplies across all markets is zero.

Clower's conclusion that (3.5) does not hold in Keynes' theory is correct. His (faulty) reasoning is as follows. Keynes introduced a behavioural postulate which Clower calls the dual decision hypothesis. Restricting the definition of commodities 1, . . . , $m$ to 'goods' and commodities $m + 1, \ldots, n$ to 'factors' (heterogeneous labour), the 'hypothesis' is that households will not plan to make purchases in excess of income obtained from the sale of labour time. Hence 'according to the dual decision hypothesis the market relevance of $\bar{d}_i(\mathbf{P})$ and $\bar{s}_j(\mathbf{P})$ is contingent on the satisfaction of the condition that realised current income be not less than planned income'.[19]

If, however,

$$\sum_j^n \mathbf{p}_j(\bar{d}_j - \bar{s}_j) < 0 \tag{3.6}$$

(which is to say the demand for factors is less than the supply), income will be given not by the willingness to work at wage $\mathbf{p}_j$ but by the willingness of firms to hire:

$$\mathbf{Y} = \sum_j^n \mathbf{p}_j \bar{d}_j . \tag{3.7}$$

In this circumstance, Clower suggests that the appropriate response is for households to undertake a second decision, deriving a revised expenditure plan by maximising (3.1) subject to (3.7) to obtain 'income-constrained' demands, $\hat{d}_i$, which are less than the planned purchases given by general equilibrium analysis:

$$\sum_i^m \mathbf{p}_i \hat{d}_i(\mathbf{P}, \mathbf{Y}) < \sum_i^m \mathbf{p}_i \bar{d}_i(\mathbf{P}). \tag{3.8}$$

Equation (3.5) (Walras' Law) must be replaced by

$$\sum_{i}^{m} \mathbf{p}_i[\hat{d}_i(\mathbf{P}, \mathbf{Y}) - \bar{s}_i(\mathbf{P})] + \sum_{j}^{n} \mathbf{p}_j[\bar{d}_j(\mathbf{P}) - \bar{s}_j(\mathbf{P})] \leq 0 \tag{3.9}$$

where the inequality holds if there is involuntary unemployment and the equality applies at full employment.

Thus Clower correctly concludes that Walras' Law does not hold in Keynes's system, though the method of arriving at the conclusion is not correct (see below) and generates several misleading subsidiary conclusions.

## THE FORMAL BASIS OF THE KEYNESIAN REVOLUTION: REBUTTAL

### Clower's Walrasian Model

Clower's 'Walrasian' model, on which his contrast with the 'Keynesian' model is based, is at variance with the general-equilibrium model at several key points.[20] Hence it cannot be used to illuminate the formal basis of the departure of Keynes from general equilibrium.

The model used by Clower is a general-equilibrium model of exchange, invalidly applied to production (hence the appearance of factors of production, a transformation function, output and profits in the Clower model). Clower is following Hicks (1939) and Patinkin (1956) in applying the exchange model to a production situation.[21]

In Walras's (1926) original construction, the exchange model pertains to an economy of transactors who begin with given initial endowments. These may include the capitalised value of consumers' services.[22] Then, faced with vectors or prices 'cried at random' each transactor determines, for each vector, how much of each commodity to retain, and how much to supply to the market from that endowment or to demand in excess of his endowment, subject to the constraint that the value of his excess demands not exceed the value of his excess supplies. The value of sales from his endowment (which includes his labour time) constitutes income with which to obtain his desired basket of goods for final consumption. Although he knows that he would not be able to meet his plan at disequilibrium prices, for purposes of *formulating his plan*, this knowledge is quite irrelevant; for he knows also that one of the price vectors cried will be an equilibrium vector (assuming existence). He does not know *which* one, and indeed that cannot be determined until he and everyone else also formulate their plans. Thus in formulating his excess demands and supplies he acts *as if* he can sell everything he decides to sell at *each* price vector cried, even though in the event only the plan corresponding to the equilibrium price vector will be relevant. He must formulate a set of plans to cover all price contingencies, for, in the language of the general-equilibrium fairy-tale, he must be able to provide the auctioneer with his information to guide him in finding the equilibrium price vector.[23]

The plan relevant to each price vector is found by maximising subject to a budget restraint, in the usual way. The constraint consists of the individual's initial endowment valued according to the price vector cried. Sales out of his endowment during the 'week' provide the 'income' with which to satisfy his current excess demands. Clower's model departs from this construction in several crucial ways.

In the general-equilibrium exchange model, there is no new production, except of consumer's services; no services are required as inputs, to be combined with other factors to produce output. Thus, there are no *firms* as such. Clower's model is dichotomised into households and firms. Transactors belonging to each sector could, in principle, be distinguished by their initial endowments. 'Firms' would be assumed to have no labour which can provide services. Endowments of 'households' would include no capital goods; they have only labour to sell. In Clower's model they are distinguished not by their endowments, but by their market behaviour: households are assumed always to have an excess supply of labour while firms always have an excess demand. This may appear to be a minor point, for the endowments could be inferred. But it is of some consequence, as it turns out.

First, by not specifying the initial endowments, Clower has not placed constraints on his functions, despite appearances to the contrary. In his model, the 'budget restraint' for households will vary with aggregate output, and this could take any value, for the transformation function, the 'constraint' for firms, is not related by input–output coefficients to any specified stock of productive inputs. This is perhaps the source of his deeply misleading usage, in speaking of his Keynesian excess-demand functions, as 'the constrained functions', implying, by contrast, that the functions in Walras's model are unconstrained.[24] They are not. But the functions of Clower's bastard Walrasian model indeed *are* unconstrained, despite equations (3.3) and (3.4).

Clower's formulation illustrates the fact that we have lost sight of the role of quantities in constraining the Walrasian equations. It is simply not true that 'quantities never appear explicitly in the market excess-demand functions of traditional theory' (Clower, 1965; 1969, p. 280). In the theory of consumer choice, excess demand is the amount an individual demands for final consumption *in excess of* his initial endowment of that good. Thus the expressions 'excess demand' and 'excess supply' encompass the exogenously given quantities represented by the vector of initial endowments, *which are the quantity constraints of an exchange economy.* The introduction of quantities into excess-demand functions cannot be the central contribution of Keynes. They were always there.

Second, unless we assume that households' endowments contain no saleable commodities, there must be some price at which some households will cease to offer their labour and begin to demand it (and, in terms of Clower's model, there will be prices at which firms find it unprofitable to produce). General-equilibrium demand (and supply) functions are schedules giving the maximum demanded (supplied) at *all* hypothetical prices, from zero to infinity. If prices take their full range, decision units may change from being 'households' (offerers of labour) to being 'firms' (demanders of labour) depending on the price vector. This crossover is ruled out in Clower's model.

Recognition of the above misspecification is avoided by committing another quite fundamental error. Clower specifies only *one* budget restraint each for households and firms: equations (3.3) and (3.4) are defined only for *prevailing* market prices. This is the only price vector considered, in contrast to the infinite number employed in deriving continuous-demand functions. In posing the maximisation problem with respect to a single price vector, Clower does not derive demand (supply) *functions* at all, but only a *point* on each demand and supply function – the single maximum quantity of each commodity willingly demanded or supplied at prevailing prices.

Furthermore, though he does not say so, this 'prevailing' price vector can only be the equilibrium price vector. Examination of his treatment of profits shows that this is the only interpretation consistent with the rest of his construction. Profits are usually assumed to be a residual to firms, yet they constitute income to households (presuming they are all distributed). Now even if the distribution of profits is immediate, their magnitude cannot be known until the output is sold. But households must know their profit income before deciding how much to buy. Clower gets around this problem first by including *realised* profits, **r**, as the relevant variable in the household budget restraint and assuming its value to be fixed. Then, when it comes to deriving Walras' Law by combining the demands and supplies of the two sectors, he appeals to the following argument (pp. 274–5): while it cannot be presumed that **r** (realised profits) and (the firm sector's profit target) are equal when they refer to individual experiments (Patinkin, 1956; 1965, pp. 11–12), 'in the case of market experiments,[25] however, it does seem plausible to suppose that $\mathbf{r} = \bar{r}$ provided that the variables $s_1, \ldots, s_m$ and $d_{m+1}, \ldots, d_n$ *have assumed their equilibrium values*' (my italics). This assumption is essential to his derivation of Walras' Law, equation (3.5).

Clower's argument concerning profits thus reveals that he has only derived the *quantities demanded* in the *equilibrium state*. It follows that, as derived, Walras' Law only holds for the equilibrium state. Other interpreters of Walras (e.g., Hicks, 1939, and Patinkin, 1956) have always insisted that Walras' Law holds at all times; in disequilibrium, excess demand in one market is matched by excess supply of equal value in another. Clower's 'Walrasian' model precludes such an interpretation of Walras' Law. If his model were formally correct, then *any* disequilibrium, Keynesian or not, would be incompatible with Walras' Law.

## The Dual Decision Hypothesis

The fact that the demand and supply behaviour of Clower's transactors is only defined for one set of prices, the equilibrium set, is an important influence on his specification of the dual decision hypothesis. The premise on which the hypothesis is based, Say's Principle (see page 62), is unexceptionable. But the dual decision hypothesis does not follow from it. Clower's hypothesis is that where

$$\sum_j^n \mathbf{p}_j s_j < \sum_j^n \mathbf{p}_j \bar{s}_j \tag{3.10}$$

a *second round* of decision-making is indicated; namely, maximise

$$U(d_1, \ldots, d_m, \mathbf{s}_{m+1}, \ldots, \mathbf{s}_n), \tag{3.11}$$

subject to the modified budget constraint

$$\sum_i^m \mathbf{p}_i d_i - \sum_j^n \mathbf{p}_j s_j - \mathbf{r} = 0, \tag{3.12}$$

that is, subject to income realised in the unemployment state.

Compare this to the decision process revealed by imposing unemployment on the decision procedure illustrated in Figure 3.1. Figure 3.2 is a simplified version of Figure 3.1, with budget lines for only two wage rates. A labour demand function, $L^D$, has been introduced in Quadrant IV.

Suppose that at the prevailing wage $W_0$, labour, in aggregate, wished to work $L^s{}_3$ hours, but firms are prepared to hire only $L^D$. Before entering the labour market, households, in aggregate, had planned to earn $Y_3$ and consume $C_3$ (point *A* on the consumption function). In the event, only $Y_0$ is obtained by the sale of labour. This fact necessitates revising downward the planned *levels* of consumption and saving from point *A* to point *B*, but does *not* entail, as specified in the dual decision hypothesis, a second round of maximising. Consumers' plans are represented fully by the consumption schedule; which, if it is a stable function of income,[26] is consistent with both full and under-employment states. This is obvious, for there is only one point on the schedule consistent with full employment, in a given state of expectations.

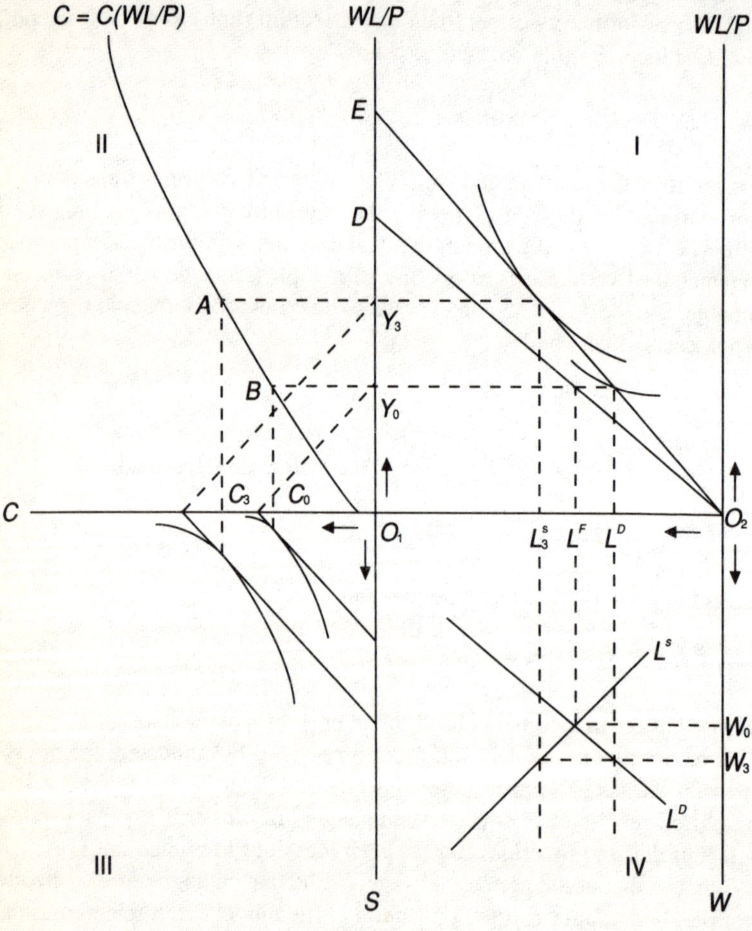


*Figure* 3.2

The consumption-saving choice is made subject to an income constraint, regardless of whether that income is the level households would have preferred, given the wage, or not. Preferred income is only relevant to the derivation of the labour supply curve. Consumption and saving are functions of income *regardless of how that income is obtained* – whether by working less at a higher wage or more at a lower wage.[27] In terms of Figure 3.2, $Y_0$ may be earned by working $O_2\,L^D$ hours at the wage consistent with $O_2\,D$ or $O_2\,L^F$ (full employment) at the wage consistent with $O_2\,E$. The consumption-saving plan is the same in both cases. If it were the case that households, upon realising that sales of labour have been less than optimal, revised their plans in the schedule sense, consumption would have to be specified as a function of the wage rate and (actual) employment as separate arguments. Consumption is then not independent of the extent of enforced leisure. This is a plausible assumption, but not the one traditionally made.[28]

The conclusion is that a second round of decision-making on consumption ($d_1, \ldots, d_m$) is unnecessary. Unemployment requires a movement *along* the individual's consumption function rather than a revision of plans (a shift in the function) as specified by the dual decision hypothesis. It follows that Clower's conclusion that the dual decision hypothesis incorporates established preference analysis as a special case (p. 289) is false. Far from having 'an established position' in 'geometrical classroom expositions of consumer behaviour' (pp. 290–1), the dual decision hypothesis is inconsistent with orthodox theory and is a misspecification.

In Keynes's sequential economy the dual decision, as specified, is, in fact, impossible. By including $\mathbf{s}_j$ in the utility function to be re-maximised, the dual decision hypothesis states that in the second round, households reassess how much labour to supply subject to the new constraint of realised income, when in fact such maximisation has been expressly ruled out. Of course they must reassess consumption levels. But the employment situation has already been settled. The labour market is *closed*; sales of labour have been realised, whether optimal or not.

These difficulties with the dual decision hypothesis stem from failing to derive demand and supply schedules, instead of points. In terms of Figure 3.2, $W_3$ is the prevailing wage, though it is not the equilibrium wage. Suppose households construct a plan based on that wage rate alone: they intend to supply $OL^s_3$ of labour and consume $OL_3$ of goods. $Y_0$, being the preferred income at some wage other than that prevailing, does not play a role in the household's planning exercise. The only consumption plan the household had entertained was the *level* $C_3$, and naturally, when income $Y_3$ did not materialise, this plan had to be revised, according, as Clower rightly says, to realised income. But in a properly specified model, that realised income would have been one of the range of hypothetical incomes subject to which households made contingency consumption plans. The only difference between the household in Keynes's world and in Walras's world is that the latter knows that one of his optima will be realised in the equilibrium solution. The former has no such assurance. It is not so much that Keynes's households take account of the possibility of unemployment as that both they and Walras's households recognise the possibility of more than one income level,whether due to unemployment or to the auctioneer's calling a new wage rate.

Excess demands are not independent of current market transactions in either world, in contrast to Clower's claim (p. 280); the neoclassical household, as well as the Keynesian, knows that income must be realised if goods are to be bought. In both, notional or hypothetical income levels form the constraints in the planning exercise, while realised income constrains the demands the household makes in the market-place. Keynes made no innovation here. The difference is that household income in the neoclassical world is endogeneously determined, whereas in Keynes's world, the logic of decision-making in a production economy results in household income, in some (not all) circumstances, being determined exogenously to the household sector. Where firms can get more than enough labour at the going wage, it is they, not households, who determine household income.

## PRODUCTION, TIME AND EQUILIBRIUM

### Production v. Exchange

In assessing the difference between Keynes and neoclassical economics, it is not really appropriate to contrast Keynes's production model with an exchange model when Walras himself provided a production model. Debreu's (1959) attempt to incorporate time shall also be noted.

The significance of the difference between production and exchange can be seen by looking again at the absurd result obtained from applying Walras' Law to the Keynesian aggregates: that unemployment would always be accompanied by excess demand for output. Responsibility for this absurdity lies with the invalid use of the theory of an exchange economy to analyse production.

In an exchange economy, all goods and services are exchanged on a par. They are alternatives: more of one good is obtained by giving up some of another. Thus the conclusion that an excess supply of labour is matched by an excess demand for goods is correct where labour is restricted to providing consumers' services. In production economies, however, labour is demanded as an input. Input demands are derived from, and change in the same direction as, final output demands: unemployment results from an insufficiency of demand. At first sight it would appear then that Walras' Law applied only to an exchange economy. Unfortunately for clear thinking however, Walras' Law continues to hold in Walras's production model, despite its foundation on the theory of derived demand, because of the model's timeless nature.

In Walras's production model, we begin with fixed factor endowments rather than an endowment of final products. Then the technical coefficients are specified and profit-maximising production possibilities computed, for each given price vector. The derived demands for inputs and the demand for final output at that price vector are then compared to the corresponding supplies, and prices *and the quantities to be produced* altered until, assuming existence and stability, the equilibrium vector is found. Thus deficient demand for a product is revealed and eliminated *before any production takes place*. In the exchange model there is no false trading. In the production model there is no false production; in equilibrium, wages and prices elicit just that amount of output which labour will both work to produce and then wish to consume, at those wages and prices. Market uncertainty has been eliminated by the costless effort of the auctioneer, and *time* abolished by assumption: 'Production . . . requires a certain lapse of time. We shall resolve this difficulty purely and simply by ignoring the time element at this point' (Walras, 1926; 1954, p. 242). In effect, by eliminating time, payment for effort is made directly in the form of final output, suitably redistributed according to workers' preferences,[29] so that any given price vector inputs and outputs are direct alternatives from the point of view of payment, as are goods and consumers' services in the model of exchange. Flexibility of the level of output and its composition at different prices makes this constraint on final payment consistent with the principle of derived demand, and Walras' Law continues to hold.

## Time in General Equilibrium

The attempt to introduce time into general-equilibrium theory was made by Debreu (1959), who succeeds only in showing that the logical result of specifying well-behaved preferences and production functions for commodities which are distinguished both by their physical characteristics and by their date of delivery is that contracts covering all contingencies can be fixed at a single point of time. Once again market uncertainty is eliminated and only a point in time matters. Walras' Law holds.

**Time and Equilibrium**

We have shown earlier that in a production model in which time enters materially, underemployment equilibrium is possible. But the point could stand elaboration.

There are two concepts of equilibrium extant in economics:

1. Equilibrium is a point of rest; forces leading to change are either absent or countervailing.
2. Equilibrium is a point at which supply equals demand.

They correspond to the distinction made by Clower in an earlier article (1960): he calls the first equilibrium and the second market clearing.

In a static system involving recontracting the two concepts come to the same thing; forces leading to adjustment are present until the market clearing-point is reached. In terms of this model unemployment equilibrium is impossible: the existence of an excess supply of labour *signifies* disequilibrium.[30] However, this inference is only correct in an economy such as that of Walras, which is not permitted to function at all unless it functions perfectly.

In Keynes's economy, where there is nothing to guarantee the absence of false production or false trading, the two terms are not synonymous. Fulfilment of the first definition of equilibrium need not imply market clearing, which is a stronger condition. Unemployment equilibrium is possible, if, despite the existence of excess supply in the labour market, there are circumstances in which no force for change exists.

In a Keynesian world, entrepreneurs estimate demand and hire labour according to that estimate. If firms succeed in getting all the labour they require and sell their output at the price they set, all their expectations have been met, and they are (by assumption) maximising profits given those expectations. Hence they have no reason to change their plans next period; they provide no force for change. Households are in a different position. They would *like* to sell more labour than they have done, but they have no power to effect a change. There is no mechanism of recontracting by which a new wage can be set: the setting of wages is up to firms (who will raise them if they get insufficient labour, but in the case just outlined have no reason to lower them). And, as Clower indeed stresses, households have no means of informing firms that demand could be stronger if employment were higher.

Although their actual consumption is less than full employment consumption, the *net* position of the commodity market depends on the amount supplied as well as demanded, and is ambiguous: equation (3.9) indicates that an excess supply of labour is compatible with either excess demand or excess supply of goods – and by implication, with zero excess demand also. The first two possibilities represent unemployment *dis*equilibria, the first giving rise to adjustment toward full employment, the second leading to deepening unemployment. The third possibility, the combination of excess labour supply with a perfectly cleared market for output, is the position of unemployment *equilibrium*.[31] If it should happen that at the actual level of income $Y$ households consume exactly what firms expected to sell, *there is no force for change, despite the fact that households are not maximising their utility from work and leisure*.

Keynes's unemployment equilibrium is an equilibrium in the first sense, not in the more restricted second sense. In the absence of recontracting or perfect information and foresight there should be no presumption that the economy has any tendency to move toward equilibrium in the second sense, or that the neoclassical result is a special case of Keynes's more general theory. In particular, in a sequence economy there can be *no presumption that Walras' Law will hold, even in equilibrium*. Walras' Law holds in models constructed so that everything of consequence takes place at a *point* of time, when all plans of households and firms are made known and mutually agreed. In an ongoing economy there is no such point in time. Arrow need not have taken his agnostic position (see introduction).

## Neoclassical Objections

Asserting the absence of adjustment forces in a market with excess supply provokes the following questions: would not firms, observing idle labour, lower wages and increase employment, and should not rational households offer their labour at a lower wage? Either action would initiate change and refute the assertion that the above state was an equilibrium state.

In reply, let us start with households. In the *General Theory*, households enter the labour market as individual units; collective bargaining plays no part in the analysis. Even if, taken as a group, they might gain by offering to work at less than the going wage, no individual has any incentive to do so. It is to his advantage to seek the highest wage he can get – until he finds that he is one of those whose labour is not required. By this time, however, it is too late. Firms have already got the labour they want. To take on more men is not profitable, even at a lower wage. The only possibility is to fire some of those they have just employed and substitute cheaper labour for them. That course of action is not feasible (for equal pay for equal work is the rule in much of the real world as well as in marginal productivity theory). To take advantage of the lower wage the firm must persuade its entire present work force to accept the new lower wage. This would be costly in terms of effort for the firm. More to the point, it does nothing to affect employment.

Employment will only be affected if firms increase the amount of labour they use. This requires either that labour is substituted for capital, output remaining unchanged, or that firms decide to increase output. The first possibility is ruled out in Keynes's short run, for the stock of capital goods is fixed. The second is feasible, for each firm in atomistic competition sees a gain for itself in expansion of output at lower cost. So let us suppose that, having observed unemployment this period, in the *next* period they somehow manage, despite the absence of a coordinating mechanism, to lower wages across the board. If the consumption demand schedule is stable with respect to the wage change, the expansion will be successful if and only if the demand and supply of investment goods also expands, in just the right proportion to compensate for the fact that the marginal propensity to consume is less than one. It is unlikely in a period of unemployment that investment will rise to compensate, particularly since the price of labour relative to capital has fallen. Moreover, the consumption schedule is likely not to be stable but to fall if the wage share falls[32] ( a complication ignored in the early part of this chapter). It is almost certain that the expansion will not be as profitable as each firm expected and that employment will fall again. The wage cut will have proved a costly and fruitless experiment, resulting in only a temporary improvement.

It matters little, therefore, whether we insist that if firms' demand expectations are met they will not revise their actions despite the observation of unemployment,[33] or whether we allow them the costly experiment of attempting to expand. In the one case we are certain to remain at unemployment until some exogenous force for change emerges; in the other, we may not end up at precisely the same position as before, but barring the precise change in the balance of output which will sustain the expansion we will, in the absence of an optimistic turn in long-run expectations, return to a point at which households are again not maximising. It is in the first case that the importance of the sequence of decisions inherent in production is most clearly seen. In that sequence, if firms' expectations with respect to the availability of labour are met, it is then only in the market for output that their expectations can be falsified and so lead to a revision of their plans in the following period; if firms have obtained their desired labour supply, the existence of unemployment provides no force for change unless firms sell more, or less, than they had expected. In Keynes's economy, an excess *demand* for labour is a disequilibrium situation: firms will compete for labour by raising wages. But in periods of unemployment, forces for change, if any, come not from the labour market, but from the goods market.

## CONCLUSION

Keynes's departure from orthodoxy consists not in any change in the theory of household behaviour, but in constructing a system of interaction between households and firms in which households do not always get exactly what they want, because they have no power to effect change. This result is not imposed *ad hoc*, nor does it rely on monopoly, irrationality, or market imperfections. These might compound the problem, but the problem is independent of any of these factors; it arises from the sequential nature of decisions inherent in the productive process in the absence of collective bargaining. By deciding to 'confine discussion to current values', Clower misapprehended the formal nature of the 'Keynesian Revolution', which involved the complete overthrow of the static method of solving a set of simultaneous equations, in favour of analysing the results of decisions which are taken in a well-defined sequence, on the basis of information available at the time and forecasts of an uncertain future.

**Notes**

1. Cambridge (England) is known for its contempt for the idea of constructing theories on the basis of 'rational behaviour'. It is not always understood that 'rationality' in this context entails being perfectly informed, about the future as well as the past, in contrast to its ordinary meaning, of doing the sensible thing given one's (limited) knowledge. Clower (1975) has recently characterised the latter as 'Marshallian reasonableness', which usefully sharpens the contrast with Walrasian 'rationality'.
2. For expressions of this view see Leijonhufvud (1973) and Laidler (1974). See also Harcourt (1977).
3. The only improvement offered by the new over the old classical view is that labour is now merely ignorant, rather than stubborn.
4. Clower (1975, p. 3) regards this interpretation of the *General Theory* as 'customary' and correct, and Tobin (1975) agrees.
5. This is not to say that unemployment never gives rise to adjustment; the existence of unemployment equilibrium does not preclude unemployment disequilibrium.
6. Clower (1975) now feels that the *General Theory* is best described as an analysis of short-run disequilibrium adjustment processes, rather than short-run disequilibrium states.
7. This is not consistent with using the tools of comparative statics. Formal

support for this assertion is found in Benavie (1972). See also Leijonhufvud (1968, p. 50).

8. Leijonhufvud (1968) is of course based on it. See also Hines (1971).
9. See for example Barro and Grossman (1976), and Mackay and Weber (1976).
10. This distinction is blurred in Clower (1965; 1969, p. 278). I understand household behaviour to be modelled by the theory of choice, and general-equilibrium theory to deal with the interaction of the plans of individual transactors.
11. See especially Arrow and Hahn (1972) and Shackle (1974).
12. 'A Monetary Theory of Production', reprinted in Keynes (1973a, pp. 408–11).
13. Shackle and Joan Robinson have said this from the beginning. It has been echoed more recently by (*inter alia*) Leijonhufvud (1968) and Clower (1975).
14. Unless you produce to order. A central property of money, of course, is that it provides a form of saving which avoids having to place specific future orders. See Keynes (1936, pp. 210–13).
15. Keynes's method was too complex and subtle to be characterised simply – hence the arguments over whether it was static , dynamic, or kaleidic, whether it analysed adjustment processes or was process analysis, and the like. Kregel (1976) is an illuminating exploration and exposition of Keynes's method which fully recognises its complexity. See also n. 12 above.
16. With given long-period expectations new investment decisions are not taken; only production decisions need be made.
17. In the *General Theory*, Keynes did not distinguish clearly between actual (*ex post*) aggregate demand and the estimate of it which must be the basis of production decisions. But in the notes for his 1937 lectures (Keynes, 1973b, pp. 182–3) he wrote '*ex ante* decisions in their influence on effective demand relate solely to *entrepreneurs*' decisions' (his italics). I am grateful to J. A. Kregel (1976) for bringing this statement to my attention.
18. In practice, plans would be made 'over the relevant range'.
19. All the shortfall in income is due to failure to sell labour, not failure to receive expected profits. He has retained the assumption $\bar{r} = r$, which was initially defended only for general-equilibrium states.
20. It is doubtful, in fact, whether we would have got in such a muddle over Keynes if we had understood Walras properly. (Cf. Keynes's comment to Hicks: 'What you are giving is a representative belief of a period when economists had slipped away from the pure classical doctrine without knowing it and were in a much more confused state of mind than their predecessors had been' (Keynes, 1973a, p. 79).)
21. This procedure is defended by Hicks (1939, p. 77) and Patinkin (1956; 1965, p. 3). Cf. Walras, who provides separate theories of production and exchange.
22. Income can then be obtained from the sales of labour services. To accord with the assumptions of the exchange model these must be consumers' services, not inputs to a productive process (cf. Clower, 1965; 1969, p. 280).
23. Note, in this connection, Clower's assertion (1965; 1969, p. 275) that economics provides only the beginnings of a theory of disequilibrium transactions plans. In fact in orthodox theory, a full set of plans to cover all price vectors is derived by every transactor. There are an infinite number of price vectors, and we mortals would find such a requirement impossible to meet. In

a land without time, however, we should not find it a difficult task.

24. Clower (1965; 1969, p. 288). This unfortunate terminology is now in widespread use.
25. Patinkin (1956, 1965). These terms are a red herring; in Walras's model there are no 'market experiments': all aggregate functions are derived from individuals' choices.
26. An initial period of dissaving, to support consumption at accustomed levels when income is reduced by unemployment, has not been included in this simple demonstration. There are no lags in adjustment, in conformity with Clower's strictures (1965; 1969, p. 273, n. 7).
27. It is an interesting sidelight of this demonstration that it can be seen that as long as saving remains positive, the community as a whole unambiguously prefers the high-wage, unemployment alternative: the indifference curve which cuts $0_2E$ yields more satisfaction than that tangent to $0_2D$, and there is no offsetting disutility from dissaving.
28. Keynes (1936, p. 90) of course, regarded income as a proxy for the level of employment, *N*, in the consumption function. But I doubt that his preference for *C*(*N*) over *C*(*Y*) was to allow for a dual decision in the sense of Clower. Employment was the variable Keynes was most concerned to explain. It was also the most volatile component of real income at the time Keynes was writing; wages and consumer prices were relatively stable. Thus while he took income and wealth to be the determinants of consumption at the microeconomic level (pp. 91–6), *aggregate* income was an unsatisfactory proxy for *N* insofar as employment elasticities differed among industries.
29. In a one-good model, this redistribution does not arise. Everyone is paid in wheat; there is no necessity to trade with someone in another line of work.
30. Note that Clower in the *Appraisal* (1965; 1969) defines equilibrium as consistency of all plans, thus ruling out unemployment equilibrium.
31. It is obvious that in the real world this condition will never be precisely satisfied, even at the aggregate level and certainly not for each individual firm. It should be interpreted as it was intended, as a condition which could obtain in the main. No more precision should be required of it than is required of the theory which generated it, and no one would expect a 'theory of output as a whole' to apply with any exactitude to the components of that aggregate.
32. This is highly likely but not certain: output, profits and employment have risen and wages have fallen.
33. See Kregel (1976) for Keynes's view that this model's usefulness lay in highlighting the principle of effective demand as the principal cause of unemployment equilibrium, in opposition to the prevailing view that unemployment was 'a short-run disequilibrium phenomenon . . . the result of booms and slumps that might result from inexact entrepreneurial expectation' (pp. 213–14).

# 4 Financial Counterparts of Saving and Investment and Inconsistency in a Simple Macro Model

## Author's Note

This chapter is the first published guidepost of my journey out of neoclassical Keynesianism. The paper challenges both the separation of *IS* from *LM* and the application of Walras' Law to the *IS–LM* model (and some other models, here excluded). The second of these concerns foreshadowed, in my own work, the analysis in Chapter 3 and work on the finance motive in *Macroeconomics After Keynes* (Chapters 9 to 12); There is also an unpublished paper called 'Keynes and Robertson on Saving and the Multiplier', which I hope one day to get round to finishing. The point made here is at the centre of Kuska's (1978) attack on balance-of-payments theory and it foreshadows some aspects of Foley (1975).

Though I still stand by my attack on the use of Walras' Law in the *IS–LM* context, today I would not argue, as I do here, as if a microeconomic perspective on saving was appropriate to macroeconomics. Nevertheless that *is* the perspective implicit in *IS–LM*, so it is not inappropriate to the problem at hand.

Writing this paper and its antecedent, a paper called 'Double Entry Book-Keeping and *IS–LM*', which was never published, I saw standard macroeconomics crumble and run through my hands. Indeed the essence of the problem posed here, how to mix economic stocks and flows, has never been resolved. Vera Lutz's 'Multiplier and Velocity Analysis: A Marriage' (1955), was quickly followed by Chris Archibald's 'An Annulment' (1956). Clower and Bushaw (1954) and Cliff Lloyd (1960) developed a stock-flow equation system. The balance-sheet approach of Godley and Cripps (1983) is to my mind a very successful integration of stocks and flows. The most radical approach is that of Schmitt (1982) and Cencini (1988), who developed the idea of economic quanta to resolve the stock-flow problem.

I turned back to the *General Theory* as a result of my disillusionment, and my career thus changed its course. From writing this paper I also learned, gradually, that economics is not about the logical consistency of models – mercifully, as very few models are logically consistent and those which are, are sterile. I learned the vital lesson that models involve compromise, and that the trick was to find the right compromise for the problem at hand. In other words – in a phrase much used in Cambridge – horses for courses.

Hy Minsky gave me a wealth of comment on this paper, and, though he was, rightly, sceptical of the notion of sectoral budget restraints except for government, he was very encouraging. Thanks are also due to the army of colleagues who were discouraging, though it would be impolite (much less impolite to them than they were to me) to name them; they made me think – and fight.

## INTRODUCTION

Financial assets play two roles in the economy. They provide wealth-holders with assets which relieve the saver of having to own and operate real capital, and they serve to transfer purchasing power from surplus- to deficit-spending decision units. Macroeconomic theory until recently has concentrated almost exclusively on the portfolio role of financial assets (including money), leaving implicit their role in financing expenditure.[1]

A fundamental reason for studying the financial aspects of models is that it is the deficit purchases and the saving decisions which permit the conflicts between plans of separate decision units and cause disequilibrium in the economic system. Such a separation of plans is not possible in the absence of borrowing. It is the existence of claims which enables potential deficit and surplus units to translate their expenditure and saving plans into effective demands for goods and for assets. The distribution of effective demand between the two groups will depend partly on the price (interest cost) the potential deficit sector has to pay to persuade the potential surplus sector to lend to it.

It is the purpose of this paper to build a framework in which the financial side of effective demand is made fully explicit, and to use the framework in a critique of the *IS–LM* model. A result of this appraisal is that when finance is considered explicitly, the model is shown to be dynamic,[2] and the 'equilibrium' solution, with the exception of the stationary-state equilibrium, holds only for an instant of time. In addition, interdependencies created by the recognition that transactions involve two markets show that the static model discussed here implies demand functions for the market omitted by invoking Walras' Law which are not acceptable.

## THE FINANCING OF PURCHASES

In a money economy purchases of goods, services, and financial assets must be financed either by giving up some acceptable asset or by issuing an acceptable claim against oneself. Therefore demand for a good, service, or financial asset, as opposed simply to the desire for it, must presuppose a willingness on the part of the demander to give up money or obtain credit and a willingness on the part of the seller of the good, service, or asset to accept the money or claim. Every transaction thus affects two markets, one being either the market for money or the market for claims.

Every macro model implicitly or explicitly defines the number of different types of assets in that model. These, along with perishable goods (including labour services), define the set of possible purchases which the decision units can make. To make a purchase effective, purchasing power must be found. The choices of assets and debt-forms available to each sector may be (but need not be) restricted to a subset of the available items. From these specifications it is possible to discover the forms that saving may take and the possible means of financing deficit expenditure.

The usual macro model deals with market aggregates – consumption and investment goods, a representative loan contract (the bond) and money, and sometimes labour services. These constitute the choice set for the economy. All goods in the set are treated equivalently. All are available to any decision unit – household or firm. Each unit having made its choice by the usual maximising procedure, the individual demands and supplies are then aggregated over those units, by commodities, to produce market excess demand or supply equations for each good.

The point of macroeconomics, however, is to cut across the detail of individual behaviour to find aggregates which share characteristics in making economic decisions, so that it becomes reasonable to treat these sectors as if they were planning units and thus to postulate *sectoral* economic behaviour. For example, in the *General Theory*, the private sector of the economy is seen as the outcome of the choices of three such groups: entrepreneurs, consumers and rentiers. The division may be simplified to a dichotomy between households and firms, the rentier being the consumer in his role as manager of the household's accumulated savings. For this dichotomy to be useful, households' behaviour must be different from that of firms. The critical assumption is that households typically save, while the business sector is usually in deficit.

As usually defined, saving is merely the difference between income and purchases, by households, of new goods and services. Saving is not a positive action; it is 'not spending'. It has no concrete form. It is not sufficient, for purposes of this chapter, to accept this abstract notion of saving. Income is a flow: it is generated continuously and cannot be stored (saved) except by the purchase of some durable asset, real or financial.

Current macro models incorporate one of two major views of saving. One definition is consistent with the assumption that households may choose freely among all assets and hence is implicit in those models which aggregate over markets. On this definition saving is a means of storing command over future consumption streams. This can be achieved, in principle, by purchasing financial assets to exchange for consumer goods later, by buying consumer durables, or by purchasing (and operating) productive capital. In terms of likely behaviour in an industrialised economy with a developed financial system, the last alternative is virtually ruled out for households choosing at the margin. The alternative definition of saving concentrates on the impact of the consumption–saving choice in the current period. Consumption is defined as purchases, by the household sector, of currently-produced[3] goods and services. Saving is whatever portion of income is not spent in this way. Durable goods purchases thus count as consumption, leaving the acquisition of financial assets (including money) as the only outlet for saving in a world where households do not directly own productive capital.

Productive-capital goods are assumed to be owned exclusively by firms. Purchases or construction of such goods is denoted as investment. In fact for our purposes 'investment' may be taken as a shorthand expression for any business sector spending on new goods, whether these are durable capital or not: the crucial element is that it is assumed that investment is a form of deficit spending: that it requires finance above and beyond the cash flow from current sales. It follows from that assumption that while individual firms may finance investment by running down accumulated cash balances, the business sector as an aggregate does not have this option.

Given the above assumptions regarding each sector's behaviour, consider how each sector finances its expenditures. We generally speak of financing expenditure 'out of current income' or 'by borrowing'. These terms require precise definition. At any point of time, a sale of goods or financial assets is made in exchange for money. If instead of a point of time we consider a period during which wage payments are made the household sector may use this current cash inflow to finance both its current expenditure and its acquisition of non-money financial assets.

A firm may similarly finance expenditure out of current income, the cash inflow from sales. Financing of expenditure on goods and services out of current income, whether undertaken by households or the business sector, represents neither a leakage nor an injection to the circular flow of income.

For the household sector however, not only consumption but also saving is financed out of current income. At any point of time, the sector's actual saving comprises not only its current additions to holdings of 'bonds' but also its additions to money balances whether or not those additions to money holdings are intended as a form of new desired saving. Within the income period, cash holdings are bound to fluctuate around their intended level: it is only the net intended acquisition of cash at the end of the period which constitutes new saving. A transaction involving the purchase of a 'bond' in exchange for money at the point of time when it occurs, is thus not new *actual* saving but a switch to a less liquid portfolio. It represents new intended saving if the money for which the bond was exchanged represented current income payments which were accepted without the intention to hold in money form into the next income period, whereas it *is* intended to hold the bond. If, on the other hand, the purchase is matched by a reduction of cash balances at the end of the current income period as compared to last period's final level, then the bond purchase is not new saving, but only a change in desired portfolio composition.

Now suppose that there are *n* financial assets (including money) in the economy. Insofar as households are saving, that saving represents a demand to add to holdings of those financial assets. By definition, income is allocated to consumption and saving, the latter being, under our assumptions, equal to purchases of financial assets and additions to money balances. A rational household recognises that a plan to save is a plan to acquire larger stocks of those assets.[4] If, therefore, the equation determining consumption and the equations for end-of-period demands for *n*–1 of these financial assets are given, the full demand function for the *n*th asset follows. If we impose on sectors the same postulate of consistent behaviour assumed for individual units, then this point holds for the household sector in aggregate.

And on our assumptions, if positive net investment is taking place, a portion of firms' expenditure is financed out of borrowing. The financing of expenditure through the issue and sale of financial paper ('bonds') in fact comprises two transactions: the sale of the security transfers money from surplus to deficit units and the money is then spent on goods and services. If both transactions occur within the income period we can speak of deficit spending financed by bond sales, although in fact the spending is financed by money obtained from bond sales. The borrower's effective demand for goods in excess of income depends on the amount of money he actually obtains, which in turn depends on the demand for bonds and the amount he wishes to supply. Consistent behaviour requires that a plan to deficit-spend be matched by a plan to supply claims. Thus if there are *m* types of securities issued by the business sector, specification of the investment function and *m*–1 of the supply functions of these securities unambiguously defines the supply function for the *m*th security. Given planned deficit expenditure, one supply-of-claims function is not independent, but may be derived from other functions in the model. A borrowing sector thus creates its own budget restraints: when the decision to deficit-spend is made, proceeds of loan flotations are estimated at that time. These estimates plus expected current income constitute the total (endogenous) 'budget restraint' of the deficit sector.[5]

We shall proceed to incorporate financing considerations, using the above framework, into the standard *IS–LM* model. It will be shown that the model is not in fact static and that the most acceptable equilibrium of that model is the stationary state. It will also be seen that the implied equations for the omitted market (the bond market) do not take a form which would be widely regarded as satisfactory.

## FINANCING IN THE IS–LM MODEL

In its simplest form, this model is concerned with aggregate demand for goods, divided into consumption and investment, for bonds, and for money. Standard demand-for-money, saving, and investment functions and the two equilibrium conditions constitute the model, described by the following familiar set of equations. Using standard notation:

$$M_t^s = M_0, \tag{4.1}$$

$$M_t^d = L(Y_t, r_t), L_y > 0, L_r < 0, \tag{4.2}$$

$$S_t = S(Y_t), 1 > S_y > 0, \qquad (4.3)^6$$

$$I_t = I(r_t), I_r < 0, \tag{4.4}$$

$$M_t^d = M_t^s, \tag{4.5}$$

$$S_t = I_t. \tag{4.6}$$

Stocks are measured at the end of the period. The market for labour and the influence of capital on production are ignored. The assumptions made in the previous section, restricting the choices of each sector, create a correspondence between the sector responsible for a given decision and the supply or demand for each good or asset: households buy consumption goods and do all the saving, which takes only financial forms. Business firms operate the productive capital stock, make the investment decisions, and finance solely by borrowing. They hold no financial assets, including money. How there can be money when there is neither a government nor banks to issue it is not explained. The stock of money is not only given, but fixed, since there is no transaction in the model for which new money could be the counterpart. We assume that this stock of money, however it came into being, is willingly held at the outset.

We make the following additional assumption. The price level is fixed, the index being set at 1 so that there is no need to distinguish between real and nominal magnitudes or between the money rate of interest and the real rate. It is also assumed that the ratio of the price of consumption goods to capital goods is fixed, so that goods-market equilibrium cannot be brought about by a change in this relative price. Consideration of financing imposes additional connections within the model. Current planned saving, given our assumptions, may take one of two forms: a demand for an increase in money holdings or demand for an increase in the value of bond holdings.[7] Thus

$$S_t = \Delta M_t^d + \Delta B_t^d / r. \tag{4.7}$$

Given our assumption that in aggregate firms do not hold idle money balances, all investment must be financed by borrowing. Consistent planning for the business sector implies matching investment demand with a plan to supply new claims. The bond is the only such claim in the model. Thus it follows that

$$I_t = \Delta B_t^s / r. \tag{4.8}$$

Sales of new bonds result in 'activation of idle balances'. This latter term does not mean increasing the supply of money (which is ruled out) but changing the distribution of money by inducing householders to spend money holdings on bonds, thus providing funds for investment.[8] The act of supplying new bonds, by pushing up the rate of interest, encourages a portfolio switch from money to bonds. It is only through issuing new securities that firms can induce an activation of money balances. If firms held money balances, aggregate investment could be financed for a time by the business sector's 'dishoarding' those balances, thus rendering them 'active'. This financing option is plausible for an individual firm; in treating firms as an aggregate it is closer to the facts to represent the sector as a net borrower.

It can be seen from equations (4.7) and (4.8) that equality of saving and investment is not a sufficient condition for equilibrium: the form of saving must correspond to changes in the stock of claims as well. In this restricted model, equilibrium is only possible in the goods, bonds, and money markets when $\Delta M^d = 0$: equilibrium exists if there is some interest rate at which all new saving flows into the bond market.

This outcome is quite plausible in any single period. But equilibrium is defined as a position which will be maintained in the absence of exogenous disturbances – maintained, that is, for more than a single period. General considerations of portfolio balance suggest that as bond holdings increase (and money holdings do not) the public becomes progressively less interested in acquiring additional bonds. One wculd predict that in order to persuade households to increase their lending to firms, higher rates of return would have to be offered. The equilibrium solution generated by the *IS–LM* model, in contrast, suggests either that there exists some rate of interest at which savers are prepared to continue indefinitely to extend finance to firms, being satiated with money holdings, or that equilibrium is reached at that rate of interest just high enough to drive net new investment to zero.

It is not usually assumed that the only solution to the *IS–LM* model is that of the stationary state. For there to exist an equilibrium with positive rates of saving and investment, savers must at some interest rate exhibit absolute 'illiquidity preference'. In the *IS–LM* model, the existence of such a rate and the plausibility of the demand-for-bonds function which would ensure such a rate has simply been assumed. The bond market having been dropped, the question has remained out of sight. And it was not a problem to loanable-funds theorists. The distinction made in the loanable-funds tradition between 'saving' and 'hoarding' implies a definition of saving which excludes net additions to money balances: 'saving' consists of making funds available to business firms. This definition of saving might appear to provide an escape from the unpalatable conclusion we have just reached, for in terms of our model, the loanable-funds definition makes saving identical with bond purchases. Equality of saving and investment is then identical with equality of new bond supply and the incremental demand for bonds.

That this escape is unacceptable has been powerfully demonstrated by Patinkin.[9] To paraphrase his argument: if investment is identified with supplies of new bonds and saving with a demand for bonds, the bond market is a mirror image of the goods market: one of the two is entirely redundant, and must be dropped. That will leave us with two independent markets, the goods (or bond) market and the money market, one of which, in turn, is dropped on the basis of Walras' Law. The model is left with one market to determine two unknowns.

In any case, this ruse is inconsistent with one of the basic assumptions of the model, embodied in equation (4.7): that savers may, depending on the rate of interest, attempt to save by acquiring additional money balances. There is only one bond demand function consistent with the model, as we elaborated in the previous section.

## THE IMPLICIT BOND MARKET FUNCTIONS

One can always construct bond demand and supply functions which will be consistent with the equilibrium solution derived from the rest of the model. We have concluded earlier in the chapter that the consistent sectoral behaviour assumption does not permit that latitude: the bond demand and supply functions follow by necessity from the rest of the specification. The question is only whether the properties of those functions are acceptable. It is obvious from what was said earlier that the properties of the bond demand function must differ from those associated with portfolio balance theory if the equilibrium solution of *IS-LM* is not be restricted to the stationary state. The bond demand function may be derived as follows:

Explicit forms must be postulated for the implicit equations (4.2) and (4.3). Linear equations are convenient:

$$S_t = S_0 + S_y Y, \tag{4.9}$$

$$M_t^d = L_0 + L_y Y + L_r r. \tag{4.10}$$

Incremental ('flow') demand functions may be inferred from stock demand equations and vice versa as long as (1) the measurement period of the flow demand begins and ends with the points of time for which the stock demand is defined[10] and (2) beginning-of-period stocks are equilibrium values. Making these assumptions we can write:

$$\Delta \frac{B_t^d}{r_t} = \frac{B_t^d}{r_t} - \frac{B_{t-1}^d}{r_{t-1}} = \frac{r_{t-1} B_t^d - B_{t-1}^d r_t}{r_{t-1} r_t}, \tag{4.11}$$

and we take the first difference of (4.10) to obtain

$$\Delta M_t^d = L_y \Delta Y_t + L_r \Delta r_t. \tag{4.12}$$

From (4.7), (4.9), (4.11) and (4.12) we have:

$$\frac{r_{t-1} B_t^d - B_{t-1}^d r_t}{r_{t-1} r_t} = S_0 + S_y Y - L_y \Delta Y_t - L_r \Delta r_t,$$

or, rearranging:

$$B_t^d = r_t \left[ S_0 + S_y Y_t - L_y Y_t + L_y Y_{t-1} + L_r r_{t-1} + \frac{B_{t-1}^d}{r_{t-1}} \right] - L_r r_t^2. \tag{4.13}$$

In similar fashion one may derive the implicit bond supply function. Let the investment function take the form

$$I_t = I_0 + I_r r_t, \; I_r < 0. \tag{4.14}$$

Then

$$B_t^s = r_t\left[I_0 + \frac{B_{t-1}^s}{r_{t-1}}\right] + I_r r_t^2. \tag{4.15}$$

One must doubt whether these bond demand and supply functions, which, it cannot be too strongly emphasised, follow by necessity from the other functions of the *IS–LM* model, are functions most economists would propose as a matter of choice. They have several unexpected and uncomfortable properties, principally (1) they depend on past values of income and the interest rate as well as current ones and are therefore dynamic, (2) the determinants include products of variables, which have no obvious intuitive interpretation, (3) they are quadratic and therefore not single-valued with respect to $r_t$ and (4) the interest-intercept of the demand function is ambiguous in sign. The last two properties, fortunately, need not detain us for long.

Both functions are of the form $B = Ar + Cr^2$. The roots are $r = 0, -A/C$. Write $A_d$, $C_d$ and $A_s$, $C_s$ to indicate the coefficients for the demand and supply functions respectively. The signs of $A_s$, $C_d$, and $C_s$ are definite. It follows from $C_d > 0$ and $C_s < 0$ that the solution to $\partial B_t^d / \partial r_t = 0$ is a minimum and to $\partial B_t^s / \partial r_t = 0$ is a maximum. From $A_s > 0$ and $C_s < 0$ we know that the interest-rate intercept for $B^s_t$ is positive. $A_d$ however is ambiguous in sign. Ruling out $A_d = 0$ as unlikely, the two bond demand functions consistent with (4.11) are shown as $B_1^d$ and $B_2^d$ in Figure 4.1 along with the bond

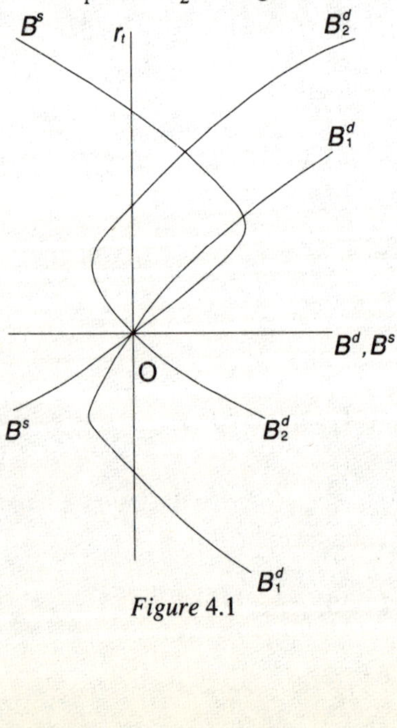


*Figure* 4.1

supply function given by (4.14). The axes follow the conventions of economists rather than of mathematicians.

The functions are assumed to have economic meaning only in the positive quadrant.[11] $B^s$ is backward-bending because it is the money proceeds of bond sales which determine firms' supply decisions. As can be seen, multiple solutions will not occur. All intersections will be stable. The only unacceptable feature of the functions with respect to the current interest rate is the implication of $B^d{}_1$, that positive bond-holding begins at interest rates adjacent to zero, indicating a trivial convenience yield on money. More disturbing than any flaw in the *ceteris paribus* response to the current interest rate is the fact that the $B^d$ function contains arguments which have no obvious interpretation.

The fundamental point is that the functions are explicitly dynamic. This exposes the contradiction inherent in a static model which is a mixture of stocks and flows. Only pure flow models *or* pure stock models are both static and internally consistent. Only if all goods are perishable are consumption and income approximately flows. But saving and investment involve decisions to hold assets through time; and in a money economy expenditure involves the transfer of an asset between transactors. If the stock demand for assets is determined by a vector of variables $X_1, X_2, \ldots, X_n$, and planned saving takes the form of an incremental demand for those assets, then saving is a function of $\Delta X_1, \Delta X_2, \ldots, \Delta X_n$. The *IS–LM* model specifies one stock demand function and the saving function, both as functions of levels of the variables $Y$ and $r$. The omitted equation, the bond demand function, must therefore contain the terms in $\Delta Y$ and $\Delta r$. Its peculiar form, involving terms in $r_t r_{t-1}$, $r_t \Delta Y_t$, and the like, derives from the model's somewhat illogical specification in which one stock and one flow function have levels of the variables as arguments.

It follows from the inclusion of functions determining stocks that equilibrium in the *IS–LM* model implies the stationary state. In equilibrium, $\Delta B = \Delta r = \Delta Y = 0$. Hence (4.13) becomes

$$B = r(S_0 + S_y Y - L_y Y + L_y Y + L_r r + B/r) - L_r r^2, \tag{4.16}$$

which reduces to

$$S_0 + S_y Y = 0. \tag{4.17}$$

Similarly (4.15) reduces to

$$I_0 + I_r r = 0. \tag{4.18}$$

It is the insistence on incorporating financing constraints which has exposed the contradictions in the *IS–LM* model. It might be argued that if it is a reasonable approximation to abstract from the influence of investment on the capital stock it is equally a minor simplification to ignore the influence of saving and investment on the bond and money markets. The two problems are similar in one respect: both involve changes in existing stocks – changes which might be presumed to be small relative to those stocks. But the case for ignoring the influence of *I* or *K* is not one of scale; it follows from the assumption of period. The time which elapses between ordering or constructing new capital and its production of additional output might be quite substantial; therefore in the short run one may concentrate on investment as demand for current output and neglect its effect on productive capacity. But the effect of a decision to float a new issue of bonds is immediate: the purpose of the flotation is to effect a redistribution of money purchasing-power as a *precondition* for carrying out an investment plan. The interest incentive required may or may not be small; that depends on demand conditions in the bond market. One cannot determine whether the effect *will* be small unless one explicitly considers those demand conditions.

In the *General Theory* the reason for ignoring financing flows was a different one: Keynes judged that the effect of these flows on interest rates would be outweighed by the effects of changes in expectation concerning the 'normal rate' (which *shift* the function relating speculative demand to the actual rate of interest).

## CONCLUSION

A well-known simple macro model has been examined in this chapter, to determine whether it is a satisfactory construction given that it is known to the participating decision units that every change must be financed, thus imposing a constraint not only on actual, *ex post* transactions but also on spending and saving *plans*.

It has been argued that the *IS–LM* model is unsatisfactory in its present form. The explicit recognition of the need to finance expenditure and find an asset form for saving leads immediately to the conclusion that the goods, bond and money markets are interdependent and that the consumption and demand-for-money functions postulated in this model imply demand-for-bonds functions which are not acceptable. The static form in which the model is expressed is misleading at best. The 'equilibrium solution' of the

*IS–LM* model is either transitory, dependent on very special conditions, or consistent only with the stationary state.

We have argued the case for specifying the portfolio demand equations explicitly and deriving the saving function. This departure from the custom of dropping the bond market generates sensible flow equations and allows for a complex relation between saving, wealth, and current or permanent income.[12]

The importance of the chapter, in my view, lies in the fact that these conclusions do not follow from special behavioural assumptions but from the recognition that trading always involves the exchange of assets of equal money value. This fact holds in both equilibrium and disequilibrium; thus it applies to the plans of rational transactors, not just to equilibrium market outcomes.

## Notes

1. The first major attempt to integrate finance and output was the work of Gurley and Shaw (1960). Horwich (1964) in his extensive study also attempts an integration, but unfortunately he misses a central implication of his own framework (see note 5). An approach similar to that taken in this paper is found in Rose (1959), Minsky (1957b), Davidson (1968a, 1968b) and Wells (1971). Christ (1967, 1968) and Ott and Ott (1965) have explored financial constraints on government policy decisions but they do not impose them on private-sector spending.
2. This point was made by Christ (1967, 1968) and Ott and Ott (1965).
3. Secondhand markets are implicitly assumed to be unimportant.
4. Clower (1965) has called this the 'dual decision hypothesis'. It is not really a behavioural hypothesis but a facet of the usual assumption of rationality in a world dominated by exchange for *quid pro quo*.
5. The need to finance every exchange – or more broadly the assumed absence of stealing, gifts, and other unilateral transfers – is the basis of Walras' Law. But compare the conclusions reached here with the usual expression of Walras' Law. The weakest statement of the Law is that equilibrium in the *n*th market is assumed if $n - 1$ markets are in equilibrium. Slightly stronger, because it encompasses disequilibrium, is the view expressed by Patinkin (1956; 1965, p. 37): he believes that Walras' Law yields a 'budget restraint for the economy', and from it the excess demand or supply in the *n*th market can be derived from the disequilibrium conditions in other markets. Our model shows that if Walras' Law is to be applied to planned magnitudes (rather than simply to outcomes) in models where disequilibrium is possible, then it refers to planning units or aggregates of those units. And if it does apply, it determines one entire behavioural function for each unit. If one follows tradition and eliminates the bond market, one does so not because its

equilibrium is assumed by equilibrium in other markets, but because both its demand function and its supply function are redundant equations. This is the point which Horwich (1964) misses.

6. We have here assumed that the interest rate does not determine the rate of saving but merely the choice of portfolio. The assumption does not materially affect any of our conclusions: it was made merely to conform to the dominant version of the *IS–LM* model, though it is worth noting that it is closer in spirit to the *General Theory* (Keynes, 1936) than is the later modification to include the rate of interest as a determinant of savings.
7. The bond demand and supply functions are specified in money terms, indicating the desire to place in securities, or to obtain, a given money sum. (For this reason the notation omits a time subscript on $r$; it is always the same as that on $B^d$ or $B^s$.) Under our assumption of fixed prices, the money and real values of borrowing are the same.
8. In a more general model which, instead of (4.3), specified

$$S_t = S(Y_t, r_t), S_r > 0, S_y > 0, \qquad (4.3)'$$

the rise in $r$ would encourage additional new saving out of a given income as well as causing a change in the desired portfolio.

9. Patinkin (1956; 1965, p. 262ff.). He is concerned with the 'Keynesian' identification of excess supply of money with excess demand for bonds, but the point applies equally to the present problem.
10. For a useful discussion of the issues involved, see Baumol (1962), especially the Appendix. He notes that there is no reason to suppose the intraperiod approach to end-of-period demand to be monotonic. The practical importance of this point depends on the length of the chosen unit period.
11. Negative bond demand could be regarded as bond supply if the assumption that households are always net creditors is relaxed. A symmetrical statement holds for bond supply.
12. In the original paper, the argument was extended to the Brainard and Tobin model, a permanent income model and a wealth model; consistent savings functions were derived for the *IS–LM* model and permanent income model from asset-holding hypotheses. (*Eds*)

# 5 A Comment on '*IS–LM*: An Explanation'

**Author's Note**

This paper was a comment on Sir John Hicks's paper '*IS–LM*: An Explanation', published in the *Journal of Post Keynesian Economics*, 1980–1.

Marshall's short period tends to be the 'excluded middle' in economic method. Production of output is the significant feature of the short period. Production fell out of sight early in the development of Keynesian economics: I learned from Augusto Graziani (1984) to think of *IS–LM* as a model of exchanges which take place after the level of output is already, somehow, determined. The similarity of Hicks's framework in '*IS–LM*: An Explanation' to that of the widely-criticised paper on the finance motive by Asimakopulos (1983) is striking. At least the framework is now proving controversial. (See the numerous comments on Asimakopulos, 1983, in the *Cambridge Journal of Economics* and in the *Journal of Post Keynesian Economics*.) I was loath to break off work on *Macroeconomics After Keynes* to write this piece. I am grateful to Paul Davidson and Geoff Harcourt for insisting that I do it.

## INTRODUCTION

Sir John Hicks has performed an invaluable service in delving into the history of the creation of *IS–LM* analysis and in providing an integration of his view of the analysis at the time of its conception with his later work on method in *Capital and Growth*. From these elements, I believe, the view expressed in *The Crisis in Keynesian Economics* is derived, and now we know more of the foundations of that view.

In scrutinising *IS–LM* analysis as a representation of Keynes, Sir John focuses on two crucial and intimately related issues: the nature of the price adjustment assumed and the question of period. I wish to comment mainly on the latter, but what I have to say I hope will illuminate the former.

## THE NATURE OF THE PRICE ADJUSTMENT

Whether explicitly or implicitly, all static analysis is confined to some period or other, if only because the nature of the supply curve depends on what is allowed to vary (Marshall). Within the period certain characteristics are fixed, and although the period may be repeated many times with values of the variables unchanged (tranquillity), it is in principle set off from the past and the future in a well-defined way.

What, Sir John asks, is the period appropriate to the analysis of Keynes's model of employment, and does *IS–LM* analysis embody an appropriate sense of period?

Sir John's answer to these questions is conditioned by his methodological approach. It is an approach which is so entrenched in the subject that it has become a 'maintained method' in the same sense as 'maintained hypothesis': that its assumptions are not meant to be challenged. I believe that the assumptions need to be challenged if Keynes, and the relationship of *IS–LM* to Keynes, is to be understood. They are (1) that variables are *determined* only in equilibrium, and (2) that 'flexible prices' imply the equality of demands and supplies. The second assumption gives rise to the common, though erroneous, understanding that it is necessary to impose exogenously-given wages and/or prices for the period if unemployment is to be a possibility. The first assumption gives rise to the particular characteristics of Sir John's 'year'.

Since the object of Keynes's analysis is to determine output and employment, it is clear that the Hicksian 'week' is not long enough, for with output largely predetermined, there is scope only for inventory changes, as Sir John says. And if output is predetermined, so, necessarily, is employment.

Sir John's proposed period, the 'year', has the following characteristics. It is long enough for current output to be adjusted to its equilibrium level. Equilibrium is defined as equality of saving and investment or, equivalently, the fulfilment of short-run demand expectations, the long-run expectations which determine investment demand being taken as given. The level of output so determined in turn determines offers of employment by means of a *rule* which relates current excess demand to employment. Adjustment is confined to output and employment (quantities), for wage and prices are fixed within the period. Adjustment of expectations, or adaptation to changed expectations, is left to multiperiod dynamics. The adjustment required for the establishment of single-period static equilibrium concerns only the adjustment of output to demand. (The role of expectations here is not entirely clear in Sir John's exposition, for reasons which I hope to make apparent.)

## PERIOD-MODELLING

I should like to approach the period-modelling of Keynes's theory slightly differently. I believe my approach to be a fair representation of Keynes, and it resolves some of the paradoxes which Sir John brings to the fore. Most of my discussion will concern output and employment; liquidity, as in Sir John's paper, comes in only at the end.

Begin by taking the period to be that for which a production and hiring decision is made: one decision, irrevocable until the beginning of the next production period. Call that period, if you like, a 'quarter', though in practical terms it will vary in calendar length according to the type of industry. In the nature of things, firms must decide their production and labour-hiring strategy for that period on an estimate or expectation of demand for the period. The profit-maximising firm will establish *both* the level of output and a pricing policy on the basis of the demand estimate, given their costs. It does not matter how unsure of that estimate they are; they must still act on it.

Their costs (the aggregate supply curve)[1] depend significantly on wages. If in the recent past they got all the labour they wanted at the going wage, and their estimate of demand for this period is not *greatly* different from previous levels, it may be reasonable for firms to estimate their costs on the basis of 'last quarter's' wage.[2] The amount of labour they need to produce to meet the demand according to standard profit maximisation, is then determined; and provided that when firms make their offer of employment their demands actually do not exceed the maximum amount of labour forthcoming at 'last quarter's' wage,[3] employment is determined, as are output and prices for the period.

There is, however, no way of knowing whether the levels of the variables are equilibrium values or not. Equilibrium will depend on demand expectations being met, and only well *after* these decisions have been made will the accuracy of the demand forecast be known: the actual volume of demand, to which the expectation must be compared, will only be known at the end of the period. Employment, in the production period, is determined by costs and forecasts of demand, not actual demand.

This fact implies that equilibrium employment takes more than one production period to establish. This is the point of Sir John's 'year': it comprises several 'quarters', so the equilibrium criterion can be applied. By incorporating into one period several evaluations of results and revisions of plans, the dichotomy between the *determination* of employment and its equilibrium level (whether full employment or not) and the assertion that employment can be determined in the first instance strictly in the minds of entrepreneurs – both uncomfortable ideas – can be avoided. They are, however, essential to Keynes, though obscured by his device (in the *General Theory*, ch. 3) of assuming that short-period demand-expectations *are* met, so that it looks as if employment is determined by actual, rather than expected, levels of demand. This assumption may create the impression that demand and employment are determined simultaneously or within a single period. However, unless one is prepared to impose on Keynes the assumption of tranquillity (in this case stability of demand) – an assumption which he was trying to overturn – simultaneity only occurs when firms hit on the right estimate of demand first time.

If expectations are *not* met, firms may, or may not, revise their expectations at the beginning of the following period. Whether they do so depends on their views concerning the stochastic component of demand or, equivalently, on their inventory policies. The more importance a firm attaches to the possibility that its misestimates are due to random fluctuations in demand, the more 'quarters' will elapse before it makes a change.

The number of production periods which elapse between falsification of expectation and a change in expectation thus varies among firms with different inventory policies and according to the perceived nature of the divergence between actual and expected demand. But since the 'quarter' is not a length of calendar time, there is no particular difficulty in this. Then we have a number of periods in which firms seek the position of the actual demand function (assuming – this is vital – that it has not moved again) by varying price, output, and employment (*P*, *Q*, *N*).

Still the 'year' is not accomplished, for in addition we have, at the macroeconomic level, the repercussions of changes in some firms' *P*, *Q*, *N* strategy on demand faced by other firms (the multiplier). These repercussions must work themselves out within the 'year' to give the equilibrium *P*, *Q*, and *N*. A 'year', therefore, is a period in which a good many decisions about the relevant variables may – indeed without excellent forecasting *will* – have been made.

## FIXPRICE METHOD

It is time to examine the application of the fixprice assumption to the 'year' in the light of the producer's strategy in the absence of either tranquillity or perfect foresight.

Within one production period the fixprice method is appropriate in the following sense: once the demand and cost expectations are made, there is for each firm only one solution which maximises expected profits. It involves a choice for the period of *both P* and *Q*. (The role of middlemen in setting prices is here ignored.) *P*, *Q*, and *N* are fixed at the beginning of the period – on, if you like, the opening 'day' of the 'quarter'. And there they stay until the 'quarter's' end. One could describe the model as fixprice (*and* fixquantity), but this fixing is, of course, endogenous.

The extension of fixprice to the longer period when quantities may change to establish equilibrium precludes, however, the possibility of profit maximisation, or perhaps a better expression is that fixprice 'adds an extra constraint subject to which profits may be maximised'. The constraint is, however, gratuitous. There is no evidence whatever that Keynes ever adopted it, and no reason to believe that the model of Chapter 21 is different from the rest of the *General Theory* (as Sir John proposed), rather than an elaboration of the elements which go into the price–quantity decision only alluded to in the rest of the book. The multiplier includes both price and quantity adjustments, as Chapter 10 of the *General Theory* makes quite clear.

Now I turn briefly to the problem of the integration of production and finance. There is no doubt that the holding period horizon of speculators is less than the production period of firms, or that transactions in 'bonds' establish a portfolio (stock) equilibrium while $Q$ is a flow. However, neither the different horizon nor the contrast in dimensions creates problems within a single production period. The rate of interest, determined by liquidity preference at the beginning of the 'quarter', along with long-period expectations, fixes the investment component of actual demand for the period; capital-goods suppliers may consider the interest rate when estimating the demand for their output at the beginning of the 'quarter'. Transactions demand, like production, must be forward-looking and based on estimates of expenditure made at the beginning of the 'quarter'.

Thus the portfolio adjustments which matter to $P$, $Q$, $N$ determination take place at the same time or just prior to the first 'day' of the 'quarter' in which those decisions are made. Subsequent readjustments of the portfolio of financial assets may affect future levels of demand or even the actual outcome in the present 'quarter', if investment is quick to react. The $P$, $Q$, $N$ decision is, however, fixed for the 'quarter' regardless of those readjustments. The difference of horizon, though real, is of no consequence.

Furthermore, since the determination of $P$, $Q$ and $N$ takes place on the first 'day' of the 'quarter', i.e., at something close to a point of time, there is no conflict between stocks and flows either. It is only the search for equilibrium $P$, $Q$ and $N$ which poses dimensionality problems in combination with the liquidity side.

Looking at Keynes in terms of production periods, several of which are needed before equilibrium can be established, has the following advantage. A one-period model, whatever its characteristics, is a very difficult framework into which to incorporate liquidity. Money is like the queen of spades in a game of hearts: no one wants to be holding it when the game is over. It is essential, for liquidity, that the game go on. There is room for liquidity in Sir John's 'year', but what is expected to happen at the end of it? We know the answer for it appears in the first of Sir John's *Critical Essays* (1967). It is an unhappy answer. Far better to structure the game so that it does go on; the production-period solution can repeat itself indefinitely once equilibrium is reached, and still liquidity may be wanted against the probability, which by construction is non-zero, that something surprising may happen.

## CONCLUSIONS

I conclude from this exploration that fixprice *IS–LM* analysis pertains to the determination of income (*PQ*) at the beginning of the 'quarter', in the special circumstance when firms estimate aggregate demand correctly, i.e., where there is no conflict between determination of income for one production period and equilibrium, assuming *actual* demand is stable. The fixprice assumption is necessary only because the model takes no explicit account of aggregate supply. Without either fixprice or the supply side, the model does not determine employment (except by a 'rule'), for employment, in the short period, is uniquely related to output, and *IS–LM* only determines income. The applicability of the model bears a relationship, but a relationship of limited scope, to Keynes's model.

### Notes

1. This is a mistake. The aggregate supply curve is costs plus expected profits (quasi rents) (V.C., 1991).
2. If for any reason labour supply conditions are believed to have altered since the beginning of the previous 'quarter' – i.e., when labour was last hired – some other estimate will be made. To take this into account would greatly complicate the analysis to no significant gain.
3. If there is excess demand for labour, the wage will have to change. Variations in wages due to this cause are permitted through the device of establishing aggregate demand and supply in wage-units: wages, like prices, are not fixed in the *General Theory*.

# 6 Keynesians, Monetarists and Keynes: The End of the Debate – or a Beginning?

## INTRODUCTION

In large part, monetarists and Keynesians, in their debate on the mechanism and efficiency of monetary policy, have accepted as ground rules the same economic model, the *IS–LM* model due to Hicks. It has been shown (Chick, 1973b; 1977, ch. 3) that short of restricting the parameters of that model to extreme values the debate cannot be settled on *a priori* argument alone. It was then suggested that the debate might usefully be couched in terms of the assumptions concerning adjustment rather than the static parameters, though this suggestion required persuading the monetarists to turn their attention to the early stages of the path to equilibrium. These points were made in the context of the ground rules of the debate as it then stood. Both the method – comparative static analysis and dynamic adjustment according to the correspondence principle – and a crucial assumption – that the mode of introduction of new money is a matter of indifference – were accepted for purposes of the argument.

It was indicated (*ibid.*, pp. 131–9) that this assumption concerning monetary changes was not satisfactory. Indeed, in 1972, Friedman paved the way for considering different modes of monetary change, in a backhanded sort of way: he argued that the mode of financing fiscal policy was important, fiscal policies being more effective if accom-panied by monetary changes than by changes in interest-bearing debt or tax changes. Here at least is recognition that monetary changes always entail a change in some other economic variable as a counterpart. Friedman's well-known, because colourful, assumption that money rains down on the economy from a helicopter has one supreme methodological attraction: it permits us to hold to the established method of analysing a change in only one variable at a time, *ceteris paribus*. Recognising that all monetary change involves some *other* change as well forces us to relinquish that method.

It was also hinted (*idem.*) that final equilibrium solutions as given by comparative static analysis were inapplicable: in the real world the effects of monetary change (or any other sort of change) work their way through time and the final equilibrium result obtained by comparative static analysis is never reached. This is not just due to the length of calendar time required: that would not be a serious problem if we could be sure that the approach to equilibrium was always monotonic, for we at least could reach conclusions about the direction of change. But there have been too many studies of monetary questions in which overshooting of the final position figures prominently (e.g. Laidler, 1968; Tucker, 1966; Tanner, 1969) for us to rest our case on that. More fundamentally, however, the path to equilibrium is likely to alter the structure of the economy, so that comparative static results do not apply.

In this chapter, therefore, the method of comparative statics is supplanted by process analysis. Because of the complexity inherent in the use of process analysis (Faxen, 1957) the effects of monetary change cannot be traced through very many periods. Nevertheless, the results from using this method are quite powerful. As a result of the analysis,

1. a new interpretation of Keynes's position on the relative efficacy of fiscal and monetary policy is offered;
2. the difference between Keynes's analysis in the *General Theory* and the subsequent 'Keynesian' position is clarified; and
3. the fundamental unity of the monetarist and 'Keynesian' positions is made more apparent (thus continuing the process begun in Chick, 1973b).

## MODES OF MONETARY CHANGE

A change in the money stock of a closed economy can come about in several different ways. There are, for a start, two suppliers of money: the monetary authorities and the banking system, supplying high-powered and deposit money, respectively. When the monetary authorities allow the supply of high-powered money to increase, an interest rate policy is being pursued, whether implicitly or explicitly. If, for example, the government, for contracyclical reasons, is running a deficit, and – also for contracyclical reasons – it is undesirable to allow the interest rate to rise, then where the deficit is financed by issuing government debt to the public, the central bank simultaneously provides the money wherewith to purchase it; that is, the form of financing by borrowing is preserved, but the usual need to raise interest rates in order to sell the securities is obviated and the net result is a rise in the money supply. As a shorthand, this process will be designated 'fiscal policy financed by new money'.

Open-market operations can of course occur even in the absence of the need to provide new government finance; these constitute the second main source of monetary change. The third main influence of the authorities over the money supply is exercised through the various means of affecting bank lending: calls or releases of special deposits, limits on the expansion of advances, and so on. Finally, the banks themselves can initiate monetary change, either because they have reserves in excess of those demanded by the authorities, acquired in a period of pessimism and uncertainty, or because they have some (though in this country quite limited) power to encourage a flow of funds to them by raising rates of interest on their liabilities or indeed, by creating new, more attractive, forms of liability such as negotiable certificates of deposit.

Keynes did not stress these differences. In a passage which, read superficially, provides the source of the Keynesian contention that money ($M$) affects income ($Y$) chiefly through the interest rate ($r$), Keynes treats the monetary financing of government deficits and bank expansion as equivalent:

> The relation of changes in $M$ to $Y$ and $r$ depends, in the first instance, on the way in which changes in $M$ come about . . . . [If] changes in $M$ are due to the Government printing money wherewith to meet its current expenditure . . . [the] new money accrues as someone's income. The new level of income, however, will not continue sufficiently high for the requirements of $M_1$ [transactions and precautionary balances] to absorb the whole of the increase in $M$; and some portion of the money will seek an outlet in buying securities or other assets until $r$ has fallen so as to bring about an increase in the magnitude of $M_2$ [speculative balances] and at the same time to stimulate a rise in $Y$ to such an extent that the new money is absorbed either in $M_2$ or in the $M_1$ which corresponds to the rise in $Y$ caused by the fall in $r$. Thus at one remove this case comes to the same thing as the alternative case, where the new money can only be issued in the first instance by a relaxation of the conditions of credit by the banking system, so as to induce someone to sell the banks a debt or a bond in exchange for the new cash. It will, therefore, be safe for us to take the latter case as typical. (1936, p. 200.)

It is not safe. Keynes, while beginning the passage by emphasising the importance of the transaction which is the counterpart of the monetary increase, ends by saying it makes no difference. We shall establish that it does.

## DEFICITS FINANCED BY NEW MONEY

Monetary finance of government deficits is not unusual in the UK. Monetary policy in the 1960s was directed towards the interest rate, often mitigating its fluctuations. To the extent that the rate was stabilised, fluctuations in the government deficit were reflected in changes in the money supply.

The important feature of the direct financing case is that autonomous expenditure and the supply of high-powered money increase together, as one and the same transaction. The government's expenditure plan is made *effective* by the creation of new cash: it could not take place without it (unless interest rates were permitted to rise). There should be no dispute, therefore, about the first-round consequences of this policy action. The monetary increase, which the monetarists regard as the active element of the policy, is simply the counterpart of the income generated by government expenditure, the aspect focused upon by Keynesians. In the first round, the government purchases goods and services in exchange for money, providing income paid in the form of money, to the suppliers of those goods and services.

Both Keynesians and monetarists should be able to agree that there is now an excess supply of money. The disagreement concerns the reaction to that excess supply. Keynesians assume that the public react solely by buying bonds; this is the foundation of their assertion that the effect of a monetary increase on income takes place through interest rate changes. Monetarists, on the other hand, would argue that the new money will raise the demand for goods. It is widely believed that this difference of view stems from contrasting assumptions about the substitutability of money for commodities and financial assets. At the extreme, Keynesians are said to believe that the only relevant margin of choice is between money and bonds, while an equally extreme classical view acknowledges only the transactions motive for holding money, thus predicting that an excess demand for money falls entirely on the market for goods. Tobin (1961, 1969) and Friedman (1956) have proposed less extreme versions which, respectively, still preserve the Keynesian emphasis on the money-bond choice and support the monetarist prediction that a change in the money supply is manifest mainly in changes in output and/or price rather than changes in the interest rate.

But in fact this question of relative substitutability, connected to the question of motives for money-holding, is quite beside the point. In the context of process analysis, which was undoubtedly the method of Keynes's analysis in the passage just quoted, our modern antagonists are referring to different stages in the sequence of events following the monetary change. Let us return to Keynes's description. In the period in which the deficit occurs, $M$ and $Y$ increase by the same amount, the amount of the deficit. The need for transactions balances rises with increased income but not *pari passu*: the Cambridge $k$ is less than one and there are economies of scale in precautionary holdings also (Patinkin 1956; 1965, pp. 82–8 and Appendix). The money not absorbed by transactions and precautionary balances will find its way into the speculative sphere. Initially there is no demand for speculative money holdings (the interest rate is unaltered). Purchases of bonds then lower the interest rates until the speculative demand rises sufficiently to take up all the new money not absorbed by income-related demands. That occurs in the period subsequent to the introduction of new money. The lower interest rate stimulates investment and raises income (and transactions and precautionary demand) still further, somewhat reversing the initial fall in interest rates. It is only to this *second* reaction in the process, the disposal of money not absorbed by $M_1$ balances, that the 'Keynesian bond–money margin' pertains.

Let us explore the transactions demand further, for it is here that the money–goods margin is important. Unlike precautionary demand, which is also used for the purchase of goods but only occasionally, transactions balances circulate continuously in exchange for goods. They are not really 'held' except on average. Some might suppose that people, or firms, would hold additional transactions balances as a luxury (Friedman, 1959), using some of their increased income to lengthen the period between trips to the market or to the bank (cf. Clower, 1969, Introduction; 1970). For simplicity, however, it is helpful to assume that changes in the money supply leave the pattern of payments unaffected. Then the increased transactions balances unambiguously would be used in the purchase of commodities, if the new money accrued to households, or raw materials and labour if it accrued to firms.

**Response of Consumers**

When household incomes rise, it is typically assumed that both consumption and saving rise. Some of the new money finances the incremental consumption; the rest, saving, may (depending on expectations of interest rate changes) be used to purchase bonds. In other words, that part of the new money which is added to transactions balances as it circulates in exchange for goods finances what Keynesians call the multiplier, creating income changes in addition to the initial change arising from the deficit.

From the monetarist point of view, the stimulating effects of government expenditure arise from the propensity of those who acquire additional money balances to spend those balances on commodities. But what is the difference? To Keynesians, increased income is an incentive to spend, and financing is rather ignored, it being assumed that income is paid in the form of money. To monetarists, money burns a hole in people's pockets, no matter how it gets there; whether it represents additional income, as in the case being considered, or is an increment to wealth, income remaining unchanged, as in the helicopter case, it raises the budget restraint. A spending decision needs money to finance it, and a rise in the budget restraint (extra money) does typically result in an increment of spending. Keynesians and monetarists should agree on this point. It is awkward for both if they do not, for if Keynesians wish to deny the monetarists' 'direct effect' they must repudiate the multiplier; and if monetarists are to sustain the importance of the direct effect, they must accept its consequence, the multiplier.[1] On this, the two sides should agree.

Conflict may still arise, however, both about the fundamental issue of causation and about the *extent* of expenditure in all rounds after the initial change. First, causation. The monetarist position is that monetary changes *cause* changes in income. So the initial fiscal action, in which money and income increase simultaneously rather than in causal sequence, does not relate to their theory. It is the subsequent rounds of income change which are relevant. Their theory would describe events as follows: each person in the multiplier chain receives an increment of income in the form of money, which money is more than sufficient to cover the old level of transactions. The excess supply of money is spent on goods, which generates income. Thus the monetary increase plays a causal role in the rise in income. From a Keynesian point of view, the desire to increase expenditure comes from the realisation of a higher level of income. The increased volume of money balances (larger pay packet) merely *enables* that desire to become effective in the market place. Its role is not causal.

Second, the *extent* of induced expenditure. Keynesians would insist that the amount was given by the marginal propensity to consume, in each round. The monetarist position is less clear, for they approach the problem as one of adjusting to an excess stock of money. There is on the face of it no simple relationship between the existence of this excess stock and the *rate* at which consumers attempt to get rid of it by spending it. This is a question of adjustment speed, for which we need to make some assumption such as equality of marginal and average income velocity (the timing of payments remains unchanged; the extra expenditure is spread evenly over the expenditure period).[2] If, by such an assumption, the two approaches were made comparable, it is likely that monetarists would assert a larger impact on the goods market than would Keynesians. This can be inferred from the monetarists' tendency to play down, and even deny, an interest rate effect of monetary change. For there to be no interest rate effect it would appear that one of three assumptions must be adopted: either (1) the marginal propensity to save is zero (with its attendant problems for stability) or (2) the rate of increase of private[3] financial assets keeps pace with the desire of savers to place money at interest, or (3) savers hold all the unspent portion of their new incomes as idle money. It is difficult to imagine modern monetarists owning up to any of these propositions,[4] particularly the last, which, ironically, is the liquidity trap.

Monetarists have avoided having to adopt one of these alternatives by changing the definitions of consumption and saving. Keynes, pursuing the effects of money flows, defined consumption as consumers' expenditure on commodities. Saving, therefore, could take the form only of purchases of financial assets or of idle money holdings. Monetarists have adopted the Fisherian schema, in which consumption is the stream of utility from commodities; saving, therefore, may take the form of purchases of claims to future utility streams, through the acquisition of durable goods. This change of concept permits monetarists to save face when confronted with the choices given above, but does not, of course, contribute to the settlement of differences with Keynesians.[5]

## Response of Firms

We now turn to the response of firms whose sales have risen as a result of government purchases. If the increase in sales is thought to be more than transitory, a revision of output and pricing plans is called for. Assuming an upward-sloping marginal cost curve in the short run, the likely outcome is an increase of both price and output. The increased cash flow from sales will finance the rise in outlays for raw materials and labour to prepare for an expansion of output. Again, these expenditures will have multiplier effects, and again, if the incremental cash flow exceeds the increased outlays, the remainder will probably be placed in short-term securities, pending an investment decision. The extent to which the multiplier consists of real output changes rather than price changes is decided here. Once again, both income and the interest rate are affected in ways which both Keynesians and monetarists should be willing to accept.

## Further Considerations

Overshooting of the interest rate is virtually inevitable, due to the fact that changes in income through the multiplier take time. Keynes short-circuits this process, leaping straight from the interest rate effect to the final equilibrium with his phrase 'at the same time to stimulate a rise in $Y$ to such an extent that the new money is absorbed'. It will not happen 'at the same time', of course. Assuming (unrealistically) that the initial monetary increase is the only one, money which goes into bonds as a temporary abode of purchasing-power will return to active circulation as income grows over time (perhaps quite a long time) and the initial fall in interest will be reversed at least to some extent and perhaps completely. It is even possible that the final equilibrium rate will be higher than the rate obtaining before the deficit is undertaken. (The reason for this ambiguous outcome can be glimpsed in what follows.)

To assume no further monetary increase is unrealistic for two reasons. First, the initial fall in interest is likely to stimulate investment, an activity typically financed by borrowing and often financed initially by *bank* borrowing (which increases the money supply) and funded later. Second, the deficit was financed by high-powered money, the bulk of which would not normally remain in the hands of the public but would find its way to the banking system, where it would constitute an increase in reserves and a base for new lending, just at the time when the demand for bank loans is increasing on account of the favourable prospects for investment. By now it is obvious that to trace out the full effects would be a formidable task. And it would only divert us from our main purpose, which is to explore the difference between new money which finances a government deficit and new money arising from bank lending.

## MONEY CREATED BY BANK LENDING

We now turn to examining the policy of money creation achieved by stimulating an increase in bank lending. Suppose, beginning in bank portfolio equilibrium, that the central bank releases special deposits. Banks have been provided with excess reserves, other things being equal. So the banks should now be willing to expand their earning assets at every given rate of return: their supply-of-loans function has shifted rightward. Assuming no previous rationing of credit (by applying exceptionally rigorous standards of credit-worthiness, for example) and given a downward sloping demand curve for loans, a fall in the loan rate is required if the *actual* volume of loans is to increase. (A stable demand curve for loans implies no change in borrowers' expectations. This is to some extent unrealistic in the circumstances postulated. We shall return to this point later.) The money supply (deposits) will not rise until loans *have* increased. Thus a fall in the interest rate (now the bank loan rate; in the previous section it was the rate on securities) must occur *prior* to and as a precondition for a money supply increase. While the interest rate in the deficit/new-money case played a role in the transmission of policy in the periods *after* the initial increase in the money supply, the role of the interest rate in the transmission of this present form of monetary policy is to convert an increase in bank reserves – which are *not* money – into a rise in deposit holdings of the private sector, which are money.

This is the point at which Keynesians evoke the image of the horse that will not drink. The argument that in a depression an increase in bank reserves will not increase loans, while seeming plausible in a verbal presentation, is harder to sustain in the face of some simple geometry. In Figures 6.1 and 6.2 let $D_{L0}$ be the demand to maintain the stock of already outstanding loans, $D_L$ the total demand for loans (hence at $r_0$ no new loans are sought; at higher rates borrowers wish to repay), and $S_L$ the banks' willingness to issue and maintain a given level of loans. $S_L$ shifts to $S'_L$ as a result of the provision of reserves. For loans not to expand, either banks are in their own 'liquidity trap' (Figure 6.1) or the demand for loans is totally inelastic (Figure 6.2). A case has been made for the former in recession, though it has been strongly challenged:[6] it has been supposed that banks react to the greater uncertainty and higher probability of bad debts by holding excess reserves rather than expanding loans. And clearly the less responsive borrowers are to interest costs the less the expansion provoked by a given fall in interest rates – though some increase in lending will still

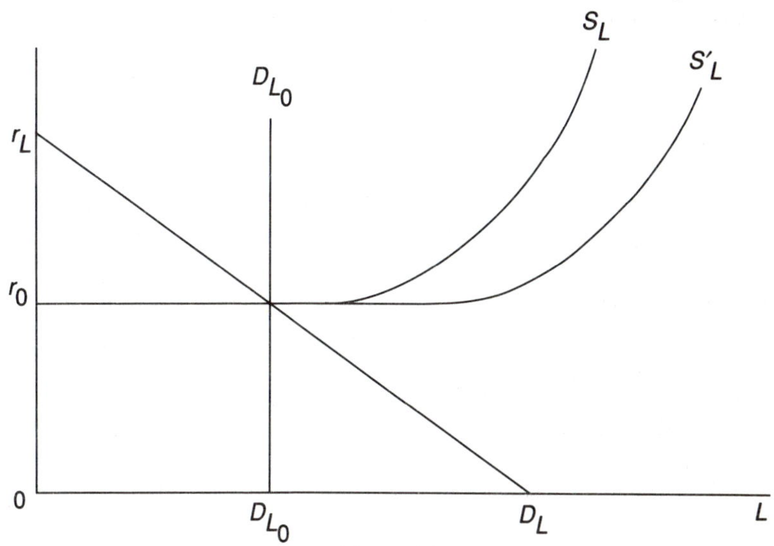


*Figure* 6.1

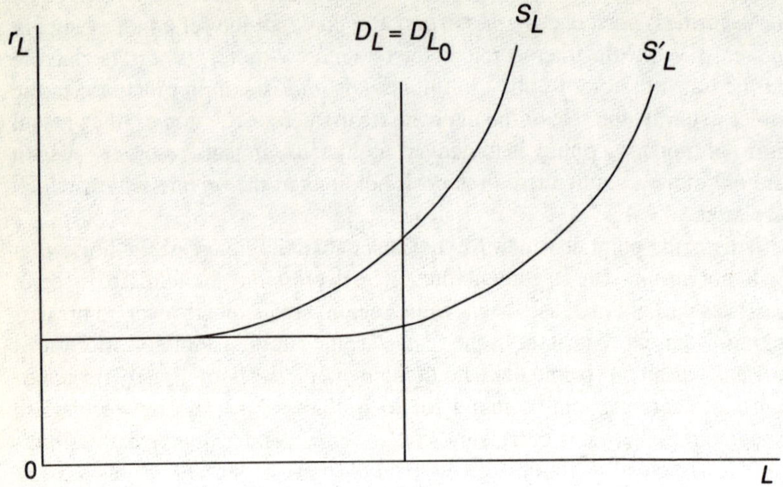


*Figure* 6.2

take place, even given unchanged expectations, as long as $D_L$ has some elasticity.

The monetary authorities have always relied to some extent on an expectation effect of a monetary policy shift. In relaxing a constraint on the banks, the authorities indicate an expansionary stance, which firms should see as favourable to profits and investment, thus encouraging borrowing. In terms of the Figures, the $D_L$ function shifts to the right, and bank lending may increase without any fall in the loan rate. Thus when expectations are allowed to change, a change in the interest rate is not *essential* to the transmission of this form of monetary policy. Its significance depends on the 'announcement effect' of policy on expectations.

The amount of new money created by a relaxation of special deposits, then, depends on the elasticities of the demand and supply of bank finance and on the extent, if any, of shifts in these functions. But for simplicity we have bypassed an important point. The effect of the monetary increase on expenditure and thus on the generation of *income* depends on the extent to which the banks' expansion takes the form of new loans (whether overdrafts or the purchase of newly issued securities) rather than the purchase of existing securities, and on the intentions of borrowers. Expansion of new loans provides funds to those who wish to deficit-spend. Those who issue liabilities against themselves can reliably be assumed not to intend to hold the proceeds of borrowing as idle money, except for the short time for which the 'finance motive'[7] is relevant.[8] However, there remains the question of whether the proceeds will be spent on commodities or on securities. In the case of firms borrowing by means of new issues of securities (which will not bulk large in bank credit in any case) it is extremely unlikely that the proceeds will go to finance holdings of other securities though for individuals purchases of securities cannot be ruled out. The preponderance of existing securities in the market ensures that most of the money channelled into securities markets will not support deficit expenditure.

Furthermore, not all the banks' expansion will take the form of new loans. They too may make purchases of existing securities.[9] It is often asserted that these purchases could have an immediate effect on expenditure, as people sell their securities to the banks in order to spend the proceeds. This is quite a reasonable supposition for a particular individual – people often sell securities to make purchases, say of consumer durables. But at the *aggregate* level it is less plausible. It supposes that security-holders in aggregate have, simultaneously with the authorities' decision to expand bank reserves, decided to spend out of accumulated wealth – that is, to dissave. Clearly such behaviour in aggregate presumes a shift in preferences. Analysis is usually conducted against the background of stable preferences; we wish to adhere to this convention. At best, sellers of securities in aggregate may be expected to spend some of their capital gains. (More of this in a moment.)

To fix ideas, represent the assets giving rise to new deposits as *OD*, *NS* and *OS* for overdrafts, new securities and old securities, respectively, and $a_1, a_2, a_3$ as the banks' marginal propensities to increase deposits by expansion of *OD*, *NS* and *OS* respectively. The *a*'s sum to unity. Then define $b_2$, $b_3$, $b_4$ and $b_5$ as borrowers' marginal propensities to use *OD*s to buy new securities, to buy old securities, to hold deposits idle, and to buy goods, respectively; $C_3$, $C_4$ and $C_5$ as the proportional allocation of the proceeds of a new issue to the purchase of old securities, idle balances and goods; and $d_2$, $d_3$, $d_4$ and $d_5$ as the proportional allocation of the proceeds of a sale from portfolio to the purchase of newly-issued stock other old stock, idle balances and goods. Relationships between expenditure and balance-sheet changes are given in Table 6.1. The following characteristics are assumed:

$$a_1 > a_3 > a_2;\ a_2 \text{ is small;}$$

$$b_5 > (b_2 + b_3);\ b_4 = 0;$$

$$c_5 = 1;\ c_3 = c_4 = 0;$$

$$(d_2 + d_3) < d_4;\ d_5 \text{ is small.}$$

*Table* 6.1 Expenditure and modes of finance

| | *Overdrafts, OD* | *New securities, NS* | *Old securities, OS* | *Deposits* | *Consumption + investment* |
|---|---|---|---|---|---|
| Change in bank assets | $a_1$ | $a_2$ | $a_3$ | 1 | n.a. |
| Money borrowed from banks | –1 | $b_2$ | $b_3$ | $b_4 = 0$ | $b_5$ |
| Allocation of proceeds of a new issue | n.a. | –1 | $c_3 = 0$ | $c_4 = 0$ | $c_5 = 1$ |
| Allocation of proceeds of a sale from portfolio | n.a. | $d_2$ | $-1 + d_3$ | $d_4$ | $d_5$ |

To the extent that deposit expansion results from new loans, expenditure on goods may reliably be assumed to increase. If $b_2$ were zero, initial expenditure rises by the same amount as the rise in the money supply. This is perhaps the sense in which bank lending is similar to public works financed by new money, as Keynes suggested. The earlier remarks on the Keynesian and monetarist positions apply.

To the extent that the banks' expansion takes the form of purchases of existing securities, those purchases will lower the rate of interest on securities to the extent required by the interest elasticity of money demand. Idle balances willingly held thus have increased, not in *response* to an excess supply of money, as in the previous case, but as a counterpart to bank expansion. It is obvious that this portion of the rise in the money supply works through the interest rate. It does not affect expenditure and income directly, except for capital gains. Here, the 'Keynesian' transmission mechanism holds, and monetarists would be hard pressed to deny it – unless, of course, they accept absolute liquidity preference on the part of the public.

In summary, monetary policy operating through a relaxation of credit conditions will increase initial transactions balances and expenditure by the amount $a_1 b_1 + a_2 c_1 + a_3 d_1$. The largest component is $a_1 b_1$, representing new bank borrowing encouraged by a fall in the loan rate and/or a rise in expectations. Idle balances will increase to the extent $a_3 d_3$, which arises from banks' purchases of existing securities from the public. The *immediate* expenditure increase will be less than the increase in the money supply to the extent $a_1 b_2 + a_3 d_3$.

Subsequent effects occur as before. The new expenditure will have multiplier effects, and further borrowing, on securities markets rather than from banks, may follow from the fall in security yields caused by the banks' demand for securities. But for any given increase in the quantity of money, these income effects will begin from a smaller first-round income change, compared with the fiscal deficit case. So if the *rate* at which the multiplier proceeds, and the *rate* at which investment responds to lower interest rates, and the *rate* at which savings are placed in securities markets are assumed to be given, then at any point in time the position of the economy will be different according to the manner in which money is increased. Differences may diminish over time, as the decisions of many periods outweigh differences in initial conditions, but the independence of long-run equilibrium from the path to reach it is a classical article of faith, not a demonstrated proposition. And in any case policy-makers are interested in the path.

## OPEN-MARKET OPERATIONS

And so the third method of increasing the money supply, which we can deal with fairly quickly. The interesting feature of an open-market operation is that it is concerned entirely with the composition of the public's financial wealth. An open-market purchase increases the supply of money and decreases the volume of bonds outstanding. Typically the rate of interest falls, to persuade bond-holders to sell to the government broker; the extent of its fall is given by the interest-elasticity of liquidity preference. There are some capital gains for those who sell – there is no initial change in income proper. Surely this is the case in which the Keynesian transmission mech-anism is most obviously appropriate and relevant.

The monetarist direct effect could play a major role if it were reasonable to assume that the intervention of the government broker determined only the timing of the sales of securities on the part of households which were intending to spend but were waiting for a favourable moment to sell their assets. But as pointed out above, this amounts in aggregate to a desire to dissave – an extreme assumption which monetarists have never explicitly endorsed. The monetarist direct effect may have a role to play, but it is more properly limited to that portion (given by the marginal propensity to consume?) of capital gains which are spent on commodities.[10]

For the Keynesian transmission mechanism to be the exclusive means of transmission, all capital gains must be ploughed back into the speculative sphere, as idle money holdings. This is not an implausible assumption. The reasoning is as follows. Bond-holders have sold to capture a capital gain. If they expect the policy to work in the traditional manner, the fall in the interest rate will encourage investment; this will increase the demand for funds on the securities market and raise the interest rate once again. Those who sold securities may be waiting for that rise, after which securities become cheap again; they are holding money idle meanwhile. If this behaviour is typical, the interest rate is the *sole* transmitter of this form of monetary policy. In any event, one can say with confidence that because capital gains are small relative to the monetary change effected by open-market operations, the monetarist direct effect is far smaller in this case than in the other two modes of monetary increase which we have analysed.

## RESOLUTION

Is it not possible to come to some agreement? It would seem plausible to suggest that when Keynes talked of monetary policy he had in mind the type most prevalent in his time (and still): open-market operations.[11] With a minor qualification this is the type of policy for which it is most obviously true that money has its chief effect through the interest rate. This fact has nothing to do with the absence of a money–goods margin of choice; it arises *because of the way money enters the system.* In an open-market operation, the government broker *poses* a money–bonds choice. What happens subsequently depends on how people spend out of accumulated wealth and capital gains, questions on which, unlike expenditure out of income, there is no widely accepted presumption of behaviour. They may not plan to spend any of it, but if they do, the amount is most unlikely to be significant.

Contrast the cases explored above with the 'helicopter' policy. The new money is clearly a windfall. No effort has been expended to earn it, so it is perceived as an increase in wealth, not income. It comes all at once, not gradually as payment for goods or services. With this increase in wealth, the incentive to save is far less than it would be if the money accrued gradually as income, where even though wealth has increased it is less obvious to the receiver. The very prudent might place some of this new 'helicopter' money at interest, but it is not implausible that most of the money will be spent on commodities. It does not matter whether the commodities are durables, which in the Fisherian income scheme count as saving: the point is that there is expenditure on goods rather than financial assets. The monetarist direct effect naturally dominates – would not Keynesians agree?

For the other cases explored in this paper, it has been shown that it is important for Keynesians and monetarists to see that there is a unity in the idea that income determines the plan to spend and money makes it possible, for otherwise each is placed in an absurd position: for Keynesians to refute the direct effect they may have to disown the multiplier, and monetarists may have to embrace the liquidity trap to prevent interest rate changes from absorbing some of the adjustment to monetary change. But the most important message is the futility of talking about the transmission mechanism divorced from the type of monetary change being considered. A debate which is not at cross-purposes is more likely to take place if the specific properties of different policy options are taken into account.

**Notes**

1. Cf. Friedman and Meiselman (1963), in which the direct influence of money on income is sharply *contrasted* to the multiplier.
2. Since the new money also represents an increase in the wealth of the private sector, the argument in the text should be equally acceptable to those using a consumption–wealth relation in preference to or in addition to the consumption–income relation.
3. An increase of government bonds has been ruled out by assumption.
4. Even the classical writers did not subscribe to them. Although at times they skated close to accepting the first proposition, it is difficult to pin them down to anything so bold, particularly in the short run, which is our concern here.
5. Friedman (1956) has argued, additionally, that the interest rate effect will be slight because there are so many financial markets over which the demand to place excess money balances may be spread. One could equally well argue that the 'direct effect' is vitiated by the existence of a multiplicity of goods. It is not convincing.
6. Morrison (1966, ch. 3) reviews this hypothesis. See also Brunner and Meltzer (1968), who apparently worked independently, as they do not refer to Morrison's study. Both studies are quite critical of the hypothesis, for a variety of logical reasons, and adduce evidence against it.
7. Keynes (1937c). His definition differs from that of Davidson (1965).
8. I have seen, not infrequently, references in the literature to borrowing in order to increase one's money holdings. Outside the (rather trivial) strict interpretation of the finance motive, this strikes me as patently absurd. Indeed in an overdraft system, overdrafts and the money supply do not expand until those granted an overdraft facility actually make use of it.
9. While overdrafts bear a higher rate of return, bank expansion usually includes some securities, to maintain liquidity. In general, banks may be supposed to be indifferent between new and old securities. In the UK they typically buy 'seasoned' securities, leaving it to the discount houses to buy at tender.
10. Friedman (1957) suggests that windfalls are spent on durables. But are capital gains which are actively sought by those 'playing the securities market' regarded as windfalls?
11. In the 1980s the phrase 'monetary policy' changed completely; from a general term encompassing interest rate policy it became associated with control of the rate of growth of the money supply essentially by fiscal means (V. C., 1991).

# 7 On the Structure of the Theory of Monetary Policy – Part I: Money Circulating *v.* Money Held*

**Author's Note**

This essay was to have been the first of three, the second exploring the treatment of income and wealth in monetarist and Keynesian theories, and the third dealing with issues of method. The first, introductory, section is to be read as belonging to the trilogy as a whole. Unfortunately, even before the present essay was published, the monetarist–Keynesian debate, so full of unresolved issues of great interest to monetary theory, moved to the political/ideological plane, thanks chiefly to Modigliani's 1977 essay, 'Should We Forsake Stabilization Policies?'. After that article the theoretical issues were no longer of interest. The monetarist–Keynesian debate fizzled out; there would have been no market for Parts II and III.

The present essay deals with the demand for money, raising, as in Chapter 4, some sticky problems of stocks and flows. By the time this essay was written (in the summer of 1977), I clearly preferred messy compromise to logical purity, as being more relevant to the untidiness of economic life.

## THE NEED TO EXAMINE 'DEEP STRUCTURE'

The theory of monetary policy as represented by the 'Monetarist–Keynesian debate' is, from a methodological point of view, degenerate. The cause of the trouble is that the subject is perceived in terms of an inappropriate classification. The two opposing opinions around which the debate supposedly revolves are defined at too superficial a level, and the fact that only two claim attention (allowing for variations within each camp), follows the tradition of Western thought to analyse by dichotomisation (good and evil, nature and culture, mind and body), which has been known to cause trouble before. In this case, to see the extremely rich set of ideas which constitute

* The author wishes to thank Michael Danes for helpful discussions and anonymous referees for their comments, and to acknowledge the usefulness, in a way too general for specific citations within the paper, of unpublished papers by John Foster (1978), Valeria Termini (1978) and Maurice Townsend (1968).

the theory of monetary policy in terms of two opposing camps requires a good deal of Procrustean engineering.

The aim of this chapter is to demonstrate the weakness of this dichotomy and to provide an alternative. Thus its topic is not the content of the debate but the fashion in which it is being conducted.

At present, the Keynesian and monetarist camps are identified, broadly speaking, by whether money is supposed to work its magic on the 'real sector' through interest rates or whether the link between money and income is paramount. The transmission mechanism

$$M \rightarrow r \rightarrow I \rightarrow Y$$

identifies the Keynesian and

$$M \rightarrow Y$$

is associated with monetarism. The proliferation of theories flying the 'Keynesian' or 'monetarist' banners has served to blur this sharp outline, but not to obliterate it.

The issue is not how sharp the distinction is, however. The point is that these postulated 'transmission mechanisms' are not *theories* but manifestations of underlying theoretical structures. Surely it is at the level of *theory* that opposing views should be evaluated. That job, I argue, has not yet been done in this field of enquiry.

If there were a one-to-one mapping between the underlying theoretical structure and the transmission mechanism which is supposed to follow from it, there would be nothing lost in characterising the two camps by their transmission mechanisms, but this is not the case. I have already shown (Chick, 1973b) that a variety of theories and their permutations reduce to one or other of these two mechanisms – indeed the book's *leitmotif* was the robustness of the conclusions to the variety of theories adduced to support them.[1]

This fact gives rise to paradoxes. For example, Tobin's approach (as in e.g., 1961, 1969; Tobin and Brainard, 1963) is a portfolio framework not dissimilar to that of Friedman (1956, 1958, 1968, 1972), yet Tobin serves as a representative Keynesian and if Friedman does not count as a monetarist I should be quite lost. One could go on: Friedman claims the quantity theory[2] as his antecedent, while Patinkin (1972) argues that Friedman's work is a development of Keynes's liquidity preference, and Brunner (1968, p. 18) states that the antecedents of the 'weak monetarist' general portfolio approach are Keynes, Fisher and Wicksell. There is also a need to reconcile the coexistence of Radcliffe theory and Tobin in the Keynesian camp; the one is concerned with adjustment of a portfolio of assets – no one ever seems to go into debt – while the other theory revolves around the problems of access to credit. Does Friedman's characterisation of 'credit' and 'monetary' theories help? And where does Keynes fit in all this?

The paradoxes arise from the method, used before now by me as well as other commentators, of evaluating each theory as a total package. When the theories are pulled apart into their components, their 'deep structure', a way to resolve some of these paradoxes is found. Table 7.1 provides a suggested structural scheme. It does not pretend to be exhaustive or definitive; it is offered as provisional and suggestive.

*Table* 7.1 Structure of the theory of monetary policy

*Theoretical Issues (Postulated Responses)*
- effect on interest, output, prices
  - neutrality
- role of interest rate in transmission mechanism
- efficacy of monetary policy

*Analytical Structure*
- money circulating *v.* money held
  - commodity and financial circulations
- income–wealth schema
  - Fisherian *v.* Keynesian
  - 'rationality' and the treatment of debt
  - consolidation and the treatment of debt
  - aggregative detail
- treatment of time
  - impact effect *v.* equilibrium
  - Marshallian periods: market period, production period, investment period
  - the unit period, temporary equilibrium
  - the 'long run' – satisfaction of expectations
- method
  - statics, 'pseudodynamics', differential-equation dynamics
  - sequence analysis

*Stimuli*
- change in outside money
  - through foreign trade
  - through government policy
    - open market operations
    - fiscal deficits
  - 'helicopter'

*table cont. overleaf*

*Table* 7.1 *cont.*

change in inside money
  change in bank reserves
  increased private sector demand

*The Environment (Changeable Aspects)*

institutional framework
  credit
    direct – stock and bond markets
    indirect – intermediaries
  money
    circulating metallic money
    convertible paper
    inconvertible paper
cyclical phases

*Assumed States of Nature*

degree of stability inherent in the private sector
inherent optimality of the outcome of private sector behaviour
role of government
individualism *v.* behaviour determined by economic class
nature of long-term trend (stationary state or growth)

---

Table 7.1 begins with the *results* of theorising, listing the main issues in the monetary debate, encompassing questions such as 'how will interest rates respond to an increase in the money supply?'. The idea that answers might differ because of the assumed source of new money is explored in Chick (1978a) and the fiscal policy counterpart has also now been treated explicitly (see especially the papers in Stein, 1976). But there are many other potential reasons for different replies: someone's answer may depend on the institutional environment, the current state of the economy, the way the monetary increase occurs, and what is assumed about the 'normal' long-term state of the economy, as well as on the more obviously theoretical aspects listed under 'Analytical Structure'. Friedman might reply to the above question that as an impact effect interest rates would go down, thus appearing to agree with Keynesians. However, because his income–wealth scheme is Fisherian, he describes services of durable goods as providing a return akin to interest on those durables. Thus he may have in mind something a Keynesian would describe as a direct effect, leaving what the Keynesian understands by rates of interest – the observable money rates – unchanged.

This example is fairly typical of the sort of problem generated by lack of explicit treatment of analytical structure and a full statement of the assumptions about the environment or the nature of the stimulus whose effects are being analysed. In addition, there is evidence of an anachronistic carry-over of ideas devised in and for older institutions, in particular, metallic-money economies.

Apart from minimising the amount of talk at cross-purposes which so bedevils this field, there is another potential benefit from the explicit concern with deeper structure: if we dismantle the theories carefully, we stand to gain possession of serviceable building-blocks with which to construct new theories suited to new problems or a changed universe, consciously deciding which pieces to use and which to discard.

A full analysis of theories of monetary policy according to their structure obviously cannot be attempted here. I have given one example of the potential usefulness of the approach. The body of the chapter will explore one element of 'analytical structure' in detail: namely, whether money is modelled as being in continual circulation or held as an asset.

## MONEY CIRCULATING, MONEY HELD

### Introduction

It will be argued in this part of the chapter that an important source of difference between theories of monetary policy lies in their implicit modelling of money's role. This may seem a curious concern, for surely nearly everyone would agree that in actual fact 'no asset is in action as a medium of exchange except in the very moment of being transferred from one ownership to another. . . . Between transactions all money is idle' (Sayers, 1960, p. 712).

The accuracy of that statement is the beginning, not the end, of one's woes. Is the money held on Monday and designated for expenditure on Tuesday 'held' in the same sense as money accumulated and held in anticipation of an annual holiday? One knows that no rational person intends to hold money forever; do we therefore say all money circulates? This question is entirely bound up with *time*; the essential problem is how best to model money's indisputable movement between agents through time, in the context (almost always) of a static model. Even if the model is dynamic the problem is not solved, for plainly money circulates in different spheres at different speeds, and at different speeds under different circumstances.

Concentration on one or another aspect of money results in theories which explain why one can expect money to be continually changing hands (it has only exchange value, is a barren asset, etc.) or why it is held (uncertainty about prices or interest rates, transactions costs, etc.). I shall argue that classical theory was almost entirely concerned with the first and modern theory almost exclusively with the second, with Keynes perhaps serving as a bridge between.

Uncovering the underlying view of money is a difficult enterprise, for at least two reasons. First, the view is almost always mixed (correctly reflecting how money behaves): elements of 'money on the wing' are hidden away in portfolio theory and even theories of circulating money allow it to rest for a time. Second, the view is usually implicit. Discussing what is implicit is by necessity highly subjective, for it involves inferring what lies behind what is written. The authors may or may not have *consciously* taken the view that I shall ascribe to them; still less have they discussed it openly. And one can never be sure that something which is not said has been omitted precisely because it was taken for granted.

That said, let us proceed, for the only alternative is to leave the question alone, and that is not right if one believes that these differences of vision are important. I shall begin with the present consensus.

## Portfolio Theories

### *In General*

Portfolio theory has become the accepted framework for the analysis of monetary policy, as demand-for-money theory has been transformed into a theory of wealth allocation.[3] There is wide agreement that the only questions with which the theory of monetary policy need be concerned are the relative substitutability amongst assets and which ones should be on the choice list. The rest is detail. This view is endorsed by, *inter alia*, Tobin (1972), Patinkin (1972). This is the evaluation in a thorough survey of the literature:

> The general view that has been emerging from the writings of both neo-Keynesians and monetarists stresses the impact of monetary policy changes on the composition of assets held by the public and the influence of these changes on interest rates on these assets and ultimately on the rate of return from investing in the production of new physical assets. There is, however, considerable disagreement as to the major variables and interest rates that must be defined in order to take account of all the ways in which monetary policy works out its effects. (Park, 1972, pp. 11–12.)

The characterisation of Keynes by Tobin (1969) and Leijonhufvud (1968) is also widely accepted. Keynes is supposed, in their lights, to have lumped all non-money assets together and called them 'bonds'; the 'portfolio' was thus restricted to two assets, money and bonds. It follows that monetary policy can only work through the bond rate. The significance of Tobin's own framework is said to be that by including real capital in the 'portfolio', the margin of substitution between money and real goods is 'reopened',[4] as if it had previously been closed. Friedman claims still greater generality; his framework (1956) includes consumer durables (and possibly also non-durables) and human capital. Indeed the scope of Friedman's 'portfolio' is the entire range of alternatives to holding money.

Are we to understand by this characterisation that there has been a steady progression toward greater realism, from the *simpliste* notion of Keynes through Tobin to the full majesty of Friedman's framework in which money impinges on all areas of economic life, and monetary policy stops not at the borders of the City but goes all the way to training college and university, where the demand to add to human capital must be backed by money? It is surely correct to say that money can buy a wide range of things, but is that adequate reason for claiming superiority for the theory which encompasses the broadest range of assets, and for regarding the developments from Keynes to Tobin to Friedman as one of progressive improvement?

I shall argue that the view that these theories differ only in their scope or in their elasticities of substitution is quite misguided. Though both the Yale and Friedman approaches share a certain superficial affinity with Keynes's treatment of money, they are far closer to each other than to Keynes. The fundamental difference is often masked by the descriptive language chosen, but the fact remains that the portfolio approach treats money entirely as an asset to be *held*. Keynes, on the other hand, was concerned with money both circulating and held (though he seems at times to forget the former).[5]

Portfolio theory is comparative-static in method[6] and based on the device of the unit period.[7] Asset demands are specified as end-of-period stocks. It is an obvious but rarely remarked feature of theory based on these foundations, whether 'Keynesian' or 'monetarist', that once the equilibrium portfolio is reached, holdings will be maintained unless there is some exogenous change in the data. Money, gilts, looms, aircraft and dining-room chairs find their place in individuals' optimal portfolios and *stay there* until something new happens. Thus portfolio theory precludes the kind of equilibrium which characterises the classical conception of money, an equilibrium in which money is continuously circulating from hand to hand in an ever-recurrent pattern. Despite the seas of ink that have been spilled on the subject of the inadmissibility of money in a world where one *tâtonnement* settles everything, Friedman-and-Tobin portfolio theory belongs to just such a world. Once portfolio equilibrium is reached, no further exchange takes place – and there is no need to hold money, even to avoid 'risk', for capital gains and losses are irrelevant if not *realised* by sale – i.e., a further exchange.

The logic of the model offers two possibilities: either the equilibrium holds only for the unit period and no one knows what will happen next (temporary equilibrium), or as protection against a quite spurious risk people hold some money till Kingdom come:

> So we are told, without a smile on the face. But . . . what an insane use to which to put it! For it is a recognised characteristic of money as a store of wealth that it is barren; whereas practically every other form of storing wealth yields some interest or profit. Why should anyone outside a lunatic asylum wish to use money as a store of wealth? (Keynes, 1937a; 1973b, pp. 115–16.)

Money in these models only has a chance to circulate in disequilibrium, to restore equilibrium after a monetary increase. It is commonly assumed that the response to a monetary increase is to lower the yield on money relative to whatever else is included in the portfolio and thus to encourage the 'substitution' of those other things for money in the portfolio. For some strange reason, common-sense language is never used at this point: why is it not said that people or firms will *buy* securities or real assets?

This reticence to speak of expenditure and portfolio readjustment in the same breath has been going on for quite a time. Keynes (1911) took Fisher to task for it in his review of the first edition of *The Purchasing Power of Money*. Fisher's rejoinder in the preface to the second edition (1931) is that this means of achieving substitution was, in effect, too obvious to state.

It is not as obvious as all that. Indeed, it is entirely possible for relative rates of return to change *without* any money changing hands. Dealers set security prices in response to their perceptions of the state of the market; they often change without any trading taking place. Similarly the yield on real capital is not entirely objective; it varies as much with the expectations of the owner as with the assets' market prices. And the market prices of assets vary with the expectations held by their suppliers, who may change prices as much in anticipation of demand as in response to it.

The allegation that portfolio theory does not model money as circulating is reinforced when one looks at the same theories in the context of an excess *demand* for money. In the opposite, customary context, that of excess supply, it is easy to imagine excess balances being spent on assets, even if this expenditure need not follow logically. However, the indivisibility and poor marketability of many assets makes it quite implausible to suggest converting these things back into money when one's putty turns to clay. Durable goods can be sold at knock-down prices, to be sure, and the fall in prices will increase the real value of the existing money stock, but people are unlikely to do this every time they want a bit more money, reversing the decision when the situation changes – 'as if a farmer, having tapped his barometer after breakfast, could decide to remove his capital from the farming business between 10 and 11 in the morning and reconsider whether he should return to it later in the week' (Keynes, 1936, p. 151).[8]

### *Tobin in Particular*

Tobin gets around this absurdity by equating shares to real capital, for one can sell equities easily. As individuals try to realise them for money, their value falls – but at least money actually circulates in the process. This device of treating equities as if they were of the same form and substance as the real capital they supposedly represent is, however, nothing but a sleight of hand. In the real world when a business firm is faced with a cash-flow problem the solution is hardly to be found in 'substituting real capital for money', nor would the firm be heartened or helped by the knowledge that its shares are falling on the market.[9]

So the story that portfolio theory models money circulating in asset markets is not convincing. If further evidence is needed, we have Tobin's explicit statement (1969, p. 334) that the significance of money in capital-account adjustment owes nothing to its medium-of-exchange function.[10]

Furthermore, any circulation of money which may be occurring in the consumption sphere is implicit and inconsequential. In Tobin's models, quite explicitly, the dichotomy between the 'portfolio', however rich, and flows of income and expenditure is absolute. An early model (Tobin, 1961) is concerned with the capital account only. Where the income account is included in the model (e.g., Brainard and Tobin, 1968), the capital account is insulated from it: changes in the rate of saving do not disturb portfolio balance, because of the assumption of homogeneity of degree one in wealth of the asset demands. Similarly, while real assets might be 'substituted for money' to restore portfolio equilibrium, substitution between money and consumer goods is not permitted. Consumption belongs to the flow sector of the model and is insulated from capital-account events.

The assumption of the dichotomy of saving and portfolio balance is, of course, truly Keynesian. So, for that matter, is the insulation of consumption from the direct effect of a money-supply change. In Keynes's model, however, the rate of interest is important because it indicates the incentive required to bring idle money into circulation as it is borrowed to finance investment.[11] In portfolio theory, this circulation is missing – as it must be, for the circulation which might occur amongst members of the private sector is debarred by the consolidation of that sector into a single aggregate.[12] So we have the irony that the Keynesian result – money works by affecting interest and investment – is derived from a theory with a very un-Keynesian view of money, by the device of restricting the assets for which money is a substitute to capital goods.

*The 'New Quantity Theory'*

In claiming the quantity theory as his antecedent, Friedman sees the link to Fisher, Ricardo, Thornton *and Keynes* (whom he cites specifically) in that they 'pay no attention to the effect on the rate of interest of shifts in the demand for money' and 'minimize changes in market interest rates as the primary channel through which changes in the quantity of money affect spending, output and prices' (1972, p. 945).

These properties are either conclusions, which tell us nothing about the nature of the theories which generate them, or they are properties which are simply assumed (to protect 'neutrality') rather than derived. (The use of the terms 'pay no attention' and 'minimize' suggest this.) Friedman's claim is a prime example of the kind of superficial association of which I complained in the Introduction.

Friedman's 'Restatement of the Quantity Theory' (1956), which is the basis of a major strand of monetarist theory, presents a paradox: while the hallmark of old quantity theory is that money is modelled as continually circulating, Friedman's quantity theory is a model of money held. Friedman himself stresses the portfolio character of his model, distinguishing it from that of the Keynesians by claiming greater breadth and generality.

It is not obvious what is to be gained by the monetarists in taking up the portfolio approach. It would be easy to accept the proposition that if people are given[13] more money, or if their money-incomes rise, they are likely to spend a larger amount of money than formerly. That is what one might call 'common-sense monetarism'. But it is far from obvious that this is what monetarists have in mind. In their use of the portfolio approach, the circulation of money in exchange, even for assets, is hard to find, and the link between money and expenditure is, to say the least, indirect.

As before, common sense suggests that 'substitution' entails the use of money as a medium of exchange in the *purchase* of assets. Confirmation that this is the meaning intended is offered, for example by Friedman (1972):

> We, on the other hand, stress a much broader and more 'direct' impact on spending, saying . . . that individuals seeking to dispose of what they regard as their excess money balances . . . will try to pay out a larger sum for the purchase of securities, goods and services, for the repayment of debts, and as gifts than they are receiving from the corresponding sources. (p. 910.)

If this is the mechanism intended, it would be well to say so, for many have complained that the monetarists do not explain 'the mechanism' by which money affects the economy, and faced with a description like the following, from Friedman and Meiselman (1963), one can see why:

> The . . . 'monetary' view can be expressed in terms of interest rates and balance sheets only by taking a much different, and broader view. It is necessary to regard households as themselves enterprises holding physical assets which they use to produce services that they consume themselves. An interest rate is a pure number relating the price of services acquired by households as being connected by an interest rate to the source that yields it. . . . On this . . . view, the conception of assets is as broad as the conception of expenditures. . . . That is why there is such a close link between the 'monetary' view and the quantity-theory approach. (p. 218.)

Common sense interprets this passage as a way of bringing in consumption expenditure. But once again it is entirely possible for all the effects on relative rates of return to go through *without* any money changing hands. There is, indeed, an additional reason for suspecting this: Friedman's definition of consumption follows Fisher[14] – it is identified as the services yielded by goods. Insofar as goods are durable, therefore, and already owned by households, consumption can take place without any expenditure at all. Clearly all that Friedman and Meiselman's household enterprises need do to restore portfolio equilibrium is convene a meeting and revalue their assets.

## Old Quantity Theory

Old quantity theory, in contrast, generates its link between money and expenditure from its theory of the properties of and the demand for money. While quantity theorists differ in many respects, money is always modelled as *circulating*. This follows from the theory's first premise: that money has no use-value[15] and is, therefore, only held as a means to an end. Holdings of money balances in this theory are akin to what accountants call a 'suspense account' – an account which serves as a way-station for funds destined for other uses.

In the modern expositions of old quantity theory the 'other uses' tend to be exclusively goods and services: quantity theory is represented as the simplest form of the transactions demand for money.

Make the reasonable assumption that the purchase of goods (which equals consumption if (i) the goods are not very durable or (ii) if we take Keynes's definition – consumers' expenditure) goes on virtually continuously, whether in a steady stream or irregularly, but in an amount which is stable and predictable over the period between receipts of income. Inflows of cash, chiefly from the sale of labour, are also predictable both in amount and in interval: the interval defines the 'income period'.[16] In these circumstances the individual holds a fluctuating balance of cash for transactions purposes: it rises to equal the whole of his weekly or monthly income and falls to the bedrock of his precautionary balances, held in case the regularities which we have assumed fail to hold in practice. His average balance over the income period will depend on the size of his income and the timing of payments. Increase the money flow to all individuals and – assuming they are satisfied with their precautionary balances – each will spend more, for there is no point in holding the extra money, as it has no utility except for what it will buy. That is the foundation for the 'direct effect' of increases in the quantity of money on the volume of expenditure.

This model of circulating money has implications for the specification of the transactions demand for money. As Tsiang (1966) insisted, in opposition to the treatment in *Value and Capital* (Hicks, 1939), in the absence of perfect knowledge of the timing of receipts and payments, the amount of money held for transactions purposes by an individual at any particular point of time is just an accidental consequence of the timing of receipts and expenditures. It does not follow, however, that transactions balances are not volitional, that is, not demanded;[17] the concept of transactions demand is perfectly cogent when specified as an average over time, even though the level of those balances is continually fluctuating.

The important thing to notice is that unless the exact timing of all purchases and receipts is known, so that each day's transactions balances may be planned and held intentionally, transactions demand cannot be formulated as *stock* demand at a *point* of time. An appeal to the literature, which is full of stock demand-for-money functions, leaves me unmoved.

The fact that the concept of transactions demand only makes sense over time is part of the reason why it has been treated so badly in the neoclassical synthesis, which does its best to abolish time: a stock approach reduces time to a point. There seems to be a difficulty in comprehending or accepting a *demand* for something which is relinquished so readily; nor, despite all those diagrams of circular flow, are we comfortable with an equilibrium in which there is continual movement – the circulation of money.[18] In modern theory, income is a flow and money a stock; the fact that income *comes in* as a cash flow is not allowed to affect thinking on this matter.

It is the stock approach to transactions demand which *ought*, in fact, to make one uneasy, for the end-of-period demand (if we knew where the end was) is zero for an individual and equal to outpayments for firms. What do the aggregate empirical estimates measure?

As a result of the shift from a flow to a stock conception of the role of money, the quantity theory became associated with the idea, embodied in the static treatment of the real balance effect in Patinkin (1956), that expenditure was uniquely related to the *stock* of money in existence. One finds that several of those who gave evidence to the Radcliffe Committee (1959)[19] felt the need to refute this idea.

The stock conception is, I think, also partly responsible for recent emphasis amongst monetarists on the rate of *growth* of the money supply: it is a way of ensuring that money is seen as continually entering the private sector, even if its movement thereafter is doubtful. It also goes some way to explaining the extreme view that Friedman (1972, for example) takes of Keynes and Keynesians over 'absolute liquidity preference':

> I [Friedman] believe that only a finding of near-absolute liquidity preference would raise 'fundamental' issues [in monetary] theory and that any other finding would not. (1966, p. 144.)

Absolute liquidity preference prevents any new money from circulating, absolutely: changes in $M$ have no effect – on $r$ *or* $Y$ – whereas if the elasticity of demand for speculative balances is less than infinite, at least *some* of that money circulates, however sluggishly, and money matters, however little.

Before turning to Keynes, a moment should be spent on the quantity-theory view of the circulation of money which was not held for current purchases. Quantity theorists assumed that it was not rational to hold money idle except for the short time between receipt and expenditure. The rest would be put at interest, either directly or through banks and other intermediaries, which also do not hold money idle. Thus in the classical conception, money saved passes through the capital markets to borrowers, who spend it immediately and return it to circulation in the commodity sphere.

This theory, which (with some looseness?) may be called a loanable-funds theory, is over-optimistic,[20] for the act of purchasing financial claims does not necessarily constitute lending: only if *newly-issued* securities are purchased does money reach borrowers, and hence move from the financial to the commodity sphere. If existing securities are purchased by current savers from previous holders, the net effect on demand is nil where sellers of securities spend all their proceeds: their dissaving and current saving are matched. Usually, of course, some of the proceeds are reinvested, but to this negative effect on goods-demand there is the counterweight of new borrowing, the proceeds of which are spent.

As mentioned earlier, there is no trace of the idea of borrowing or the issue of new securities in either Friedman's or Tobin's version of portfolio theory: indeed, there cannot be such within the private sector, as its members' balance sheets are consolidated for aggregate analysis. It must be concluded that neither theory shares the property of money circulating, either for goods or for financial assets. So much for old quantity theory. Tobin might be relieved, but surely Friedman has something to explain.

**Keynes**

Now we come to Keynes – the Keynes of the *General Theory*.[21] As with so much else in that book his view is not entirely consistent, in a way that is itself revealing.

Looking first at his theory of the demand for money we note that he took over Marshall's (1923, ch. 14) transactions demand without fuss[22] and, as Marshall counts as a quantity theorist, we might as well accept that money was modelled as circulating in exchange for goods and labour services.[23] It is in the financial sphere that Keynes differs from the quantity theory, and for a purpose – to refute Say's Law. To do this, it had to be shown that money could be withdrawn from circulation and held idle, not just temporarily, while awaiting imminent use in the purchase of commodities or investments, but in significant volume for a significant period of time. The only justification for holding money idle which to him made sense was that there were times when the return to be obtained from putting money at interest was in danger of being destroyed by capital losses.

The interest rate influences the demand for money in Keynes not as its opportunity cost but as a proxy for the expectation of changes in the rate in the near future: the higher the current rate, the greater the preponderance of opinion that it is likely soon to fall. Those who hold securities which they expect to fall in value do not diversify – they 'plunge' – into money, a capital-safe asset.[24] Since people's expectations differ, *some* money is likely to be thus held idle, in aggregate, over a wide range of interest rates. This demand for money is an unwillingness to hold financial assets whose value varies with the interest rate,[25] not an 'unwillingness to hold the existing capital stock', as Tobin would have it.

The extent of this unwillingness determines the criterion which an investment project has to equal, but if the return on investment fails to meet the test, it is the entrepreneurs who are unwilling to expand the capital stock – or even, perhaps, maintain it. Alternatively, liquidity preference determines the cost of borrowing, as new securities must compete with those already existing. By this device of separating transactions from the flow of new demands for and supplies of loanable funds, Keynes sharpened the contrast with the then prevailing orthodoxy, in which saving was not a withdrawal but continued to circulate by providing loan capital.

If new securities did successfully compete, money would circulate through borrowing, back into the spending stream. Keynes, however, played this down, perhaps to maintain his sharp contrast with loanable-funds theory. In Chapters 11, 12, 13 and 17, he analyses money's role in an entirely portfolio-theoretic way, with the exception of the second sentence of Chapter 13, where borrowing breaks into the discussion. The whole treatment of the financing of investment is cursory: the finance motive for holding money does not appear in the book, but in a later article (Keynes, 1937b).

Add to this playing-down of borrowing the concentration on the innovation in liquidity preference theory (speculation) at the expense of what Keynes could assume was old hat (transactions) and you have the foundations of the sort of 'stagnant pool' theory of money of which I have been complaining.

The development of portfolio theory out of Keynes, while understandable, is not, however, legitimate. The quotation cited earlier fully indicates Keynes's scorn for the idea that money had a *permanent* place in an individual's portfolio: he would have rejected totally the diversification demand of portfolio theory. No *individual* devotes funds to financial investments forever,[26] certainly not to money holdings. Speculative money balances are held until expectations change or the money is wanted for transactions in goods, whichever is earlier. To an individual, one of these two things will happen eventually. With enough time, interest rates do not even have to change for idle balances to be disgorged: if a given interest rate were to persist for a long period, it would come to be regarded by everyone as 'normal' and the speculative demand for money would disappear. The only legitimate *full equilibrium* demand for money is the demand for money which circulates – precisely what modern theory, despite its obsession with equilibrium, ignores!

Although Keynes regarded his additive specification of the demand for money as nothing but a simplification,[27] it was, perhaps, quite a good idea, for the dimensions in which the transactions and speculative demands should be measured are not commensurate. Beyond the technical point of measurement, there are differences in the postulated *response* of transactions and speculative demands which also reflects conflicting time horizons: transactions balances, average holdings over time, respond gradually to changes in income, a flow which takes time to accrue, while speculative holdings, a stock demand, can move in and out of securities markets virtually instantaneously. Keynes's additive formulation avoided a direct confrontation of the different time horizons involved, but his theory of the transmission mechanism was much influenced by their existence.

*Keynes's Transmission Mechanism*

One cannot blame Keynes's interpreters for taking him at his uncompromising word:

> The primary effect of a change in the quantity of money on the quantity of effective demand is through its influence on the rate of interest. (1936, p. 298).

Let us see how he arrives at this conclusion. Unfortunately the relevant passage is quite long (1936):

> [If] changes in $M$ are due to Government printing money wherewith to meet its current expenditure . . . the new money accrues as someone's income. The new level of income, however, will not continue sufficiently high for the requirements of $M_1$ [transaction and precautionary balances] to absorb the whole of the increase in $M$; and some portion of the money will seek an outlet in buying securities or other assets until $r$ has fallen so as to bring about an increase in the magnitude of $M_2$ [speculative balances] and at the same time to stimulate a rise in $Y$ to such an extent that the new money is absorbed either in $M_2$ or in the $M_1$ which corresponds to the rise in $Y$ caused by the fall in $r$. Thus at one remove this case comes to the same thing as the alternative case, where the new money can only be issued in the first instance by a relaxation of the conditions of credit by the banking system, so as to induce someone to sell the banks a debt or a bond in exchange for the new cash. (p. 200.)

On the face of it, this is a very strange passage. Although it begins with the statement '[the] relation of changes in $M$ to $Y$ and $r$ depends, in the first instance, on the way in which changes in $M$ come about', Keynes ends by seeming to say it makes little difference. Plainly it makes a difference in the initial stages: in the first example, the printing of money enabled the government to make an income-generating expenditure; in the second, the banks lower lending rates to encourage borrowing. A concern with the impact effect yields the monetarist or Keynesian transmission mechanism depending on the mode of introducing new money into the economy, but the passage following 'at the same time' suggests that more than impact effects are involved.

Despite appearances, Keynes's first example does not allow of monetarist interpretation, at least not that of 'common-sense monetarism'. In the second sentence, the possibility arises that the now-larger money supply could stimulate spending. But no: $M_1$ balances adjust passively to the income change: even when money is exogenously supplied, income, not money, determines spending, and $M_1$ balances are acquired only as needed to *facilitate* spending.

It follows that with a direct effect of money on spending disallowed, the weight of money's influence on income falls on what happens when the excess of money over transactions needs finds its way into securities markets and affects $r$. The cases 'come to the same thing' for the very reason that the money aspect of income is ignored when speaking of spending.

In one sense this way of thinking is fair enough. Whoever got the money had to work for it; it came into the system to pay for some income-creating transactions. So it can be analysed as equivalent to a rise in wages, employment or profits, and the behavioural postulates involving expenditure are unaffected. And it forestalls such silliness as including an excess supply of money variable in expenditure functions along with income. But it is ironic that in a book which goes far to integrate money and the real sector, Keynes, in taking the hyphen out of money-income, began the separation of stocks and flows which in Tobin is explicit and complete, and encouraged discussions (and *implementations*) of 'demand management' policies without regard to their financial consequences – a flaw we needed monetarism to point out. It would not have happened if the *basis* of transactions demand in the fact of the circulation of money had been kept at the forefront of our thinking.

Circulation of funds through borrowing has survived rather better, if not at Yale. Despite the lack of emphasis Keynes gave to the interest rate as a cost of keeping funds moving in financial markets, some interpreters have placed such a strong emphasis on this aspect[28] that Friedman and Meiselman identify the 'Keynesian' view as the 'credit' approach. It is interesting to look at it through their eyes:

> The . . . 'credit' view . . . typically concentrates attention on paper claims dealt in on reasonably well organised markets or created and held by

> recognised financial institutions: government securities, open market commercial paper, industrial bonds and equities; loans by commercial banks, insurance companies, and other financial intermediaries; real estate mortgages, and the like. These claims are as a class precisely the ones used to finance the kinds of expenditure that are generally included in autonomous expenditures: government deficits, residential construction, business investment in plant, equipment and inventories. This is why there is such a close link between the 'credit' view and the income–expenditure approach. (1963, p. 218.)

The gross unsuitability of some of the listed paper claims as vehicles for speculation shows that the portfolio aspect of Keynes has almost disappeared. Apart from that, however, the description is spot-on and brings us nicely to Radcliffe. Before going on, dare I make the obvious point that autonomous expenditures are autonomous partly because they, unlike consumption, are not financed out of money-income?

### Radcliffe (for a moment)

Compare the treatment of financial markets in the Radcliffe Report (1959). Rather than concentrate on existing financial assets as transmitters of monetary impulses, as Keynes did, Radcliffe denied any importance to the stock of money, while being passionately concerned with its velocity – velocity not in the commodity sphere, which would have been too suggestive of quantity theory, but, through credit institutions, in the financial sphere. Hence we have the irony that while vigorously anti-quantity theory in its orientation and conclusions, Radcliffe shares with it the explicit concern with money circulating: money flowing from lenders to borrowers finances expenditure which in the absence of these flows would not take place. There are portfolio elements in Radcliffe as well: the ability of financial institutions to grant credit depends ultimately on the willingness of the public to hold those institutions' liabilities.[29] Thus the portfolio choice in Radcliffe influences spending through its influence on the balance sheets of lending institutions – quite a different framework from the other theories we have discussed.

## SUMMARY AND CONCLUSION

As a summary, Figure 7.1 gives a visual interpretation of the verbal presentation of the theories to which I have referred. Symbols should be obvious

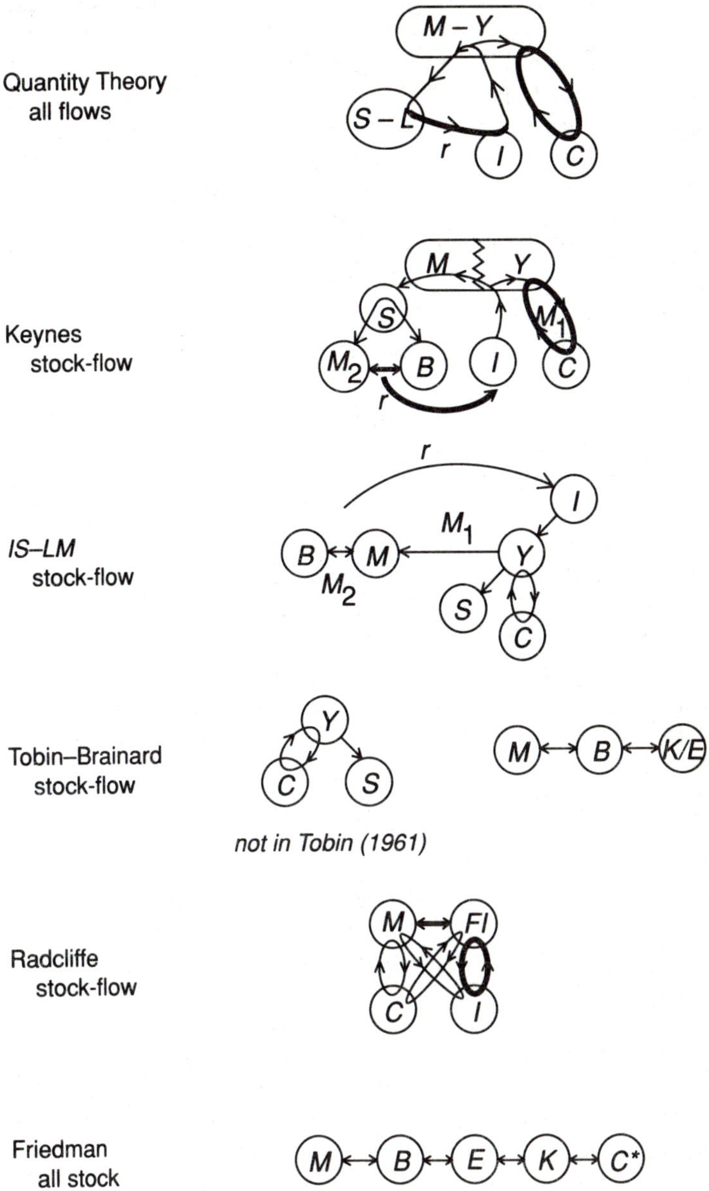

Quantity Theory
all flows
M – Y
S – L
r
I
C
Keynes
stock-flow
M
Y
S
M1
M2
B
I
C
r
IS–LM
stock-flow
r
I
M1
B
M
Y
M2
S
C
Tobin–Brainard
stock-flow
Y
C
S
M
B
K/E
not in Tobin (1961)
Radcliffe
stock-flow
M
FI
C
I
Friedman
all stock
M
B
E
K
C*


*Figure* 7.1

except $L$ for lending, $E$ for equities, $FI$ for financial intermediaries, and $C^*$, stocks of durable goods which produce the services called, in Friedman's scheme, consumption. Horizontal placements of symbols connected by arrows indicate portfolio choices; spheres of circulation are indicated by circuits linking vertically displaced variables. Important links are drawn bold.

In the (old) quantity theory, money-income circulates in exchange for consumer goods and, circulating through financial markets, finances investment; it thus affects both interest and prices. Ultimately, only prices are affected, because the purchase of goods is the ultimate use of money.

Keynes's theory establishes a border between money and income. Their only direct link is the transactions demand for money. Expenditure is affected by money if and only if money comes into the system as income, and then the monetary aspect of the transaction is suppressed: the classical circulation of money becomes the circular flow of income facilitated by $M_1$ balances. Any effect of money, *as* money, on income is indirect, operating through its action in the financial sphere. Thus the Keynesian transmission mechanism emerges. Even *fiscal policy* financed by new money, has the $M \rightarrow r$ connection built into it, though it occurs as a post-impact effect. Money ceases to circulate and have its effects as and when *and for as long as* it is held as $M_2$ balances. The Keynesian transmission mechanism applies in a more obvious way to the case of open-market operations. The difference with the monetarists arises from Keynes's correct modelling of the holding of funds ($M_2$ balances *and* bonds) as consisting of a surplus of money-income over what was required for current purchases of goods, while monetarists suggest that the money introduced by an open-market purchase may find its way into the goods market.

In the *IS–LM* version of Keynes, stocks and flows are further disconnected, as there is no direct relationship between saving and investment on the one hand and assets on the other; this reflects the absence of money circulating by means of borrowing and lending, leaving only the implicit circulation of $M_1$ balances.

The Yale model, in the more complete version (e.g., Tobin and Brainard, 1963), shows complete bifurcation into stocks and flows. The primacy of investment in the transmission mechanism is maintained by the narrowness of the portfolio, though the possibility of its operating through equity prices rather than bond prices is 'opened up'. (It is argued in the body of the paper that this possibility was never absent in Keynes.)

Radcliffe is not a complete theory. Its chief elements are the portfolio choice between money and financial intermediaries' liabilities and the finance, chiefly through these intermediaries, of all types of expenditure.

The Keynesian link to income via investment is retained by virtue of the fact that borrowed finance is more often required for investment than for consumption.[30]

Friedman, like Tobin and Keynes, has generated many models. Here, as in the verbal analysis, I take the 'Restatement' to be the underlying model. The transformation to a stock theory is complete: even $C^*$ is not consumption, for that needn't have much to do with whether one *holds* money or not. In Friedman, holding money is an alternative to holding the durables which *generate* consumption. Money in this model can go everywhere – if it goes anywhere at all. Thus money influences income as a whole, not just investment.

In conclusion: no theory is so simple as to be capable of description by a single attribute; the frequent need for reference to other elements of analytical structure than the one discussed here is proof enough of that. It is not claimed that this detailed examination of one element is an adequate basis for understanding in full how the theories of transmission are generated. But the exercise would be pointless if the distinction between money circulating and resting tells us nothing. The conclusion that I draw is one which should make biologists happy: namely that hybrids are usually more robust animals. The weakness of classical pure-flow loanable-funds theory is probably better understood and more widely accepted than what I believe to be the equally extreme weakness of pure-stock portfolio theory. Yet I am not convinced that Keynes's hybrid is quite the right mixture: his construction is tailored too closely, perhaps, to the need to refute classical theory and to take account of the turbulent stock-market behaviour which had immediately preceded the writing of the *General Theory*, and the inadequate integration of the financing of investment into a full macroeconomic theory still needs remedying. Of the theories discussed here, Radcliffe is an alternative hybrid, but it may in fact be time to breed another.

## Notes

1. Many believe, or at any rate say, that there are *no* genuine theoretical differences, that everyone, despite superficial differences, subscribes to the same model (e.g., *IS–LM* plus an expectations-augmented Phillips curve). Those who hold that view can only conclude that the differences to be resolved are purely empirical. If that is the case, theoretical controversy is wasteful; energy should be directed entirely to empirical work based on agreed criteria. Others have argued that the issue is the role of government (e.g., Modigliani, 1977) or that what divides the two camps is their world-view (e.g., Mayer, 1978). Hahn (1980), however, is still looking to theory for explanation.

2. Just what the quantity theory was or has become, is, I think, not at all clear.
3. For a survey of this development see Johnson (1962).
4. Cf. Park (1972); 'the Keynesian analysis considers only substitution between money and bonds important, but ignores entirely the substitutability between money and real assets or real expenditures' (p. 54).
5. Robertson (1940): 'Mr Keynes was so taken up with the fact that people sometimes acquire money to *hold* it that he had apparently all but forgotten the more familiar fact that they often acquire it in order to *use* it' (p. 12). (Only 'often'?)
6. Here we impinge on other elements of analytical structure. It cannot be helped, as they are not entirely independent.
7. Multiperiod portfolio theory exists, but it is not used in monetary policy discussions.
8. And how does one cash in one's stock of human capital? One can pay money to take a training course, but one cannot unlearn something to realise its value. One may reassess one's 'present value' – that is, regret having taken the course; but one is not paid for regret.
9. The usual defence of the asymmetry brought about by assets' poor marketability is to say that one borrows on the strength of future income or uses durable assets as collateral. This is, assuredly, more realistic than supposing that portfolio reorganisation must involve forced sales, but there are problems with this defence, nonetheless. First, it is the only place in the story where borrowing and lending are allowed to enter (activity on securities markets is apparently in already-existing assets), and a theory that you borrow to realise the cash value of assets but never to buy them is hardly satisfactory. Second, if capital markets were as perfect as a symmetrical application of the theory would require, it is difficult to imagine the need for money at all.
10. It is interesting that money's medium-of-exchange function is so played down by both Tobin (1969) and Brunner and Meltzer (e.g., 1972) despite their earlier contributions to the theory of transactions demand.
11. This is beautifully analysed in terms of 'monetary' and 'credit' mechanisms by Friedman and Meiselman (1963).
12. This fact is particularly jarring (though true nonetheless) in a model which places the entire weight on the 'supply price of capital'. This phrase seems (and certainly ought) to mean the price at which loanable funds can be obtained.
13. The 'helicopter' ensures that as a consequence of getting more money no one has less of something else – or has to work.
14. In raising this point we again touch on another element of analytical structure from that currently under discussion.
15. Some seem to find this assumption odd, given that the theory was current in the time of metallic money. Surely, they say, gold and silver have use-value in industry and the arts. Precisely. When not being used as money, the monetary metals do have use-value; when they are minted, and become money, their utility lies not in their metallic properties but in their ability to command other commodities – their exchange-value. The 'utility of liquidity services' is the modern term for exchange-value, although it is used in an attempt to restore a sense of use-value to money, for reasons too deep to explore here.

16. In the reverse pattern experienced by firms, the date of wage payments defines the period.
17. This conclusion is in answer to a quite different question to that raised by Hicks (1967, ch. 1) in his challenge to the volitional content of transactions demand. Hicks's question was not whether balances are held by accident or by design, but rather whether they are held by choice or by necessity.
18. Somewhat to my astonishment, the objection has been put to me that since money *is* a stock and is *measured* as a stock, both the demand for money and monetary equilibrium must be of a stock dimension. Now, the water in one's central heating system is also a stock and measured as a stock, but one would not, I think, say that the system was in equilibrium only when the water stopped flowing and was all 'willingly held' by various radiators and the tank. It is easy to agree that the system is not in equilibrium when the stock of water is rising, but that was not, I think, my objector's point.
19. See, e.g., the memoranda of evidence of Dow, Kahn and Kaldor (Radcliffe Report 1960).
20. Though perhaps not for its time, when second-hand markets in claims were not highly developed.
21. There is quite enough to do without exploring the *Treatise* or the *Tract*.
22. He made a slight but potentially significant alteration in separating the transactions demand for money from the precautionary motive. Transactions needs are regular and predictable. Thus money demanded for transactions purposes is continuously circulating and being run down to zero at the end of each income period. (Therefore the notion of an average balance demanded can be applied quite strictly.) Precautionary balances are held against less regular cash flows and enter the commodity circulation sporadically. Thus they are typically positive even at the end of the income period. For those who define equilibrium in terms of end-of-period stocks this feature is very comforting. Apparently only Robertson (1940, pp. 25–6) has made use of this point.
23. Marshall's exposition *can* be seen as portfolio-theoretic, but not in the sense of this paper.
24. Much has been made of the fact that speculators would be better advised to hold interest-bearing deposits and short-term assets. I urge those who find this a telling criticism to keep in mind that the significance of the speculative demand lies in its implications for long-term interest rates, which influence investment; then to have a look at Keynes (1936, p. 167, n. 1); and also to consider whether the rates of interest on short-term assets at the time Keynes was writing (three-month Treasury bills ran at an annual rate of considerably less than one per cent from 1933 to 1938) were worth chasing, or even safe from capital loss themselves, given the speculator's time horizon.
25. Equities could (I think should) be included along with 'bonds'. Keynes analysed them along marginal efficiency lines, as if they were real capital, a retrogression from the *Treatise*. The change of method is explained in Keynes (1936, p. 151).
26. To account for the behaviour of the rich, call a bequest an expenditure.
27. 'Money held for each of the three purposes forms, nevertheless, a single pool. . . . The same sum can be held primarily for one purpose and secondarily for another. Thus we can – equally well and perhaps better – consider the

individual's aggregate demand for money in given circumstances as a single decision, through the composite result of a number of different motives' (Keynes, 1936, p. 195).

28. Some have even been accused, for their pains, of ignoring the effects of changes in *r* on asset valuations – a reflection of the separation in thinking between the portfolio approach to asset choice and the flow-of-funds approach to the investment decision, though they are the same when properly formulated.
29. This aspect was confusing; it led to Radcliffe being thought a variant of portfolio theory. See, e.g., Johnson (1970).
30. With consumption loans now so important, perhaps 'is' should be changed to 'was' in the final clause (V. C., 1991).

# 8 Money

The ordinary person knows what money is: it is the stuff one used to buy things with. While money has taken many different concrete forms, both across societies and over time, its defining feature is general acceptability: people are always glad to take it, whether they intend to keep it for a time as a form of saving or to spend it.

The economist, looking at money from a macroeconomic perspective, sees in those two possibilities of disposal what D. H. (later Sir Dennis) Robertson called 'money on the wing' and 'money at rest': money as the medium of exchange which facilitates the circulation of goods and services, and money as the store of value which allows its holder to postpone specific expenditure decisions, thus leaving producers uncertain about future demands for their goods.

In a financially sophisticated society, other assets are close substitutes for money in both these functions. Assets may be ranked by the ease and speed with which they can be converted into money without significant loss of value. The better substitutes are called liquid assets. Money retains distinction, however, in being the asset acceptable as the final means of payment: one may use, say, a credit card ('plastic money'), as the medium of exchange, but one discharges the debt thus incurred with one of the assets which counts as money.

Money itself is not homogeneous. At any point in time in any society there are several different concrete expressions of the functions of money, if only because transactions differ greatly in size. Copper coins coexisted with gold or silver coins to cover small transactions, just as coins and notes coexist with bank deposits in modern economies. Over time, as public confidence in new forms of money develops, a practical definition of money will come to include those new assets. Central banks now collect data on several more or less inclusive monetary aggregates.

Government has done much to establish the general acceptability of particular assets. The sovereign's head on coins was designed to testify to their metallic content. Private coiners were prepared to pay a fee ('seignorage') for this stamp of uniform quality, which enhanced the coins' acceptability. As late as the 1930s, both J. M. Keynes and Irving Fisher hesitated to regard bank deposits as 'proper money', reserving unqualified acceptance only for notes and coin issued by government. As privately-issued forms of money such as bank deposits have usurped coin as the dominant form of money, the precondition for acceptability has been confidence in the convertibility of deposits into state-issued money – notes and coin. This convertibility came to be supported by central banks, providing state money as lenders of last resort. This function of central banks greatly adds to the unification and stability of the monetary and financial system.

Since no single monetary asset is acceptable in all transactions, the criterion of *general* acceptability requires further clarification. There are major acceptors who influence the course of monetary evolution. The state may declare some assets legal tender and may declare what it will accept in payment of taxes. The necessity to raise that particular form of money is an important influence on economic behaviour as long as the exchange of one kind of money for another at par is not assured. Similarly, the use of particular forms of money in the payment of wages both reflects and enhances, in a self-reinforcing manner, acceptability based on social consensus.

These examples represent the polarities of an important debate on the foundations of money: whether money is a creation of the state or of private consensus (see Frankel, 1977). In a modern Western economy, both influences are important. Bank deposits would not be acceptable by workers in payment of wages if deposits were in turn not useful in carrying out transactions, or if deposit money were not convertible in terms of notes and coin at par. Maintaining the par value of state and bank money is a prime objective of prudent banking, but it is underpinned by the actions of the state.

Nor would it be possible to pay wages by cheque had the Truck Acts not been repealed, though that action was taken only when bank deposits had reached a high level of social acceptability. Similarly, it is doubtful if a cheque on a bank deposit would be acceptable in payment of taxes if its value in terms of state-issued notes and coin were uncertain. There is a mutuality of state and social support of money in the modern Western economy: the dichotomy erected by philosophers of money, between state money and socially accepted money, needs to be replaced by an appreciation of the interactive support of the two forces in a modern economy.

# 9 Unresolved Questions in Monetary Theory: A Critical Review*

**Author's Note**

For the spring term of 1971, Mary Douglas, then Professor of Anthropology at University College London, put together an interdisciplinary seminar on Means of Payment. It was an exciting and rewarding intellectual adventure, resulting in some lasting friendships. I was invited to put the economist's point of view; this paper was the result. It was also delivered to a rather stormy session of the ESRC Money Study Group the following year.

I wish to dedicate this chapter to the memory of Phyllis Kaberry, intrepid anthropologist, dedicated teacher and wonderful story-teller.

## INTRODUCTION

Clower has made a sweeping accusation: 'The literature of monetary theory overlaps or verges on virtually every other branch of economic analysis; yet it does not contain a single coherent characterisation of . . . [either a] money commodity . . . [or a] money economy' (1969, p. 7). Though they attracted the attention of Aristotle (and doubtless others before him) and have left a voluminous literature since, the basic questions of monetary theory remain unanswered: What is money? What causes money to become established? What assets are likely to be used as money, and what causes them to fall into disuse? What are the private and social costs and benefits of the existence of money? What are the effects of changes in the quantity of money and how much control does or ought society exercise over the money supply?

* The author wishes to thank the participants in the Economic Anthropology Seminar on Means of Payment at University College London for their comments and suggestions, especially Mary Douglas, Gerald Cohen, Morris Perlman and Charles Goodhart. The comments of Yoram Barzel, Thomas Rymes, and members of the Money Study Group are also gratefully acknowledged. Responsibility for the outcome is entirely the author's.

This chapter reviews critically some of the controversy over these questions; the net result supports Clower's assessment of the current state of knowledge while suggesting some new lines of enquiry. Certain aspects of received ideas about the role of money are found less than satisfactory or less rich than they might be. Further, it is suggested that our concentration on money's role in exchange has limited our understanding of the operation of money economies. Money not only affects the efficiency with which we conduct trade, but also influences the rate of capital accumulation, the commodity composition of output, and relative prices.

## THE DEFINITION OF MONEY

### Definition by Function

It is unpromising to begin by admitting that despite centuries of debate the *object* of monetary theory has never been successfully defined. Other economists might take a rather more optimistic view, and argue that there is in fact a consensus: that money is whatever serves as the means of payment. This consensus is the outcome of a long discussion attempting to define money according to its functions,[1] in which traditionally four functions were commonly regarded as delimiting money: money served as means of payment, store of value, unit of account, and standard of deferred payment. It came to be accepted that the latter two were simply the same function with different time horizons, and that the unit of account could be separated from the first two functions, both in principle and in practice. (The British guinea provides an example of a pure unit of account.) Then the distinction between the means of payment and store of value functions was attacked on the grounds that nothing could serve as a means of payment that was not also a store of value, for things which had no value would not be acceptable in exchange.[2]

Now, anything we call a good has value. But most economists would attach different probabilities to the emergence of a perishable good or a durable asset as money. This point has two implications. First, it indicates that the question of time horizon has been avoided. Things have value for different lengths of time, depending on their intrinsic properties and the volatility of their demand. For how *long* must the money asset serve as a store of value? For how long, on average, are people willing to hold money 'idle'? The longer is this holding period, the more durable the asset which serves as money must be. Societies which typically do not *save* by accumulating money could use a less durable form of money. Second, since all assets are stores of value, that function is not sufficient to distinguish money from other assets.[3] Thus the medium-of-exchange function has come to be regarded as money's unique feature.

The interchange between Professors Clower and Shackle at Sheffield (Clayton *et al.*, 1971) challenged this consensus and brought out points of considerable interest. Clower argued for the inclusion of trade credit in the definition of money, on the grounds that it is a medium of exchange. Trade credit is distinguished from other claims in being accepted directly in exchange for goods, in contrast to forms of credit which involve *borrowing money* – issuing a claim in exchange for a loan of money which is then spent. The concept of trade credit relevant to this discussion comprises not only book credits extended among firms to pay for supplies, but also the credit given by retail shops to customers and (perhaps bulking largest of all, though virtually ignored in the literature) the credit given to firms by labour: labour services are provided in exchange for a claim on the firm (accrued wages), which is discharged periodically by a transfer of money (wage payments). Trade credit, thus broadly defined, is in widespread use, and is of considerable significance to the process of exchange.

Clower's expansion of the notion of medium of exchange, carried to its logical conclusion, carries the implication that any good which is *acceptable* in exchange can be regarded as a *medium* of exchange. In defining the medium of exchange, the *extent* to which a given asset is accepted is crucial. Money is identified as the asset *most* generally acceptable in exchange in a money economy. The question of including trade credit then rests on empirical evidence or judgement concerning how generally acceptable it is, relative to money.

Shackle's reply returned the debate to theoretical issues. His argument was based on defining money not as the medium of exchange but as the means of payment. Payment is effected when the transaction is finally closed, the debt discharged, and no further contact between the parties required or expected. If money is proffered for goods, payment and exchange coincide. But if trade credit is offered, there must be another exchange later on in which the credit is extinguished by a transfer of money or by a reverse flow of goods. Only then is payment effected.[4] Trade credit may be a medium of exchange but it is not a means of payment; indeed, it is used to *postpone* payment. Hence, trade credit should not be included in the definition of money.

In the event, their interchange and the discussion which followed were essentialist; but there is a fundamental lesson to be learned from it. The problem is not to discover the essence of money but to decide on criteria for useful aggregation of the economy's assets. Aggregation must be determined by what we are trying to explain: if we wish to understand the phenomenon of *exchange*, something which takes place at a point of time, trade credit shares the property of money that within its established sphere it is accepted as a matter of routine, even if it is not 'demanded to hold', that is, even if it causes temporary balance-sheet disequilibrium.

Shackle's distinction raises the time horizon problem once again. Exchange is instantaneous; time is not involved. But payment may be delayed. The time lapse between exchange and payment will depend on the terms of trade credit and the willingness to hold money idle.

Even if we were to agree to define money as the means of payment, we are left with the serious problem of identifying the assets which serve that function. Functional definitions of money do not suggest a unique mapping from money, the abstract concept, to any real-world counterpart. What is expected in final discharge of debt is largely determined at any point in history by social convention.[5] In choosing an aggregate we must fall back on pragmatic judgement of general acceptability in payment, as we have done in identifying the assets which serve most widely as the media of exchange. The concept of general acceptability is not clear-cut; it may refer to the range of transactions for which the asset is acceptable or the range of traders to whom it is acceptable. But once it is realised that even an agreed definition of money will not help to identify the relevant assets, a pragmatic approach is easily accepted and these ambiguities are not a cause for worry.[6]

Acceptance of the pragmatic approach, however, raises a fundamental difficulty which has not been generally recognised. If the assets which serve as money are to be identified empirically – that is, historically and *ex post* – we are unable to explain or predict either the acceptance of an asset as money or its disappearance from monetary use. We can only describe what *is*: whatever is used as money is defined as money. We cannot predict the limits to which a given monetary system can be pushed before the monetary assets become unacceptable. Hence it is impossible to analyse the breakdowns associated with hyperinflation, the future of a new instrument such as credit cards, or the effects of other financial innovations. We need to know *why* certain assets become and remain 'generally acceptable'. The first is widely believed to depend on certain characteristics which make some assets particularly well-suited to serve as money. To understand the second we need to develop an explanation of confidence. Money relies on confidence – confidence in its continued acceptability by virtually everyone in the economy. We shall take up these points in turn.

**Characteristics of the Money Asset**

Attempts to avoid the circularity involved in defining money as whatever acts as money have concentrated on describing certain properties which make some assets more suitable as media of exchange. Yeager (1968) and Miller (1965) have focused on transactions costs: money assets are those which, when offered in exchange, minimise the costs associated with trading. Their definition, however, does not suggest why certain assets are more suitable than others for saving transactions costs, nor does it contribute to our understanding of just what these costs are. Whichever asset is established by social convention will effect exchange at least cost.

A similar inconclusiveness besets Bronfenbrenner's (1945) definition: that money is the asset with the highest 'liquidity'. His discussion is of interest because it indicates a link between liquidity and transactions costs. Liquidity has three dimensions: a liquid asset has a high probability of yielding a high percentage of its original value without an undue lapse of time. A perfectly liquid asset is an asset which in exchange is *certain* to yield its original value, immediately. The dimensions are a probability, a percentage, and a time horizon. If money is generally acceptable, offering it in exchange for goods maximises the probability of getting a good price (paying a low price for the commodity) within any given time span. Use of any other asset in transactions is more costly 'because' it is less liquid. It can be seen that this is no real advance on the *ex post* definition of money: the most liquid asset is the one which is (already) generally accepted. But it highlights the connection between uncertainty concerning prices and 'illiquidity'. We shall return to this theme later.

The only non-circular approach to predicting which assets will serve as money is to list a series of properties which seem to make an asset suitable for general acceptability: durability, recognisability, portability, divisibility, relative inelasticity of supply, and the like. This approach does not help to *define* money. It is a description of the asset most likely to fulfil the monetary role, assuming that one can recognise money when one sees it. If it were found that these properties were possessed to a considerable extent by most monies, then perhaps one would have a theory of how money 'emerges', but a perusal of a book such as Einzig's *Primitive Money* (1948) quickly persuades one both of the tremendous variation in the intrinsic physical properties of the money assets used in various societies and of the difficulty of agreeing on whether an asset is, in fact, functioning as money. Our list of the 'properties of money' is plainly culture-bound; it is really a description of gold. One may conclude that while methodologically respectable, the 'properties' approach has not been empirically fruitful.

In most economies, there is more than one money asset (for example, deposits, notes, and coins). The properties of these assets differ and so do the areas in which they are used, and it is plain that these are systematically related. The asset which minimises transactions costs in one exchange may be inefficient in another. It would be absurd (or impossible) to pay for a house in pennies (portability is lacking) or a bus ticket with a £10 note (indivisibility). These are obvious examples, but detailed study over a wide range of experience might provide more subtle insights into the suitable properties of money assets than we have at present.

## The Origin of Money

The origin of money remains a mystery, and, somewhat surprisingly, an area of lively controversy. There are many subtleties to intrigue and entertain one, most lucidly set out by Ellis (1934)[7] though the disputants can be dichotomised into those who ascribe the origin of money to social custom and those who place primary emphasis on the role of the state.

Keynes, for one, was unwilling to be detained by these philosophical, and largely essentialist, arguments. While Yeager, Miller, and Bronfenbrenner never really made it clear whether they were explaining the emergence of a money asset or the continued use of an established one, Keynes's treatment of the first was brisk: to him, money was necessarily a 'creature of the State', whether directly or indirectly. A government may establish an asset as money directly, by declaration of legal tender status. When a government merely ratifies and reinforces accepted custom, it still plays a supportive role, maintaining confidence in a money already established.

The question of the origin of money loses its mystery if the creation of money is an explicit decision of a conscious agent. But societies lacking any established government or hierarchy have been known to develop money;[8] hence it is not generally valid to attribute 'moneyness' as necessarily conferred by some outside force or conscious collective social decision. But Keynes's main concern in his discussion of money in the *General Theory* (1936, ch. 17) is to explain not the origin but the continued use of money, taking the existing monetary framework as given. His central point was that for confidence in money to be maintained, prices of goods must be more stable in terms of it than in terms of some other asset or good: the convenience of using money in trade depends on prices (including the price of labour) stated in terms of money being highly stable, and thus predictable. The stability and predictability of prices is what makes one willing to accept in transactions an asset for which one can find no direct use. This very willingness to accept serves in turn to maintain price stability, just as accepting unanticipated changes in inventories of goods serves to even out price fluctuations in single markets. Thus, the liquidity of money makes it generally acceptable and its general acceptability makes it liquid.

A test of Keynes's theory could, in principle, be constructed at the level of individual prices. It would involve a comparison of the historical stability of the money price of, say, blankets with the apple price of blankets, where prices are defined not simply by converting the money price of blankets to an 'apple standard' but by taking the price of blankets which could obtain when apples are offered in exchange, and comparing the variability of this price with the price variability when money is offered.[9] If barter is as inefficient as economists suppose, one would expect to find a wide variation in the apple price of blankets, and a small variation in the money price of blankets when examined on a cross-section basis. One is unlikely, however, to find useful data. When barter trades do take place in money economies, the price established is typically not independent of the parties' knowledge of the money prices of the two goods. Perhaps one can only hope for evidence from economies in which the convention of monetary exchange is less firmly entrenched.

In part, the stability of money prices follows from the breadth of markets in which money is the accepted medium of exchange. Holding money involves speculating on the course of future prices. But unlike a 'warehouse receipt', which is a claim to a specific good in the future, money is a claim to (nearly) all future goods. The risk lies in the variability of the overall price index rather than the price of a single good. Holding money is like holding a diversified portfolio, so far as price risk is concerned. Its value is not much upset by changes in *relative* prices. But when the general level of prices changes rapidly, as in hyperinflation, the stability of the value of money is undermined, confidence is lost, and money eventually becomes unacceptable.[10] The question of how much inflation a money economy can tolerate will be discussed below.

Keynes's discussion of the necessary condition for the maintenance of confidence in money is not essentialist, but is a theory that the relative stability and predictability of money prices is the source of money's continued acceptability. Typically, the maintenance of price stability (and hence confidence in money) requires some degree of central control over the supply of money; if left to the market, a monetary system may be self-sustaining for a time, but is likely to break down under pressure either from over-issue of money or from under-supply. We shall return to this theme.

If money emerges and is maintained, it can be assumed that it serves some useful purpose, privately and socially. It is to the question of social and private costs and benefits that we now turn.

## COST AND BENEFITS OF THE EXISTENCE OF MONEY

### Synchronisation and Trading Costs

There are two entirely distinct sources of the influence of money on the functioning of the economy. Its existence or absence has an impact, and so do changes in its quantity. Recent work concentrates on transactions and information costs in an attempt to discover the sources of private and social gains from the existence of money.[11]

The comparison of a moneyless (and creditless) barter economy with a money economy has become established as a hypothetical exercise designed to discover what money's contribution is. The following argument has become 'generally accepted'. Trading is costly in time and effort. (It is assumed not to be a pleasant activity in its own right.) Costs are incurred because information is not perfect: one must locate people who wish to trade and establish prices. Call these activities search and haggling. Reducing the time spent searching and haggling frees resources for more trade, for production and for the enjoyment of leisure. It is said that money does this by overcoming the problem of establishing a 'double coincidence of wants': someone can always be found who will accept money. Money also increases convenience by allowing a separation of acts of purchase from acts of sale (where these terms are defined by the direction of money flow); money allows non-synchronisation of payments and receipts for individuals, which again facilitates transactions. The benefits of infrequent trade are then related to the costs of holding inventories or postponing purchases. Carrying costs on inventories or the loss of utility involved in postponing purchases (and hence consumption) have been termed waiting costs (Clower, 1969, p. 9). The optimum frequency of trading is found by minimising the sum of trading (transactions) costs and waiting costs. Money lowers transactions costs, for the reasons just outlined, without affecting waiting costs substantially. Hence the existence of money increases both private and social utility.

The analysis has been stated from the individual's viewpoint. From a social standpoint the existence of money can be regarded as part of the infrastructure. Like roads or an electricity grid, money's existence raises the capacity of that economy to produce and distribute to final buyers. The superior productivity of a money economy[12] may have at least three sources: some of the time formerly occupied in trading can be diverted to production; there can be much greater specialisation of labour,[13] given the improved ability to obtain one's desired consumption goods by exchange;[14] and money facilitates roundabout methods of production by providing a generally accepted intermediate good.[15] Further social benefits may accrue from the reduction of inventories of final goods resulting from more frequent trade;[16] the social costs of holding stocks may also be lowered by changing the distribution of inventory holdings within the economy. These gains would be offset at the individual level by the (private) cost of holding a barren asset; but at the social level it is only the (quite low) cost of storage and the (sometimes considerable) cost of security that count.

There are some unsatisfactory features of this description of the social and private benefits of money, however. Money is not *necessary* to permit a divergence in timing between purchases and sales. Any debt instrument (for example, trade credit) can perform that function.[17] Uncertainty about the price or availability of such credit could provide a rationale for money where transactions costs fail.[18] If transactions costs are to be a sufficient condition for the existence of money, we must explain just *why it is* that money makes trade more efficient. Some authors argue that the main gain comes from reducing the cost of setting prices by haggling. But haggling is not a phenomenon restricted to barter economies; all of us are aware that it occurs in money economies as well. Haggling time may be reduced in money economies, however, for reasons connected with money's role in overcoming the 'double coincidence of wants' problem associated with barter trade.

The double coincidence of wants is, in fact, a complex concept. One can easily appreciate that in random encounters the values of goods to be exchanged would not be equal at *established* (conventional or yesterday's) prices, but prices in barter are negotiable. In principle, there should always be *some* price at which a good offered for exchange would be acceptable, if prices were sufficiently flexible: the problem is not that one cannot find anyone who wants to buy one's wares, but that one is unwilling to lower the asking price sufficiently. Effecting an exchange would simply be a matter of finding the appropriate exchange rate, were it not for the seller's reservation price. In the determination of reservation price, the seller's imputation of the value of his goods in *other* potential exchange situations than the one he is presently facing is an important factor, along with the articles' use-value to himself.

## General Acceptability and Multilateral Trade

The need to calculate a reservation price by reference to a wide range of markets suggests that money's distinctive cost-reducing role is probably due, once again, to its general acceptability. The exchange economy using credit or direct barter is characterised by *bilateral* exchange and credit arrangements. Trade credit transactions are bilateral by transactor and barter transactions are bilateral at least by the goods entailed and possibly by transactor as well.[19] Money, on the other hand, is acceptable for a wide range of goods among a large group of persons. This suggests the usefulness of looking at money as a device which fosters impersonal, multilateral trade. If the opening up of multilateral trade is money's chief contribution, then the extent to which a given money asset is used in an economy is important, as are the 'exchange rates' between different money assets and between money and various forms of credit. What determines the limits to the circulation of money, and how are these boundaries maintained or altered?

These questions can be analysed in a framework used by Clower (1967), which I shall call an exchange matrix, Table 9.1. It has been generalised to take account of two facts from which he abstracts: (1) that there are always at least two media of exchange, money and trade credit, and (2) that even in a money economy goods do exchange for goods, but typically at worse terms of trade than could be got by using money. (A similar matrix dealing exclusively with final payment, omitting all forms of credit, can be constructed, but the points I wish to make can be made without it.) Let $A_i$, $i = 1, \ldots, j, \ldots, n$ indicate goods or assets available to be exchanged, in principle.

Let $P_{ij}$ denote the price at which the $i^{th}$ good exchanges for the $j^{th}$, in units of $A_i$. Let $A_1$ and $A_4$ be different forms of money, $A_5$ be trade credit and the rest be commodities. 'Transactions costs' due to indivisibility, perishability, identifiability (quality assessment), and the like, as well as transport costs to and from 'the market' have entered into the demand and supply functions that determined relative and money prices. The costs may be

*Table* 9.1 The exchange matrix

| *Exchange of* | $A_1$ | $A_2$ | $A_3$ | $A_4$ | ... | $A_n$ |
|---|---|---|---|---|---|---|
| For $A_1$ | 1 | $P_{12}$ | $P_{13}$ | $P_{14}$ | ... | $P_{1n}$ |
| $A_2$ | $P_{21}$ | 1 | $P_{23}$ | $P_{24}$ | ... | $P_{2n}$ |
| $A_3$ | $P_{31}$ | $P_{32}$ | 1 | $P_{34}$ | ... | $P_{3n}$ |
| $A_4$ | $P_{41}$ | $P_{42}$ | $P_{43}$ | 1 | ... | $P_{4n}$ |
| . | . | . | . | . | | . |
| . | . | . | . | . | | . |
| . | . | . | . | . | | . |
| $A_n$ | $P_{n1}$ | $P_{n2}$ | $P_{n3}$ | . | ... | 1 |

pecuniary, such as transport and insurance costs, but they also include non-pecuniary costs such as walking to market, time taken to set the price, and so on.[20] The relative (goods-for-goods) prices in this matrix are not derived from the money prices we typically observe; prices differ according to what is offered in exchange. We have, however, assumed them to be single-valued for any pair of goods: there is no bid–ask spread.

The transactions costs incurred in trade depend on the assets exchanged: some pairs of goods are inherently more difficult to trade than others. Some exchanges may be prohibitively expensive (the price, as here defined, is infinite); these exchanges will not be observed. More generally, where there are positive but finite prices for all trades, one expects to observe 'disorderly' cross-rates of exchange. It is supposed that transactions costs are minimised by offering money in exchange for any commodity. If money saves transaction costs, then, taking $A_2$ and $A_3$ as typical commodities, $P_{12}/P_{31} > P_{23}$; that is, one expects to acquire more of good 3 by first selling good 2 for money and then buying good 3 with money: it is cheaper, in value for time spent, to work at one's usual job for money and pay for a restaurant meal in money than it is to wash dishes in payment for the meal.

Given differences in the costs of exchange using different assets as media, transactors will attempt to purchase with the more favoured asset first: one expects to observe more exchanges involving money than barter exchanges. Clower (1967) takes this point to the extreme in his concept of a 'pure money economy', where 'money buys goods and goods buy money, but goods do not buy goods'. This implies that all prices except the $P_{1j}$, $P_{4j}$, $P_{i1}$, and $P_{i4}$ are infinite.

Even where the two forms of money are convertible at a fixed exchange rate with no commission, so that $P_{41} = 1/P_{14}$, a good's price may differ according to the type of money tendered. Then $P_{21}$ is not necessarily equal to $P_{42}/P_{14}$. If $A_1$ is inconvertible into $A_4$ and the two forms of money have different trading efficiencies for different goods, then the costs incurred in obtaining final commodities will depend on the relative amounts of the two monies owned at the outset of trading and on one's preferences among commodities. Further, if only $A_1$ is used in exchange for $A_2$ and $A_3$,[21] other goods only exchange for $A_4$ and $A_1$ is inconvertible into $A_4$, the matrix can be decomposed into subsectors between which there is no communication, as indicated by the dashed lines in Table 9.1. Within each sphere, the quantity of the relevant money asset possessed constitutes the budget restraint (ignoring trade credit for the moment). Purchasing power depends on having the right kind of money or, as a second best, being able to offer a commodity within the same trading sphere as the desired commodity. (Formally, $0 < P_{ij} < \infty$ with these exceptions: If $i = 1$ and $j = 4, \ldots, n$; or $i = 4, \ldots, n$ and $j = 1$. In these cases $P_{ij} = \infty$ or 0.)

These situations are more obvious in international than in domestic trade. Different currencies have well-defined boundaries to their circulation (though it was not always so). Some currencies are inconvertible; money only circulates across the boundaries by administrative permission, and where that is lacking, trades for money become prohibitively expensive; barter trades are observed instead. Through inconvertibility, the price matrix of the domestic economy can be to a considerable extent isolated from prices obtaining elsewhere, thus affecting patterns of consumption and the allocation of resources semi-independently of relative prices in the money sphere of the 'outside world'. The Eastern European countries do this quite consciously.

Limits to the circulation of money also exist within a national economy: money typically does not determine either effort or consumption within the family household. Reflection will, I believe, suggest to the reader that activities might be quite differently distributed if payment at prices prevailing in the money economy were made.

Flexible exchange rates allow exchange across the former barriers, but as the cross-rates of exchange vary, the limits within which a given money asset circulates will alter, due to changing relative prices. Hence by manipulating an exchange rate a sector can be more or less isolated from the larger economy, its borders being determined by the costs of using one or another money.

Even where monies are convertible at fixed exchange rates, exchange rates between these different monies and goods are not uniform.[22] At the national level, the examples seem rather droll and trivial, having to do chiefly with the physical properties of different monies. But at the international level divergences are due to the fact that relative price structures differ, country by country, because of different tastes and endowments. This fact is recognised in the special allocation of resources and credit facilities in the pursuit of export earnings. Where a seller has the ability to determine the acceptable form of payment, considerable excess costs may be imposed on those requiring a certain type of money.

The general point which has emerged is that the boundaries to the circulation of money are determined by the costs of using it in different types of transactions, in addition to any political or administrative barriers. The boundaries are not fixed: they will be altered or transcended if the incentive is great enough. We shall see in a moment that the same point holds for the boundaries between money, trade credit and barter. The exchange matrix provides a fully general model.

Analysis based on the exchange matrix supports the conjecture that an important contribution of money is its encouragement of impersonal, multilateral trade. Many authors have made the point that having a common unit of account simplifies the calculation of prices. But this assumes that prices are independent of the characteristics of assets being exchanged; it ignores transactions costs. When these are admitted into the analysis, money has a more important, and subtler, role to play in price-setting than that of numeraire. In a barter situation, traders are restricted to those who are interested in their goods or with whom credit transactions are possible.[23] This may be a fairly narrow set of persons, about whom a fair amount of information must be known. In contrast, nothing need be known about the person who offers money. The broadening of trade which the impersonality of money permits increases the chance of being able to effect a favourable exchange. Furthermore, in barter transactions, the agreed price is strongly influenced by the preferences of the participants. With a broader range of traders, more supply and demand information is pooled, and because each transactor is involved in trading different commodities, information is pooled across markets also. This contributes to eliminating the disorderly cross-rates of exchange which characterise barter transactions. In addition, money lowers transactions costs: because of its homogeneity, divisibility, and so on, transactions costs play a smaller and more uniform role in trades for money than in barter transactions.

An important result can be stated: the net effect of these forces is the *unification of the price matrix*. In performing this function, money must be more than simply a unit of account; it must actually be used in exchange.[24] The more widely a single medium of exchange is used, the fewer disorderly cross-rates are observed. For the individual, a uniform price matrix improves the precision with which he sets reservation prices and estimates the value of his wealth. He is more certain of his budget restraint. At the social level, multilateral trade narrows the limits within which prices are negotiable. Thus the use of money improves price formation, lowers the cost of haggling and mitigates uncertainty by reducing the variability of prices.

Calculation of reservation prices is an important link between markets. The exchange matrix cannot capture fully the process of setting these prices, because of its timeless nature. Nevertheless, its generality provides further insights into properties of the money economy.

The reservation price on non-money wealth is determined by its liquidity (a reflection of its range of acceptability, among other things). The fact that the expected realisation price rises with the time devoted to seeking a buyer is what makes a transactor retain his real assets, seeking to use more liquid assets instead, starting with money. But if one runs out of the favoured media of exchange, the option of using less efficient media (for example, real assets) is open. If the constraints of money exchange are sufficiently severe, barter is an alternative, albeit a more expensive alternative. This suggests a *hierarchy of budget restraints*, money and trade credit being used first, and other credit arrangements or barter terms being negotiated if the desire to trade makes the extra cost worthwhile. Where there are few barriers to the use of money and credit, barter will be employed only rarely. National economies, especially those of the 'advanced' countries, have few such barriers, but they enter importantly into the conduct of international trade. Consider the substantial barter trade between hard and soft currency countries.[25] The generalisation of the exchange matrix to include illiquid assets and credit raises the question of the time horizon implicit in the notion that money already possessed constitutes the budget constraint (Clower, 1967), for credit can almost always be arranged at some price, just as barter can always be undertaken, if the parties are prepared to incur the costs.

The expansion of credit is, of course, the usual way of transcending a shortage of money in the short run. Money is probably only important as a budget restraint for small, recurring purchases: the money in one's wage packet may determine one's beer consumption but it is unlikely to be the operative constraint in the purchase of a car; a firm may pay its wage bill out of the cash flow from sales, but is hardly expected to finance a new plant that way. It is worth enquiring whether, for the exchanges which typically use money, the social conventions of a money economy lead to a budget restraint which, at the personal level, is more rigid than it need be. It takes imagination and some courage to break those conventions and attempt a barter or direct trade credit contract, even if one is willing to bear the economic costs of disadvantageous terms of exchange in order to transcend one's immediate liquidity constraint. One wonders whether budget constraints in non-monetary economies using personal credit in exchange might not be very much more elastic at the individual level, while being less elastic in the aggregate because of the lack of financial intermediation and potential innovation in that sphere.

There are possibilities of releasing the restraints of money, even leaving aside credit and assuming the quantity of money to be fixed. It has often been pointed out that a given quantity of money can (within broad limits) effect any volume of exchange, depending on the price level or money's rate of turnover. Thus, in principle, the quantity of money in the economy is a matter of indifference. And so it would be if prices could be changed by fiat[26] or payments patterns altered whenever necessary. In practice, these changes (like all changes) are costly. Lowering the price level requires deflation of demand, which will not leave output unaffected. The net result is that while a given unit of money buys more goods than before, the real quantity of money has fallen, for there are fewer goods to buy. The second method of releasing a monetary constraint is feasible and, in fact, lies behind the development of financial institutions. Altering the timing of payments is one possible method. It requires cooperation and the collection of considerable information (Fleming, 1964), and may involve bargaining. Financial innovation is a more important source of change. (For example, goldsmiths issued claims on gold; these claims themselves performed a monetary function and increased the amount of 'work' the gold could do.)

When the monetary constraints become onerous, the costs of releasing them are worth incurring: Minsky (1957a) suggested that a major effect of restrictive monetary policy is the promotion of financial innovation. In complex economies financial innovation is going on virtually continuously, though at different rates, making the process difficult to observe and to relate to the degree of monetary stringency. These innovations are seldom reversed. They constitute a long-run progressive relaxation of monetary constraints on activity. One can be less sure of the long-run effects of changing payments patterns. It has been suggested that synchronisation of payments and receipts is inconvenient, but not doing so is also inconvenient, for it requires larger money holdings to effect transactions. If synchronisation becomes closer in response to tight money, it may loosen again when money becomes easier (it should if the previously chosen pattern was optimal). Alternatively, having found a 'more efficient' payments pattern the new pattern may be maintained, indicating that the previous pattern was suboptimal but the costs of changing it had been too high.

## The Money Asset, Costs of Production and Employment

Still addressing the question of the influence of the existence of money, rather than changes in its quantity, let us ask whether the choice of the money asset(s) matters for reasons other than technical efficiency in facilitating exchange. Two reasons for an affirmative answer have been put forward: the resource costs of producing a given stock of money will not be the same for all assets, and the ease with which the supply can be increased will also differ. The latter relates to the connection between the monetary standard and employment.

The case for the superiority of paper money (debt money) over commodity money has been argued on the grounds that commodities cost much more, in terms of real resources, to produce (Johnson, 1969). Replacing commodity money with paper would 'release' the commodity from its monetary use, resulting in a once-for-all gain which is larger than the cost of producing the replacing paper. Later additions to the stock of money will be produced more cheaply than it would have cost to produce additional commodity money.

This argument takes 'cost of production' rather literally, and, in doing so, overestimates the social gain. It is not enough simply to produce debt money; people must be persuaded to hold and use it. A major cost of debt money, additional to its physical production, is maintaining confidence in it. We do not really have much idea of what creates or sustains confidence, must less what it costs. In gold-standard economies confidence depended on maintaining convertibility, at a fixed rate of exchange, of paper money into gold – which was cheaper than using gold coin, certainly, as long as it worked. But a 'run' would bring the whole system down. And the causes of a run are not plain.

All fractional reserve systems, in which confidence in one kind of money is based on its convertibility into some other sort, share this property of vulnerability. The cost of operating these systems must include the risk of severe disruption if they fail. These systems are by their nature not very stable, and instability may manifest itself far short of a 'run'. The basic problem arises from the fact that the supply of the monetary aggregate is not independent of the demands for the aggregate's components. If people switch to holding more of the reserve asset, the total quantity of money will change, with effects on prices and/or output. It is to reduce the effects of this potential instability that social control, in the form of establishing a lender of last resort and regulating banking, has been established in Western economies.

Low costs of production of money, if derived from a small input of labour, are not *necessarily* an advantage. The ability of money-production to absorb labour is the basis of the argument that the choice of monetary standard has a direct bearing on the ability of the economy to maintain full employment. If demand and prices fall, the value of a commodity money rises, and it becomes more worthwhile to produce it. Expansion of the production of money in response to the incentive of falling prices simultaneously absorbs the labour from the contracting areas of production and provides the purchasing power needed to maintain demand. Hence, it is concluded by some (e.g. Burstein, 1963, ch. 8), that except for brief transition periods, unemployment should not be observed in commodity money economies, in contrast to paper money economies.

It is misleading, however, to argue this case in terms of the type of monetary standard. The central question is whether the quantity of money can be significantly affected directly by those who organise the productive energies of the economy and determine employment.[27] In the economy just described, the private sector controls the source of money supply (for example, gold mines) and decides the rate of production of money. Consider, in contrast, an economy in which the volume of money, either commodity money or paper, is exogenously given; say it is determined by government policy. Now there is no automatic mechanism whereby a shortage of money encourages a rise in supply, whether by diversion of some resources into producing it, or by increasing the demand for bank loans. In the absence of a change in policy, a shortage of money will be accompanied by a rise in its value (a fall in prices) rather than an increase in its quantity. The fall in prices leads to a fall in output, and adjustment is achieved at the cost of unemployment and forgone consumption. The essence of Gurley and Shaw's (1960) distinction between inside and outside money rests on this question of control: there is nothing the private non-bank sector can do to stimulate the production of outside money, but changes in inside money can be induced by the private sector's offering claims on itself to the banking system.

Which sector should control the money supply is a real question, for the temptation to oversupply is continuous. Over-supply leads to unstable prices which, if sufficiently extreme, will render the money unacceptable. Here lies the positive value of having a money asset with a low elasticity of supply: the expense of increasing the money supply protects against the temptation to increase it too rapidly.

This section has been concerned with the social costs of various sorts of monetary systems – resource costs of producing money, costs of maintaining confidence, and costs of instability and periodic unemployment – to be set against the social benefits of budgetary flexibility (as compared with creditless barter) and efficient price-setting and trading. It is obvious that we have only the vaguest notion of the magnitude of these costs, most notably the cost of maintaining confidence. We do not even have a coherent theory of what determines confidence, particularly in systems in which the quantity of money is neither determined exogenously nor regulated internally by centralised social control. Confidence can be established or reinforced by actions of 'the authorities'; we return to this point in the final section of the paper.

## CHANGES IN THE QUANTITY OF MONEY

### Effects on the Economy

In monetary theory, as developed in Western advanced economies where the existence of money is taken for granted, the main theme is the effects on the economy of variations in the *quantity* of money, rather than reasons for the existence of money or properties of its optimal form. The literature is extensive but inconclusive, and it cannot be summarised here. Perhaps it is inconclusive because the effect of a change in the quantity of money is contingent upon the state of the economy at the time of the change and upon who issues the money and in exchange for what. The first contingency is familiar. An increase in the money supply at a time of full employment is expected to be reflected mainly in price changes, but it may stimulate output in a slump. The latter contingencies are usually denied by monetarists and ignored by Keynesians.[28] A change in the quantity of money, however, never occurs in isolation: it always comes into the system in exchange, as half of some transaction, and its effects depend partly on what that other half is. An expansion of government-issued money may result from an increase in the government's purchases of new goods and services, a direct stimulus to demand, or from an exchange for interest-bearing debt outstanding, in which case the effects are more roundabout. Bank money is expanded through increases in bank lending, so the effect of the change depends partly on what the borrower does with the proceeds of his loan.

In particular, the rate of capital accumulation, or more broadly the distribution of output between consumption and investment, may be influenced by changes in the money supply. This is easiest to see in an extreme form, in a hypothetical example. Suppose that bank loans were only given for the purpose of building new productive capital. Suppose that when the loan is made there is spare capacity in investment-goods industries. Output will rise, the initial rise taking the form of new capital goods. If the industry is at full capacity, the borrower is in the position, because of his possession of money, to bid away resources from others. Prices of capital goods will rise as a result. The net result is a shift in the composition of expenditure and output towards capital goods, a rise in the general price level and altered *relative* prices. The effects would be different if the banks had granted consumption loans.

## The Limits to Monetary Change: Confidence Once Again

Macroeconomic theory usually ignores changes in the composition of output, for they are seen as less important than changes in aggregate output and prices. But these are important for what they reveal of the power structure of an economy. The general willingness to accept money confers on those with authority to issue new money the power to preempt resources. If the government issues an acceptable money, it is in a position to run a deficit any time it chooses. At full capacity its action may cause inflation, but meanwhile, it has successfully bid away real goods and services from the private sector. Inflation, when induced by increases in those forms of money issued by governments, is strictly equivalent to a tax. A country whose money is a reserve currency is also free to run a deficit internationally, acquiring commodities in exchange for new international reserves whose future purchasing power is not assured. Banks have similar powers, at one remove. American Midwesterners perpetuate the populist slogan, 'Banks are institutions with the power to steal.' That expression is somewhat inaccurate: banks enable those who borrow from them to 'steal'. It is only as borrowers exercise their demands that the money supply rises and permits prices in general to rise to a new level. By being first in the market, they can buy *before* the new money causes prices to rise.

Money is a great convenience in a large society, and it is the more convenient the wider its acceptability. But it is precisely money's general acceptability which confers market power on those who can, by issue or borrowing, create new money. But undue exercise of that privilege is damaging to price stability, and, as argued above, price stability is necessary for the maintenance of confidence in a particular money. Theory also suggests that the preferences of asset-holders will provide checks on the rate of growth of money. History, on the other hand, shows both that the checks are not very effective and that considerable inflation is compatible with the continued use of money. These anomalies reveal that the determinants of limits to the rate of growth of money and of confidence have not really been established by monetary theory.

The theorem that asset-holders' preferences constrain monetary growth to that which, in some sense, the public desires, derives from the multiplier theory of money creation,[29] in which the preferred ratio of cash to deposit holdings indicates the cash drain the banking system can expect from expansion.[30] It is presumed that banks will not expand beyond the point at which cash reserves will meet the demand for cash. The underlying supposition is that confidence in deposits is based on convertibility into cash.

Demonstrable ability to convert does promote confidence, and the threat of conversion provides *some* sanction against over-expansion. Britain's international currency experience in the 1960s, resulting in 'Stop-Go' episodes, attests to this. If banks wish to remain in operation and countries wish indefinitely to remain reserve currency countries, convertibility acts to restrain the rate at which banks and governments create new money. But to generalise to the proposition that the holders and users of money can, in general, limit its rate of expansion is false. Convertibility is only useful in its potentiality. Its actual exercise is destructive; a run on a bank is punishment for, not prevention of, over-expansion. No bank asks actual or potential depositors (with itself *and the other banks*) to approve in advance an expansion of earning assets, though the consequent new deposits must be held by someone. Over-expansion, resulting in unduly large cash drains, are usually cushioned by the lender of last resort, thus validating the expansion. And the experience of expansion of overseas dollar holdings in the late 1960s is evidence that the sanction is, in fact, weak and if it begins to be effective, may simply be overruled.

Once convertibility has been abrogated, control of the money supply rests almost entirely on the issuer. The ability of the residents of a fiat-money economy to control the money supply is tenuous indeed. In democracies they have the power to vote the government out of office, taking away its money-issuing powers, if its management of the money supply is not to the society's liking – a solution which sounds extreme when stated so uncomprisingly but which sometimes does have some bearing on events. Has inflation never been an election issue?

Monetary mismanagement is seldom the central election issue, however. And it may well be that all governments have a propensity for 'fiscal irresponsibility' anyway. Ultimately, we say, one can always refuse to hold money. But in the case of fiat money, not convertible into any other sort of money, there is no alternative money one can demand which would put pressure on government to slow or stop monetary expansion. One can only 'refuse to hold money' by buying goods or other debt instruments. An individual will continue to *accept* money; one would be foolish not to, for one can always exchange it for something else, even in a period when its value in terms of goods is declining. 'Refusal to hold money' in this case then refers to the speed with which one takes action to spend it. An entrenched government need not be too concerned with maintaining confidence in money: it is using the proceeds of money issue to finance its expenditures; prices rise as a result, but it has obtained the goods and services it wishes. And the citizens have no option but to hold the new money, even if they have no confidence in it.

As the price rises continue, however, larger money issues are necessary to buy an unchanged volume of goods and services (Friedman, 1971). If at the same time the public has begun to anticipate inflation and is raising the speed with which money circulates, which will accelerate the rate of inflation, the rate of issue necessary to maintain the same command over real resources increases still further. Eventually, the costs of issuing the required amount, given the level of prices and the rapidly diminishing sphere in which money now circulates, are large enough to make continued issue not worthwhile: one has reached the 'currency reform' stage of a hyperinflation.

The 'social saving' embodied in paper and bookkeeping money must be balanced against the system's fragility and the difficulties of restraining monetary expansion. The exercise of checks on money issuers takes fairly dramatic and destructive forms. In many situations, the system may be contained far short of the extremes which I have outlined, partly because confidence is expensive to maintain in periods of 'excessive' expansion, and the *threat* of loss of confidence, bringing failure to the banks and expulsion from power for governments, may be sufficient to ensure some measure of restraint. History does not, however, inspire optimism for the long run.

## CONCLUDING REMARKS

From an aggregate perspective, money is an illusion. Even commodity money exchanges for 'more than it is worth' as a commodity. But money works as long as everybody (or almost everybody) believes in it. The construction of a complex financial system is a compounding of the illusion. The real value of money, ultimately, is only a reflection of a society's productive capacity. The illusion may greatly improve that capacity, as long as confidence is maintained.

The illusion and its benefits are bought at the price of conferring substantial market power to those with a franchise to produce money and of accepting great disruption should the system fail. Hence, the question of whether society benefits from the existence of money is clearly not independent of the power structure it wants or is best for it. Who should have control of the money issue? Once that question is answered, it is difficult to reconsider: the power to issue money, like incumbency in office, helps to retain that power. An established money asset is exceedingly difficult to dislodge. This fact gives money-issuers great latitude in their management of the quantity of money before any sanctions become effective. In most countries it is established that private banking systems should be subject to some form of centralised control. The question of the accountability of treasuries and central banks is still open.

**Notes**

1. 'Money is defined by its functions: anything is money which is used as money: "money is what money does"' (Hicks, 1967, p. 1).
2. I wish to cite Harry Johnson here, but cannot recall the appropriate reference, if indeed there is one: he may only have made the point verbally.
3. An exception to this view is Rosenstein-Rodan (1936), who attaches preeminence to a more precisely and narrowly defined store-of-value function.

4. With this point of view it is possible to unify what now appear to be two disparate concepts, the exchange economy and the gifts economy, and to say something about the time horizon implicit in exchange and credit, and the risks attaching to credit, in the gifts economy or sector. If gifts are not free, but imply a social obligation to repay, a gift is simply an informal credit arrangement, with a time horizon and expected repayment dependent on social institutions.
5. In the Middle Ages foreign coins often circulated, as they did again in the early days of the United States. Today national currencies have very rigid boundaries.

   Even within nations, social custom determines acceptability. In the United States, shops carry considerable change so as not to lose custom for lack of it, while in Italy a customer knows and accepts that producing too large a note means he will wait, while a small boy scurries down the street to break the note. The traveller who does not offer the exact bus fare in New York will not ride; drivers carry no change, for fear of robbery. In England one discovers that the sphere of acceptability of bank cheques is still influenced by social class, though this barrier is gradually breaking down. It is not only in primitive societies that social organisation influences monetary circulation.
6. I am indebted to G. Cohen for correction and clarification of the issues involved in this paragraph. Any remaining errors are of course my own.
7. See also Menger (1892).
8. A well-known modern case is described in Radford's study (1945) of the development of cigarette-money among prisoners of war.
9. This concept is developed further in the next section.
10. It was pointed out by Lerner (1952) that hyper*de*flation, if it were to occur, might also bring down the monetary standard, not because money becomes unacceptable but because it ceases to be offered.
11. See, *inter alia*, Brunner and Meltzer (1971), Clower (1969), Ostroy (1973).
12. This assertion may appear at variance with the celebrated conclusion of growth theory (Tobin, 1965), that a money economy exhibits a lower rate of capital accumulation than a moneyless economy. This is because money provides an alternative mode of saving. The sources of increased efficiency raised here played no role in Tobin's analysis. [Tobin reaches his absurd conclusion because he considers only the portfolio aspect of money and uses comparative statics where the method is not appropriate (V.C., 1991).]
13. Any debt instrument (e.g., trade credit) can allow specialisation to develop. In fact, given that for technological reasons things take different lengths of time to produce, specialisation would be impossible without money. (The barber cuts the farmer's hair every fortnight for 'trade credit' which is paid at harvest time.)
14. The number of feasible trades should increase; money permits some exchanges which were previously too costly to arrange.
15. I am indebted to Yoram Barzel for pointing out that direct trade in intermediate goods would, in all likelihood, be even more difficult than trade in final consumption goods.
16. Mary Douglas (in conversation) has characterised the economies with which anthropologists deal as ones in which production and consumption are very closely related. There is presumably less to be gained from the introduction

of money into such economies, which is one explanation of its relatively infrequent occurrence, even when there is exchange. Where socially-determined (authoritarian or cooperative) distribution systems are used instead of exchange, clearly money has no role to play. Some economies use an authoritarian distribution system within their boundaries but exchange with other economies, usually conducting this trade with money.

17. Brunner and Meltzer (1971) have also made this point.
18. See the discussion in Goodhart (1975, ch. 1, especially pp. 3–5).
19. This depends on market organisation. See Clower (1969, pp. 11–13).
20. Prices may also differ according to the identity of the transactors and their and the commodities' geographical locations. The costs of overcoming space are meant to be taken into account; individual skill in bargaining power is not. In order to avoid side issues, I am by-passing some rather difficult problems here. These costs are partly borne by the seller, partly by the buyer; their incidence will affect the final price. For present purposes, let us suppose the incidence is fixed by social custom and is not subject to negotiation.
21. Strictly, more than two goods are required to justify the intervention of money. The simplification avoids overuse of symbols; it does not change the basic point.
22. The proposition that a system of fixed exchange rates is equivalent to a common currency (Tower and Willett, 1975, p. II–9) does not hold when transactions costs are admitted. See also note 24.
23. Without credit, this would amount to trading under the condition that budgets must be bilaterally balanced. This very restrictive situation has been analysed by Ostroy (1973). See also Niehans (1969).
24. To my knowledge the only recognition of this point in modern literature is Marget (1942, p. 67 and 1935, especially p. 170, n. 5). In contrast, Brunner and Meltzer (1971) attribute money's efficiency in providing price information solely to its unit of account function. My point poses an amusing paradox for general-equilibrium theory. Prices are 'orderly' in terms of a numeraire. But if there are intrinsic differences between goods, giving rise to transactions costs, the numeraire commodity must enter into all exchanges. We would call such a commodity money. But as is well known, there is no reason for the existence of money in general-equilibrium theory. In fact there is no indirect trading of any kind. As Brunner and Meltzer (1971) put it, each trader engages in one 'double coincidence of wants' exchange. 'Multiple coincidence' might have been a better expression, but the point stands: there is no need for a medium of exchange. But that is not all. For this one great trade to be feasible, the intrinsic properties of goods, especially indivisibility, must be ignored. In a world of putty there is only one price. Indeed, there is no reason to trade.
25. [Counter-trade, as it is called, has been increasing, even amongst Western countries (V.C., 1991).]
26. The French currency reform of 1960 is an illustration of the irrelevance of the quantity of money when all prices are changed at once. More interesting cases are found in the history of the use of the device of 'imaginary money' (Einaudi, 1936); the quantity of circulating money could be made appropriate to the needs of circulation by changing its value in terms of the 'imaginary' unit of account, that is, prices could be changed by decree.

27. On this point, Keynes (1936) is quite clear. The low elasticity of production which he argues is one of the two distinguishing characteristics of money is not due merely to the technology of producing money:

> Money has . . . a zero, or at any rate a very small, elasticity of production, *so far as the power of private enterprise is concerned*, as distinct from the monetary authority. . . . Money, that is to say, cannot be readily produced; – labour cannot be turned on at will *by entrepreneurs* to produce money in increasing quantities as its price rises in terms of the wage-unit. (1936, p. 230. Italics added.)

28. See Chick (1973b, pp. 126–38), and the references cited therein.
29. This is a central conclusion of Tobin's celebrated article (1963).
30. An exposition of the bank credit multiplier can be found in almost any textbook in monetary or macrotheory. For a critical exposition see Goodhart (1975, pp. 129–36).

# 10 Monetary Increases and their Consequences: Streams, Backwaters and Floods

**Author's Note**

The intellectual origins of this paper, read to a conference in honour of Ivor Pearce, are explained at the beginning of the text. Ivor made my three months at Southampton University truly memorable. As theorists we are diametrically opposed but in arguing his point of view, Ivor's sense of intellectual honesty and of fair play meant that we remained, and still remain, warm friends. I also benefited from the presence at Southampton of Jan Kregel, whom I had known from 1968 or so, and of Kerry Schott, who later became a colleague at UCL for a time. Kerry, particularly, patiently listened to my thoughts and helped me to develop them.

## INTRODUCTION

The origin of this chapter is the series of conversations I was privileged to have with Ivor Pearce while a visiting lecturer at the University of Southampton in 1977. The discussions centred around monetary aspects of expansion, something Dennis Robertson had argued with Keynes and on which the monetarists should have drawn fire from the Keynesians, but for some reason they have not done so.

Ivor contended that the Keynesians were misguided to think there could be investment in advance of saving that was not inflationary. This was because such investment was only feasible if accompanied by monetary expansion, and while 'the new money may go into a backwater for a time, ultimately it will come out and that is inflationary'.

This statement, which serves as my text and the germ of the chapter's title, was accompanied by a diagram describing a large circle, the circular flow of income – in *Treatise* terms (Keynes, 1930) the industrial circulation – with a smaller one, representing the financial circulation, attached to it. The financial circulation was the 'backwater', for goods prices are not determined there. Prices and output are determined in the industrial circulation, which I shall refer to as the 'mainstream'.[1]

At the time I agreed with Ivor (much to his surprise, I think) that the standard Keynesian multiplier story was absurd. I have since become acutely aware, however, that (like so much else) in Keynes's hands the story is less absurd than it later became. Much hinges on the variety of possible interpretations of the word 'finance'. Once the different meanings of this word and of 'saving' become clear, the conflict between the key proposition of loanable-funds theory – that investment not financed by prior saving is inflationary – and Keynes's insistence that rises in investment always precede saving (and may, but need not, be inflationary) is diminished if not entirely resolved.

In gratitude to Ivor for stimulating my research and thinking on this issue[2] let me proceed as follows.

The question of whether an expansion of investment (or any other autonomous expenditure, but I shall say 'investment' throughout) is necessarily inflationary (or can ever be completely non-inflationary, as in the 'Keynesian' model) can be broken down into two parts: (i) whether an increase of investment above a previous short-run equilibrium level must by necessity be financed by new money, and (ii) whether that new money (or other source of finance) need be inflationary, and by what mechanism. These questions occupy the first three sections of the chapter.

To conclude, I will comment briefly on the relevance to today's financial environment of the two major approaches to monetary aspects of macroeconomics. (I refer of course to liquidity preference and loanable funds.[3] There are signs that the latter is making a comeback.[4]) Both are found inadequate: new approaches are needed.

## THE FINANCING OF INVESTMENT

The first question, then, is whether an increase in investment must by necessity be financed by new money.

It was Dennis Robertson (1936) who faced this question most explicitly. Robertson assumed, implicitly and without discussion (for his terms of reference would have been widely understood at the time), that 'saving' meant funds available for the finance of investment, so that 'if . . . we are prepared to forget about the period of transition, we can declare the problem of the finance of the process of investment to be self-solving' (pp. 117–18). The equality of saving and investment at the end of the process would be sufficient to ensure that the funds were there.

But common sense suggests that one cannot wait until the end of a process to find the finance that is needed to start it off. Adopting a period analysis to analyse the transition, Robertson demonstrates what we expect: that a rise in investment must be financed by new money if the velocity of circulation is constant (which he assumes). This leaves open the possibility of finance out of idle balances (a rise in velocity), which presumably would entail a rise in interest rates. (An increase in bank finance might also increase interest rates; this complication is left out.)

Did Keynes ignore the need for and the implications of the monetary preconditions for expansion? Not entirely, but he certainly did not spell them out; he was so offhand in his indicative remarks that it is not surprising that the problem was overlooked.[5]

Notice that in the last paragraph but two I did not qualify 'saving' and 'investment' by '*ex ante*' or 'intended': to Robertson saving was entirely volitional and the qualifying words are superfluous. Keynes's notion of aggregate saving – actual income not consumed – is, by absolute contrast, an entirely *ex post* concept.[6] Thus it is not surprising that the concept *ex post* saving does not appear in Robertson's analysis and has no relevance to it. This explains why he does not credit the 'Keynesian' contention that adequate saving is present at every stage of the expansion and thus investment is *continuously* financed by saving.

The background of Keynes's thinking did not become explicit until the publication of his 1937 and 1939 articles. It must be emphasised that Keynes's analysis applies to a single rise in investment, or a sustained rise of finite length considered as one event, whereas in Robertson's example the elevated level of investment continues indefinitely. (There are subtle reasons for this difference which will be made clear later.) The two approaches are, however, not as incongruous as they first appear.

Where Robertson distinguished two stages – obtaining the finance to start the process off and the eventual (equilibrium) finance by saving – Keynes (1937b, 1939) distinguishes three stages:

1. Obtaining a loan *before* making the investment expenditure.
2. Expenditure of the proceeds of the loan.
3. Establishing the permanent holding of the investment in question.

The first stage entails the fleeting but vital securing of a loan (from any source, but let us take bank credit) to provide purchasing power in advance of investment expenditure. The proceeds satisfy the (evanescent) finance motive for money, to be extinguished in Stage (2). There is no increase in saving in Keynes's terms at this stage (for actual income has not increased and consumption has not fallen), though there may have been on Robertson's definitions, if saving is responsive to interest rates. If the entrepreneurs satisfy the finance motive by establishing an overdraft facility, there is no distinction between Stages (1) and (2), as the overdraft does not come into being until it is spent (Keynes, 1937c; 1973b, p. 223).

In Stage (2) the money held on finance motive is spent and thus becomes income. Assuming the money came from bank credit, the recipients of the entrepreneurs' expenditure now hold deposits not previously in existence, through no conscious decision of their own. Keynes would account for this as saving, equal to the new investment; it being involuntary saving, Robertson would exclude it from his definition.

As the multiplier effects of this single rise work themselves out, there is an opportunity to fund the bank loan or whatever is required to finance the firm's *balance sheet position* as affected by its acquisition of new capital. When this process is complete we have reached Stage (3):

> It may . . . help to clear up misunderstanding to point out that whilst [*ex post*] saving takes place concurrently with investment (in the sense of the first acquisition of this capital good by an entrepreneur) the flow of funds (i.e. of money) available for investment (in the sense of the first acquisition of [a claim on] this capital good by a *permanent holder*) takes place subsequently. (Keynes, 1939; 1973b, p. 284; italics added.)

The 'flow of funds' available for investment is equivalent to Robertson's (voluntary) saving. This, Keynes argues, does not finance the *purchase* or construction of capital goods but rather the *holding* of the new, larger volume of capital goods. This voluntary saving, whether in the form of securities or money, gradually displaces the involuntary holding of new deposits as the multiplier process unfolds. These holdings, though at first involuntary, will count as saving in Keynes's terms.

Some investment *is* financed (in the balance sheet sense) by saving in the end, but a rise in investment cannot be financed by saving in Keynes's sense in the beginning. (We shall see later that financing by Robertsonian saving, though possible, is also tricky.)

Robertson's analysis appeared to show that new money was the *necessary* form of finance of expansion, but this necessity depends entirely on his assumption of a fixed velocity of circulation. A sale of securities to holders of idle balances will, when the proceeds are spent and income is altered, raise velocity, so that quintessentially Keynesian possibility is perfectly possible, if the restrictive assumption is relaxed.

## THE POSSIBLE CONSEQUENCES OF INCREASED INVESTMENT

Now we come to the second point: whether the new money or newly active money must necessarily be inflationary – 'The new money may go into a backwater for a time, but ultimately it will come out, and that is inflationary.'

Once again the argument comprises two questions: (i) will the rise in investment (or its monetary accompaniment) be inflationary initially?, and (ii) what happens to the money after that? Let us again examine the new-money case.

The question of whether or not an expansion of investment would be inflationary initially is essentially a question of technology and the effects of competition for resources, not a very 'monetary' problem really. Surely we can agree that the effect on prices depends on costs and firms' pricing policies. In general one would expect that a rise in the level of investment would cause the average of prices to rise in the short run even with unemployment keeping wages stable, insofar as the capital-goods industries exhibit rising marginal costs.[7]

Whether one wants to call this inflationary, however, is debatable, since if costs rise expansion is impossible without price rises. Keynes would not have called these rises 'true inflation': that term was reserved for price rises associated with *no* rise in output. Insofar as the expansion in the capital-goods industries raises costs and prices in the consumption-goods industries, there is some reduction in real consumption as compared to what was planned, which has variously been called 'forced saving' or 'automatic lacking'.[8]

It can be seen that for a rise in investment to be completely devoid of consequences for prices requires both stable wages and constant returns (see Keynes, 1936, ch. 21, for a demonstration). These are assumptions that Keynesians found necessary to impose and then justify to maintain their fixed-price model of expansion. Keynes did *not* impose them.

Having analysed the effect of an extra demand on resources represented by new investment backed by new or newly active money, one can inquire as to the influence of this money in subsequent stages. One assumes that the excess over the now larger transactions-needs goes into the backwater. As far as I could see during our discussions in 1977, we agreed on the following: *for as long as* the money was in the backwater it added no further inflationary impetus. Ivor's point was that *when it came out* it would be inflationary. Just *how* great was this secondary inflationary influence of monetary finance, depended on how much went into the backwater, how long it stayed there, and how much excess capacity there was when it came into the mainstream. I now think this is not correct.

Consider first the quantitative aspect of the question. In a depression (i) the volume of transactions in the mainstream is relatively low, so a good deal of money may go into the backwater, (ii) the rate of interest is low at such times, so much of the new money is held *as* money, or (iii) to be more realistic, it is held as bank deposits but banks are having difficulty finding sound borrowers, so (iii) comes to much the same thing as (ii). The answer is different in a boom.

Second, consider the question of time – the *length of time* the money stays in the backwater. In the early post-Keynesian reviews and articles, Tobin, Leontief and others argued, against liquidity preference theory, that a positive speculative demand for money would not be sustained indefinitely. They failed to notice that *Keynes explicitly agreed with that* (Keynes, 1936, pp. 208–9). So it is no criticism. But does their argument mean that monetary finance will inevitably have a delayed inflationary impact?

I think it could be said that the conventional reasoning concludes 'yes' for it is assumed that when the speculative demand for money is reduced to zero, the money will come out of the backwater into the mainstream – that is, jaded speculators will buy goods instead – and that raises monetary demand, to be divided as before between increased prices and output. In 1977 I had gone along with this reasoning; it is, if not incorrect, at least limited and possibly misleading.

Notice that I had translated the statement about money flows in the backwater into demand-for-money terms. The demand for money is a very partial characterisation of the activity in the backwater, however: it is curious that the Keynesian or Keynes-trained mind sees only money there, despite the fact that there can be no speculation without securities as well. The backwater consists of *all* transactions in 'idle' funds (i.e., funds withdrawn from the mainstream), whether held in money or in securities.

Similarly, the mainstream comprises not only goods and services but also the money flows that permit that output to be produced and 'circulated' (sold). This point is remembered well enough in any textbook discussion of the circular flow itself, but forgotten when the subject is the mainstream activity known as the multiplier. (We forget that when money circulates in exchange for goods and services, Keynes calls it 'income'.) This distorted image allows Keynesians, even those Keynesians who acknowledge that investment requires monetary accommodation, to envisage the multiplier as a purely 'real' expansion rather than an expansion with implications for both prices and output.

I was aware enough of that distortion, but not of my own distortion of the financial circulation. Let us therefore try to analyse the 'backwater' more carefully, keeping in mind not only that the backwater comprises dealings in all financial assets but also that these are held for a variety of purposes: the speculative demand for money and speculative, precautionary and 'investment' demands for securities. (An 'investment' demand for money is absurd. It is not obvious whether precautionary money demand belongs in the mainstream or the backwater.)

The reasoning of Tobin and Leontief suggests that money will inevitably leave the backwater. The foundations of their supposition are, I suspect, microeconomic: no *individual* (with finite life and no heirs) will hold financial assets – whether money *or* bonds – indefinitely. Eventually all financial assets are converted for use as transactions balances in the mainstream, leaving aside errors owing to uncertainty about prices, length of life, and so on. But an individual's behaviour is no guide to aggregate speculative demand. An individual does not speculate alone, neither do others think as he does – otherwise there is no one to speculate with but the government broker. And when our individual leaves off speculation others are entering the game.

What counts for inflation is *aggregate* movements out of idle money. The length of time society as a whole is willing to hold money idle in the backwater has to do with the degree of instability of interest rates and the attendant uncertainty, as well as the level of interest rates. There is nothing in the *General Theory* to suggest any time horizon for which a given state of speculative demand might prevail. Money may go into the backwater for a long time or a short time but if the rate of interest is stable enough, it becomes obvious that there is no longer any point in holding money speculatively, whatever the level of the interest rate.[9]

The most obvious alternative to speculative money-holding, however, is not for bears to switch into goods (which involves a shift in the aggregate consumption function not due to the alteration of any economic variable) but for them to join the bulls and long-term investors, holding securities and earning interest. (The demand-for-money approach has made it difficult to perceive this alternative.) If that is what they do, the money *remains* in the backwater (though it is not held as money).

If the money is to 'come out' into the mainstream, either society as a whole must decide to save less and consume more, or speculators, seeing insufficient sport in the backwater, switch their attention to commodities, foreign currencies or land. As we have learned from experience, if inflationary expectations take hold, speculators may be joined by long-term investors in turning their attention to real assets; this will, naturally, add to inflationary pressures.

There is no reason, however, to predict that these alterations in behaviour will occur with the sheer passage of time: the money need not 'come out eventually'. That it may come out, that the contents of the backwater always have the potential to create inflation in the mainstream is, however, in no doubt, and the larger the backwater the more potential is stored there, like water behind a dam.

## THE IMPLICATIONS FOR LOANABLE-FUNDS THEORY

It has been established so far that there are two possible sources of 'inflation' (or at any rate price rises!) owing to money-financed new investment: the initial effect of the rise in mainstream activity and a potential, subsequent effect if money should come out of the backwater owing to a net shift out of financial assets by wealth-holders. This shift is not 'dishoarding', and only on very careful definitions is it 'dissaving'. It is a phenomenon absent from loanable-funds theory, where 'saving' is identified with lending at interest.

In the loanable-funds view, indeed, there is no proper backwater. The theory deals not with holdings of assets and portfolio shifts, as liquidity preference does, but with *additions* to assets and liabilities: with borrowing, lending and hoarding. All saving is destined to be lent and since there can be no lending without borrowing, investment is, in effect, financed by direct borrowing from savers unless there is new money. And few people borrow in order to hoard (unless interest rates have gone badly awry, as in the days of 'round-tripping'). They borrow to spend. Thus the money that went into the backwater as lending 'comes out' almost instantaneously as expenditure.

If expenditure in excess of current cash flow (income) is financed by other people's saving, there is in total neither more money nor less in the mainstream. The deficit spending by entrepreneurs on investment is matched by consumers' financial surplus, in other words, the 'inflationary' pressure created by a rise in investment is matched by an equal withdrawal of purchasing power from consumption. This is J. S. Mill's model in which there is no general glut or deficit and only relative prices change.[10] Thus the initial overall inflationary effect is absent.

The possibility of a subsequent inflation, created by money flowing out of the backwater, is also ruled out by loanable-funds theory, for financial transactions do not constitute a semi-autonomous backwater: the flow of money in the industrial circulation is not significantly affected either in volume or in velocity by flowing through the tributary for a time.

In this theory the proposition that equilibrium is characterised by the equality of (voluntary) saving and investment also implies that (voluntary) lending equals desired borrowing. Investment, if it is to rise without a change in the index of overall prices, must be currently financed by the current flow of saving.[11] It can be seen that a 'non-inflationary' rise in investment in this framework can only occur if there is a simultaneous, spontaneous rise in the propensity to save/lend: saving occurs at the expense of consumption.

In contrast, Keynes (1937b, 1939) argued that an increase in investment *cannot* be financed by preexisting or simultaneous saving. At the macro level, preexisting saving cannot be 'stored up', and contemporary saving would only be available if there were, quite by accident, a revision of spending plans. Otherwise, current saving can do no more than support the *current* level of investment. The logic of this contention is reinforced by the recognition in liquidity preference theory of transactions in existing, as well as new, financial assets. This is what establishes the partial autonomy of the backwater from the mainstream and refutes the classical, saving/investment theory of the rate of interest; once existing financial assets are acknowledged, portfolio shifts can affect the rate of interest too, and may even dominate its determination.[12]

To see how the inclusion of existing assets affects the flow of funds to investment, consider the possible fate of a sum of money (in loanable-funds terms, saving) that its owner seeks to place in an interest-earning asset. He is indifferent, at a given rate of return, between new and seasoned issues.[13] Further suppose that there are no new issues that period. The price of existing assets is bid up and a current owner of securities sells, making a capital gain. The saving does not flow to investment and, viewed from a macroeconomic perspective, the capital gains will not return to the mainstream either. An individual may take this profit and spend it, but society as a whole cannot realise financial capital gains unless they are 'backed' by real capital accumulation.

The rate of interest has fallen, the opportunity cost of advances (as opposed to investment) for banks has declined, and now entrepreneurs *may* obtain cheaper bank credit as a result, but an attempt to take advantage of *direct* borrowing at the lower interest rate by floating securities will simply reverse the process and force rates up again. The opportunity for direct borrowing is lost so long as saving money-flows are not *simultaneously* matched by a flow of new issues. Timing is everything. Saving 'stored' in liquid form is no more of an advantage to borrowers whose timing is off than is 'prior saving' embodied in holdings of securities.

The source of finance that *can* break the necessity for perfect timing is, of course, bank credit (or, more generally, intermediary credit). As earlier explained, bank credit *creates* saving in Keynes's sense of the world; it also enlarges the size of the backwater and thus increases its inflationary potential.

In the context of the 1930s, inflationary consequences of bank-financed investment were not the first thing on Keynes's mind. The problem was rather the backwater's capacity to be an 'infinite sink of purchasing power'. Both potentialities exist. Which potentiality predominates depends, I think, chiefly on the rate of expansion of autonomous expenditure and the indirect finance needed to effect it. When this is relatively rapid, there is no time for the short-run effects on prices to be offset by the long-period effect of greater productive efficiency,[14] and if inflationary expectations build up, the likelihood of secondary effects coming from the backwater is increased. The significance of intermediation, or indirect finance, is that a divorce of investment from prior or simultaneous saving (in the money-flow sense) is possible. This kind of divorce, like another sort, has become easier over the years, due, as in the other case, to changes amounting almost to an institutional change, but unmatched by a *formal* institutional change. I suggest that Keynes's reversal of causality from the classical priority of saving to priority of investment is not, as it was portrayed, a matter of absolute theoretical correctness but rather a reflection of *de facto* institutional changes that established the ability of the banks collectively to create credit (and saving in Keynes's sense) in advance of saving in the loanable-funds sense. These changes were the steady displacement of state-created money by bank-created money in transactions and the consolidation of the many, semi-isolated banks of early days (each of which stood to lose resources substantially when it expanded its loans) into a coherent system of a few large banks whose reserve losses were likely to be small.

On the basis of this explanation and the undeniable existence of transactions in seasoned financial assets, there can be no turning the clock back to loanable-funds theory.

## IMPLICATIONS FOR THE FUTURE

There is, however, the question of turning the clock forward, which I believe is long overdue.

Up to this point I have tried only to expose some of the implicit assumptions and conceptual confusions in the monetary theory we inherit. The purpose of doing that is not to adjudicate in favour of competing existing theories if both are shown to be deficient. And I believe both are deficient in the present-day context.

Liquidity preference theory was designed to determine the rate of interest and to demonstrate the power of turbulence in the backwater to have real effects on the mainstream. The context was one of overall stability of the money supply, to which the bank loans required to effect changes in the level of expenditure were minor and transitory additions. Money introduced into the financial circulation by open-market operations could be expected later to be withdrawn by the same means, and new bank lending in the mainstream would be extinguished when the project it supported was funded.

Since Keynes's time the money supply has lost its stability; it has become, in comparison to the past, a flood. The financial circulation cannot contain it, for the numbers of those content to hold money-denominated assets when they can hold real assets is reduced to those confined by transactions costs. Speculation is in land or foreign exchange, not bonds. Meanwhile, high rates of interest have driven firms to seek finance from the banks, where they can borrow on shorter term in anticipation of a fall. New issues have virtually dried up in recent years (not a promising development for the supporters of loanable-funds theory) and as much as 37 per cent of corporate borrowing in 1980 was satisfied by the banks (Bain, 1981, p. 116). The Bank of England seems to have been ever more accommodating, to the point of acting as lender of first resort. (Poor Bagehot!) What is to stop the banks from extending loans beyond their reserves in such a system? There are temptations enough when the Bank is exerting some restraint.

It may be attractive to blame the authorities for the whole of the monetary debâcle we know we are in the middle of but cannot see accurately. It is doubtful that it is all their fault. Attention is focused on the growth of the money supply, but it is highly significant that we are no longer sure what the money supply is. While monetary theorists debate the primacy of the medium-of-exchange function or carp at liquidity preference theory for the narrowness of its asset structure (they should read Keynes, 1936, p. 167, n. 1), the financial system has transformed itself into something we can barely penetrate.

Think how simple finance looked to Hume: paper credit was not thought of as money at all, just a claim on gold. As late as 1930 (in the *Treatise on Money*) Keynes distinguished between 'money proper' and bank money.

The clear expectation embodied in this view of bank deposits (or notes) is that one can get back into money proper without much delay. Transactions in money proper, especially metallic money, are transfers of something tangible: when one person has the gold the other has not.

As long as the banking system was fragmentary and not integrated, banks shared in this property of transferring assets: that is what the cloakroom metaphor was all about. This stage of the evolution of banking had passed long before the implications were recognised in monetary theory. Similarly, the loanable-funds approach was continued beyond the time when borrowing and lending were to a great extent direct and banking had just emerged from its primitive phase. Finance in that approach is seen chiefly in its relation to the mainstream. The underlying vision of liquidity preference theory is a breakthrough, in suggesting the semi-autonomy of the financial nexus. For us now that is only the beginning of useful theory.

Consider the evolution of financial systems. For intermediation to be profitable, there must be an element of *delay*: notes supplant gold only because people leave their gold for a *time*. The whole history of financial innovation is one of putting greater and greater distance between the transactor in the mainstream and the actual need for 'money proper' – until finally even 'money proper' is only credit.

Thomas Crump, an anthropologist writing recently (1981) on money, develops the idea of the 'pure money complex', comprising those institutions whose dealings and balance sheets can be understood in the twin dimensions of money and time. This is the unifying principle underlying the financial system. This principle gives us new words for what we know already: that historically, when there is not enough money, an innovation stretches the time dimension.

Institutions in the pure money complex 'make money' (i.e. profit) out of money and time. Money and time each being homogeneous, it is extremely difficult to trace what is happening inside the pure money complex. One of the few attempts even to describe the problem – the Radcliffe Report (1959) – was greeted by the profession as a failure rather than the courageous document it was. At roughly the same time, Gurley and Shaw (1960, especially pp. 140–9) were saying that the habit of consolidating out financial assets and liabilities was a mistake. The need to consider the 'interior of the matrix of claims' is now urgent if we are to prevent financial disaster and/or inflation.[15] (There is a short-run trade-off between these two events, as the 'lifeboat' operation illustrates.)

We have at least become aware of the tendency towards vague and elastic repayment times, to judge by the frequency of articles on roll-over credits and debt-rescheduling. One can, if one is not afraid to look, see in these facts that a basic presumption of capitalism is gradually being undermined: the presumption that debt is to be repaid at a definite time and that default carries consequences.

If the 'moment of payment' never *does* arrive, expenditure is free of any connection, however tenuous, to the rightful claim on resources that money is supposed to represent. Then it is not surprising that prices go on being put up, and people pay them. Inflation is described by Crump as 'hypertrophy of the pure money complex' – a phenomenon we need to understand in order to stop.

Ivor Pearce's sound-money proposal (Pearce, 1982; Heathfield and Pearce, 1982) can perhaps be seen as a way of putting constraints on the time dimension of the pure money complex, by impairing the profitability of ever-increasing delay. We are a long way from the sort of society whose financial dealings are intimately related to saving, where interest was the reward for delay and the thing delayed was consumption.

**Notes**

1. In a general-equilibrium framework, neither the notion of separation nor the implicit priority embodied in my terminology would be appropriate. I must stress, however, that I am not using a general-equilibrium framework, for it does not capture the interactions that I am trying to describe and analyse.
2. Thanks are also due to Augusto Graziani of the University of Naples.
3. If follows from my rejection of the general-equilibrium system to which both these rich theories have been reduced that I am free also to question whether they would be equivalent in equilibrium even if the definitions on which they are based were congruent (I shall argue that they are not).
4. See especially Leijonhufvud (1981).
5. See for example, Keynes, 1936, p. 119, last paragraph, and p. 200. See also Kahn (1931): 'The intelligent co-operation of the banking system is being taken for granted.'
6. 'As for the concept of *ex ante* saving, I can attach no sound sense to it' (Keynes, 1937b; 1973b, p. 210). See also Keynes, 1973b, pp. 183–216. On the micro/macro foundations of the conflict between Keynes's and Robertson's definitions, see Chick, 1983, ch. 9.
7. Assuming the affected industries to have a degree of monopoly power, modify the statement by adding 'not reversed by a fall in the elasticity of the new demand curve as compared to the old at the relevant points'. For this defensive pedantry, apologies to those for whom it is not necessary.
8. The latter term is Robertson's (1926) in his attempt to distinguish varieties of 'forced saving'.
9. More precisely, whatever the size of the differential between the deposit rate and the rate on risky assets after allowance for risk.

10. If they are to move absolutely symmetrically, rather implausible restrictions have to be placed on cost functions of the expanding and contracting industries. I have never understood why it has been asserted that 'output-as-a-whole' will remain as before. This is a problem Mill and his contemporaries and followers have not to my knowledge faced.
11. This may explain why D. H. Robertson formulates the multiplier in terms of a continuous 'flow' of investment and specifies equilibrium in terms of the ability of a stable flow of saving to support that flow of investment.
12. The backwater is not completely independent, for the level of mainstream activity can cause sales of securities or release of speculative money holdings to augment transactions balances. It is autonomous in a way that the financial circuit in loanable-funds theory is not, in that events can occur there that are not initiated in the industrial circulation but that nevertheless affect it – for example, a change in 'bearishness' can affect the rate of interest.
13. There are practical reasons why he is not strictly indifferent.
14. If bank credit supports projects that do not improve efficiency, such as speculation in property (1972) or projects that have a long pay-off period, this counterweight is absent or delayed.
15. Hyman Minsky has been saying this for a long time. See Minsky, 1982.

# 11 Some Methodological Issues in the Theory of Speculation*

**Author's Note**

An undergraduate asked me why Friedman said speculation was stabilising but in the hands of Keynes, speculation was a destabilising force. (Good question!) When, in my reply, I went off into the philosophy of physics, I am sure she wished she hadn't asked. I am grateful to Edward Amadeo of the Catholic University of Rio de Janeiro for inviting me to give a paper at the History of Economics Conference in Toronto. For the occasion I developed my comments to the student into the paper which follows.

## INTRODUCTION

The speculative demand for money and securities which formed such an important part of Keynes's *General Theory* (1936) has not featured in recent summaries of monetary theory, even those by post-Keynesians (Moore, 1978; Rousseas, 1986; Arestis, 1988). Yet who could doubt the importance of speculation in foreign exchange or the significance of speculation in the 1986–7 stock market boom and its subsequent (October 1987) crash.

Defining speculation has never been straightforward, even if, like art, one prides oneself on recognising it when one sees it. According to both Keynes and Friedman, speculators are buyers and sellers of securities who act on expectations; but Keynes's hypothesis of the way speculators form their expectations is remarkably simple, even primitive. Each speculator has his/her own notion of what constitutes a 'normal' rate of interest. If the actual rate is higher than this normal rate, that person expects the rate to fall; if it is lower, he/she expects it to rise. Therefore the higher (lower) the actual rate of interest the greater the (probable) weight of opinion that the rate will

* The author wishes to thank an undergraduate student for provoking the thoughts which led to this chapter; Edward Amadeo for encouraging their development; William Darity Jr., Xeni Dassiou, John Driffill, Gabriele Galati, Christopher Torr and Richard Vaughan for useful bibliographical suggestions, comments and stimulating discussion. I have a general, and very large, debt to Christopher Torr's work on the issues at hand.

fall (rise) and the larger the demand for securities (money) on speculative account. This theory has the advantage that the current rate of interest, which is observable, stands as a proxy for a concatenation of personal expectations which are not observable, either individually or collectively.

The theory has been disliked – not only for the *ad hoc* character of its hypothesis of speculators' behaviour but also for its subjectivity, its assertion of individuality (Tobin, 1958; Leijonhufvud, 1968[1]) and perhaps most of all for its threat both to the concept of 'rational markets' and to belief in the market's stability.

Milton Friedman, in a famous article (1953), attacked the prediction of instability. He purported to show that if speculators were to make a profit it could be demonstrated that they reduced the amplitude of the 'underlying' fluctuations in exchange rates. Though Baumol (1957) and Telser (1959) disputed this result, they did not challenge the underlying methodology.

Tobin, as everyone knows, claimed (1958) to 'improve' on Keynes's theory by getting the same inverse relation between idle money and the rate of interest from investors' attempts to balance risk and return, with no need for individual differences in expectations. Even if all agree on the characteristics of each security, a market for securities (and money) can be created between those with different preferences between return and risk.

There is in Tobin no specification of the process by which the distribution of interest rates (or security prices) is generated from time series data. In his answer to Friedman, Baumol modelled the 'underlying' path of exchange rates by a sine wave, without discussion. In the context of fluctuations of security prices, the sine wave represents a stylised fact: movement over the business cycle, as governed by productivity and thrift.

By contrast, specifying the generating function is at the core of rational expectations: the essence of rational expectations is to find the expectations mechanism which is consistent with the 'theory', i.e., the assumed generating function, so that expectations are fulfilled except for random variation.

In this chapter, the approaches to speculation of Keynes, Friedman–Baumol–Telser (FBT), and rational expectations (with Tobin's model coming in occasionally) are compared in three respects: (i) the motives of speculators, (ii) the relationship of speculators to other market participants, and (iii) the nature of the market within which speculators operate. A comparison is then made between the methodology of each approach and methodological changes in physics. FBT's approach reflects the methodology of classical physics, rational expectations has affinities with early interpretations of the Heisenberg Principle, and Keynes's methodology, it turns out, is the most modern.

## THE MOTIVES OF SPECULATORS

There are those who would argue that any asset-holding involves speculation, as future prices, absolute and relative, are uncertain. This approach strips speculation of any specific meaning. It is possible, however, to distinguish speculators from other market participants by differences in motivation and source of profit. Speculators are those who buy and sell securities and/or foreign exchange with the aim and intention of capturing short-term capital gains and avoiding capital losses. Their time horizon is rather too short to pay much attention to interest rates on particular assets, as differences in these are dominated in the short run by changes in capital values.

Their behaviour stands in contrast to 'long-term investors', who place funds in securities markets (at home or across the exchanges) with the aim of accumulating wealth by earning interest and, if possible, long-term capital gains. Thus a central question is whether a particular approach admits of *differences* in motive between speculators and other market participants, where both groups are in the market to make money but do so by different means.

Keynes's stance was perfectly clear: *speculation* he defined as 'the activity of forecasting the psychology of the market', in contrast to *enterprise*, 'the activity of forecasting the prospective yield of assets over their whole life' (Keynes, 1936, p. 158). Speculators have a short time horizon and are motivated, therefore, by capital gains rather than by interest: speculators engage in a 'battle of wits to anticipate the basis of conventional valuation a few months hence, rather than the prospective yield of an investment over a long term of years' (p. 155). In this description speculators are tied to the market. Their problem is how to deal with what Pesaran (1984) has called 'behavioural uncertainty': the need to forecast the behaviour of other market participants (which would not be a problem if everyone behaved alike).

Elsewhere in the *General Theory* Keynes speaks of speculators 'knowing better than the market what the future will bring forth', suggesting either superior 'insider knowledge' or the use of a different and superior information set than that used by other market participants. Diverse (or divergent) expectations may exist both within the group identified as speculators and also between them and other market participants – indeed the stability of the market depends on diverse opinion.

The coexistence of two types of agents – speculators and 'others' – is also implicit in FBT. These authors took as their starting point regular fluctuations in exchange rates, comparable in the present context to fluctuations in interest rates which vary over business cycles, rising in booms and falling in slumps in accordance with 'fundamentals' – the forces of productivity and thrift, Keynes's 'enterprise'. Baumol's contribution to this debate represented these fluctuations by a sine wave. No generating function was specified.

While to Keynes the game of speculation involves forecasting the opinion of other market participants, FBT's speculators operate by forecasting these 'fundamental' fluctuations. Friedman's demonstration of the stabilising effect of speculation rests on the assumption that successful speculators are those who foresee the turning-points of this function and sell just before the peaks and buy just before the troughs. By acting against the 'fundamental' market pressure they thus dampen the fluctuations: thus profitable speculation is stabilising.

Baumol's contribution was to point out that speculators could make just as much profit by selling and buying just *after* the peaks and troughs, which would tend to accelerate the upswings and downswings and might even increase the overall amplitude of the series. His difference with Friedman derives from his assumption of extrapolative expectations in contrast to the regressive expectations of Friedman. The basic premise of an independent, objective time series of interest rates, on which speculators play but which is not permanently affected by speculative activity, is common to both. This raises the problem of identifying those at whose expense the successful speculator makes profits. The government broker is not active. Who is left but the unsuccessful speculator? Speculation, in the FBT model, is thus seen as a zero-sum game requiring a steady supply of new 'gulls' to replace those who had learned their lesson.

A further problem arises from the definition of speculators as 'those who forecast': how is speculation to be distinguished from arbitrage? This problem was raised at the time of the Friedman debate by Eastman and Stykolt (1956). It has not been resolved.

Tobin found the proposition of diverse expectations amongst speculators, and implicitly also the existence of different strategies in securities markets, uncongenial: if there is one best way to make profit, why does not everyone adopt it? He resolved this problem by appealing to a trade-off between return and risk, towards which people had different *preferences*.

The agents in Tobin's model are distinguished not by *motives* but by *preferences*. Depending on one's 'taste' for risk or safety one is a risk-averter, a risk-lover, or a 'plunger'. The latter is so attracted to risk that he/she carries undiversified portfolios, 'plunging' from securities to money as circumstances change. The tone of the article leaves little doubt that this 'taste' is to be regarded as slightly mad, the only 'normal' behaviour being risk-aversion. Plunging is, of course, exactly what Keynesian or FBT speculators do![2] I have argued elsewhere (Chick, 1983, p. 204) that plunging is not mad at all, but is rational behaviour for speculators, as far as their speculative assets are concerned.[3]

In distinguishing between motives and preferences I have in mind that motives vary from person to person for *economic* reasons: an agent may have a long time horizon (associated with the 'enterprise' motive) if he/she is, say, saving for retirement; a desire for capital gains may be motivated by, say, favourable tax treatment of capital gains; one speculates only if one has both the taste for it and also the time to devote to it; others may prefer to let their paper gains and losses cancel out; and so on.

Suppose that someone wanted to speculate in the context of Tobin's model, where interest rate behaviour is represented by a stable and symmetrical probability distribution, a normal distribution. If autocorrelation is not a feature of its generation, then clearly, everyone's rational expectation of the future rate of interest, whatever its date, is the mean of that distribution. And if the date is far enough away, even autocorrelation has no importance. Both speculators and long-term investors will agree on this. Therefore there will be no trading generated by the speculative motive: when everyone's expectations are the same, everyone will wish either to buy or sell; transactions languish for lack of anyone to trade with (Chick, 1983, pp. 213–17).[4]

Despite attempts by rational expectations theorists to incorporate 'behavioural uncertainty' (see, e.g., Frydman, 1982; Townsend, 1983), or differences in knowledge (Grossman and Stiglitz, 1980) and to distinguish market participants by the extent or accuracy of their knowledge, individual differences of behaviour have been judged (Tirole, 1982; Runde and Torr, 1985) inconsistent with the notion of rationality embodied in the rational expectations approach: the only 'motive' which has met with universal approval by other practitioners of the school is to discover the 'true model' and form one's expectations in conformity with it. (See the summary of this issue in Torr, 1984 and 1988.) While this is presumed to be everyone's motive, thus leaving no room for divergent roles – let alone diverse expectations – amongst agents in a particular market, bringing expectations into line with 'the truth' presents one of the thorny problems in the rational expectations literature: convergence.[5]

On the matter of whether a separate class of economic agents called speculators can coexist with others pursuing different aims, rational expectations has so far given a negative answer:[6] there is only one form of rational behaviour, namely conformity with the true model. Tobin, while superficially differing from this position in allowing for different behaviours, does not actually address the sort of expectations which speculators must form. We have seen that speculation is out of keeping with Tobin's parameterised risk. The expectation required to be formed by the Keynesian or Friedmanian speculator concerns not the overall behaviour of a time series as captured by statistics (the mean and standard deviation) describing a stable distribution of its outcomes, but rather a specific expectation of the value of the variable for a specific day or range of days in the future. Rational expectations theory allies in this respect with Tobin: the problem is to form correct expectations of the variable's probability distribution conditioned on the information available to the present date (Lucas and Prescott, 1971).

The above investigation has produced strange alignments: Keynes with Friedman against Tobin and rational expectations. In the next section, which explores the relationship of speculators to other market participants, we find different affinities. (A dualist will find this paper most uncongenial.)

## SPECULATORS AND OTHER MARKET PARTICIPANTS

In the FBT model, speculators enter the market sporadically, near peaks and troughs, and have only a transitory effect on the underlying sine wave. When they cease to be active the determination of the rate of interest reverts to whatever deeper model gives rise to that wave.

By contrast, in rational expectations, all actors are included as part of the system whose behaviour constitutes the true model. Mainstream economics before rational expectations tended to treat certain difficult parts of the economic system as exogenous: the government, for example, was seen as impinging on 'the economy' – that is, the private sector – from outside.[7] Rational expectations theory reminds us that such a dichotomy is mistaken: the government, by acting, *changes* the expectations and hence the behaviour of the private sector, and changes thereby the world it is trying to affect. If rational expectations were able to countenance two different sorts of behaviour, and diverse expectations within the class called speculators, the influence of speculation would have to be included in the model of interest rate determination which all rational agents are trying to discover.

Keynes, while not treating this matter formally, is in agreement with rational expectations on this crucial issue: in contrast to the treatment in FBT, speculators' actions affect the future course of interest rates, and their actions have real effects, since the rate of interest affects investment. How *much* effect speculators have is a matter of *degree*, not of principle:

> Speculation may do no harm as bubbles on a steady stream of enterprise. But the position is serious when enterprise becomes the bubble on a whirlpool of speculation. (Keynes, 1936, p. 159.)

Shackle has been the most percipient and radical interpreter of Keynes's theory of interest. He altogether doubts the possibility of a stable equilibrium for that variable: he describes it as 'inherently restless'. This restlessness derives from the behaviour of speculators, as follows:

> If we consider the influence of speculation in isolation, there is no one expectation about the immanent behaviour of the interest rate . . . which if held by everyone would cause the rate to remain constant for more than a short time. . . . [U]ncertainty about the future . . . is itself an autonomous cause of change. . . . [I]f the same opinion as to the immediately future behaviour spreads to everybody, the rate of interest will change at the moment when this belief takes hold. Unless, indeed, the belief is that it will rise just fast enough for the corresponding price-fall of securities to cancel the accruing interest; but in this case it will remain constant, and falsify the belief that is holding it constant, whereupon it will fall. (Shackle, 1968, pp. 51–3. Italics in the original suppressed.)

(Note that Shackle does not suggest that *trades* will take place, only that *prices* – or interest rates – will change.)

Not even the tension of opposites, between bulls and bears, can be counted on to maintain a steady rate of interest:

> [If the rate of interest] is held constant by the existence of two camps holding opposite opinions as to its immediate future movements, one or other of these opinions must be wrong. The action of those who find their opinion falsified will cause the rate of interest to change. (*Ibid.*, p. 53.)

Shackle's exploration of the dynamic effects of speculation illustrates by sharp contrast just why Tobin's static model cannot cope with speculation: speculation is inherently a dynamic phenomenon, which affects subsequent market behaviour. In Tobin's model it would alter the distribution of prices.

Keynes noted that

> In a static society or in a society in which for any other reason no one feels any uncertainty about the future rates of interest, the Liquidity Function $L_2$ . . . will always be zero in equilibrium. (1936, pp. 208–9.)

Shackle's examples suggest that this equilibrium is like those – made such fun of by Joan Robinson – which were impossible to get into unless one was already there: when speculators disappear, the rate of interest will be stable and if the rate of interest were stable they would disappear, but until they stop trading, the rate of interest is 'restless' and there is always something for them to speculate about.

Note the sharp contrast with FBT, where the 'fundamentals' reassert themselves and speculation has no lasting effect.

## THE NATURE OF THE MARKET

Neither Keynes nor Friedman *et al.* specifies the source of the underlying fluctuations in terms of any rigorous model; as noted earlier, the ups and downs of security prices or exchange rates were taken as stylised facts. If their cause can be reduced to supply and demand for the securities or currencies themselves, then one has little scope for speculation unless speculators have superior knowledge, for arbitrage, based on knowledge of this 'true model' will ensure that only random fluctuations remain (Samuelson, 1972). This is not a proposition which originated with rational expectations, though it is entirely congenial to it: once participants know the determinants of supply and demand, there remain only random errors, about which no (further) expectations can rationally be formed.

The question for rational expectations in the present context would seem to be the meaning and content of the 'true model'. In FBT the 'truth' is (non-speculative) 'fundamentals'. The idea that there are determinants of the rate of interest which are, in the end, quite unaffected by speculators' behaviour might seem a suitable candidate for treatment by rational expectations. The economist's 'model' to which agents in a rational expectations theorist's world must adjust appear to have a status similar to the 'laws of nature', which man ignores to his/her peril but which are completely independent of his/her actions. Torr uses the example of fishermen and the tide tables; the tables are useful to the fishermen, but whether fishermen pull their boats sufficiently up the beach to be safe from the tides is of no interest to the sea.

A model of interest rate determination which is unaffected by the actions of speculators is like a theory of the tides. It places speculators at one remove from the 'real action', denying Shackle's description of the continual reassessment and alteration of expectations which results as much from speculators' actions as from changes in the 'fundamentals'. To the extent that speculators' expectations feed off the market itself rather than being based on a different information set, a rational expectations approach would have to build in not only the expectations of the speculators but the effect of those expectations on the subsequent behaviour of the market, which in turn alters speculators' expectations.

Such a world would not only be non-ergodic (see Davidson, 1982–3, for the importance of this property to rational expectations): this is a world in which anything can happen, depending on the *sequence of actions* as well as the formation of expectations. Whether supply and demand 'fundamentals' could even be fitted into such a scheme, let alone serve as its base, is doubtful, for supply and demand are based on the presumption of stationarity (see the discussion in Torr, 1988).

The sort of market which Shackle describes is now the subject of literature on multiple equilibria and of 'bubbles'. At least one attempt to incorporate bubbles into a rational expectations model was defeated by the mathematical difficulty of the enterprise (Blanchard and Watson, 1982). The conceptual status of these features within rational expectations is a matter of unsettled controversy (Kindleberger, 1988; Calvo, 1988), even where the notion of multiple equilibria is limited to those generated by different initial conditions, whereas what is at issue here is path-dependency.[8]

## DIFFERENT WORLD-VIEWS: A COMPARISON WITH PHYSICS

It seems to me that there is a striking analogy, in terms of world-view, between the three conceptions of the relation between speculators and the rest of the market as outlined in this chapter and the evolution of thinking in physics about the relation between the observer and the thing observed, with the speculators playing the role of the observer and 'the [rest of the] market' the thing to be observed. The Friedman–Tobin model works within the world-view of classical physics. The rational expectations model is reminiscent of the early understanding of the Heisenberg Principle, when the difficulty of pinning down electrons was perceived as something which in principle could be overcome by more refined methods of measurement. The Keynes story, in which the behaviour of speculators influences the subsequent path of the decision variable, conforms to the modern understanding of the Heisenberg Principle, in which the observer (here, the speculator) influences the outcome of the experiment.

In classical physics, the observer faces an objective world which can, in principle, be understood if one can discover the 'laws' by which it is governed. The observer seeks to discover these laws by asking questions about aspects of this 'world', taking measurements, and formulating theories. These activities are believed to leave the 'world' unaffected, apart from minor damage which might be caused by an observer's measurement procedures. The Friedman-Tobin speculator, like the observer in classical physics, observes 'fundamental' fluctuations and even makes use of them, without altering their course materially. Such difference as they make has its parallel in the damage inflicted by measurement procedures.

Modern physics accepts a probabilistic description of the position and/or velocity of particles, in contrast to the classical assumption that – if only we could observe them accurately – particles are discrete entities moving along determinate paths. This is Heisenberg's Uncertainty Principle. This principle has passed through two distinct stages of interpretation. (For an account aimed at a wide audience see Bohm, 1980.) In the first stage, it was still believed that there was an objective universe, but that the observer's inability to describe the position or momentum of particles except in probabilistic terms was attributable only to the irreducible element of unpredictability in every measurement procedure.

This early interpretation was held, most notably, by Einstein. The conclusion drawn from it was that there was no reason *in principle* why deterministic laws of the universe (comparable to the 'true' model of the economy) did not exist; the only reason that they were not discoverable was the crudeness of human measuring procedures compared to the object of measurement.

It would, therefore, be a mistake to believe that because rational expectations presupposes stochastic processes it has affinities with modern physics (Drakopoulos, 1987). It is rather to this early interpretation of the Heisenberg Principle that the rational expectations story has affinity. In rational expectations a certain amount of irreducible randomness is accepted, and discovering the true model is impeded by its existence, but in principle the true model is discoverable.

It is – surprisingly or not, depending on your priors – the methodological stance of Keynes and Shackle which is closest in spirit to the methodology of modern science, which accepts a more radical interpretation of the Heisenberg Principle. In this version of the principle, it is accepted that the observer influences experimental outcomes. The analogy to this proposition, applied to the present problem, implies the full interaction of speculators and others in the market.

The result of accepting their interaction is that one's view of the operation of the market is fundamentally altered from what it would be if speculators were not there: the observer and the thing observed are one, and the answer one gets depends on the questions asked. (There is a nice application of this principle in Stoppard, 1988.) There is an irreducible quality of uncertainty about the nature of the thing 'observed' (in the present case, securities or foreign exchange markets) which is not captured merely by including an error term.

That economists in the nineteenth century modelled their work by analogy to physics is well known and in some quarters deplored. To raise the question of a similarity between three stages of methodological development in physics and the methodological basis of the three models at the core of our present discussion is not to suggest that modelling economics after physics is necessarily a good idea. I would, however, tentatively suggest that modelling economics on a physics that has been superseded for over 60 years (Heisenberg published his paper in 1927) is particularly foolish. It might be helpful to take on board the now-established ideas of 'modern' physics before Chaos overtakes us.

## Notes

1. To Keynes's (1936) little xenophobic jibe that monetary control is 'more precarious in the United States where everyone holds the same opinion at the same time' (p. 172), Leijonhufvud (1968) replied, perhaps defending the conformism of his adopted country, that 'In England . . . everyone thinks for himself and most people, therefore, arrive at the wrong conclusion' (p. 190).
2. Plunging does *not* imply, as so many people have said (see, e.g., Dennis, 1981, p. 106), that the plunger, when he/she is in bonds, holds no money; money is still held for transactions purposes. Nor does it imply that plungers (or speculators) are *certain*. They must, however, be decisive in the face of uncertainty; thus they act *as if* they are certain.
3. It is not, of course, rational to 'plunge' with all one's assets. Since Tobin writes as if the whole portfolio is involved, (see the previous note for one aspect of this point) his antipathy to plunging is understandable.
4. Prices may change, however, perhaps a great deal, in the hope of finding someone willing to trade. This may invalidate Tobin's distribution, but that is neither here nor there, as the theory was never suited to the speculation problem, which is my point. It is now accepted in some quarters at least that Tobin's theory is about precautionary and investment portfolios, not speculation. (See, e.g., Harris, 1981.)
5. The problem of convergence is that even when everyone knows the true model this knowledge is not sufficient for a rational expectations equilibrium – the transition to rational expectations cannot be made unless each actor knows that others also know the model and have rational expectations about it. This is a modern version of Joan Robinson's dictum that it was impossible to *get into* equilibrium: one has to have *been* in it from the time of the Fall of Man (Robinson, 1978). It also repeats what we know from Walras: that for equilibrium each actor – or an 'auctioneer' – must know the response of everyone else to the proposed vector of prices.

6. An approach which seems to be consistent with this possibility, however, is that of Shiller (1978), who shows that the Sargent–Wallace model (1973) can have multiple solutions. Shiller's alternative solution, which Sargent and Wallace did not mention, includes a variable *j* which cannot be forecast.

> This means that *any* unforecastable economic variable or the innovation in any variable may enter the solution! If all individuals conclude that the change in the Dow Jones average should be used in [the forecasting function] as *j*, then they will be rational in assuming so. If they have 'hunches' which can be translated into the variable *j*, then if they forecast via [the forecasting function], their hunches will yield rational forecasts. (Shiller, p. 33)

(It is the general price level next period which is being forecast.)

7. See Schott (1984) for a critique of this approach in terms of the theory of the state.
8. It is perhaps better to look elsewhere for formal models of speculation. Path-dependent multiple equilibria are at the core of catastrophe theory, for example. There is at least one catastrophe-theoretic model based on interaction between speculators who 'follow the charts' and 'fundamentalists' (Zeeman, 1974).

# 12 The Evolution of the Banking System and the Theory of Saving, Investment and Interest*

**Author's Note**

Alain Parguez has upheld the cause of post-Keynesian economics at the Institute of Statistics, Mathematics and Applied Economics (ISMEA) in Paris for many years. In 1985 he invited me to speak at a conference there. Through overwork and general muddle, I only had time to prepare a very unsatisfactory paper which, when I arrived, I tried to beg off delivering. Alain, full of charm and persuasiveness, refused to allow me this easy way out. I managed to get my time of presentation postponed to the following day and sat down, feeling somewhat doom-laden, to listen to the other papers. During a presentation in French, which I barely understand, my mind wandered to liability management, a phenomenon which had been much discussed in the UK but only in a money-and-banking frame of reference. What difference did it make, I wondered, in the larger framework of macroeconomics? Suddenly I thought I had the answer. Building on work I had done for *Macroeconomics After Keynes* (1983) and putting my answer together with the evolution scheme (which I had invented during a graduate student's supervision) I gave, next day, something like the chapter which follows. I could never have adopted such a high-risk strategy without a very supportive host and audience. The chapter is therefore dedicated to Alain Parguez, who, I think, does not know this story.

The paper has two direct descendants (Chick, forthcoming, and Chick and Dow, 1988) and one close relative (Chick, 1988).

## INTRODUCTION

The theory of saving and the rate of interest can – or at any rate should – never be independent of the state of development of financial institutions.[1] In Chick (1983, ch. 9) it was argued that the reversal of causality in the saving–investment nexus proposed by Keynes (1936) should not be seen as

---

* The author wishes to thank Sheila Dow, Basil Moore, David Llewellyn, Otto Steiger, Brian Tew, and members of the seminar at the University of Buckingham for their helpful comments and suggestions. The final product is the author's responsibility.

correct theory in triumph over error but as a change in what constituted correct theory due to the development of the banking system.

The purpose of this chapter is to carry this perspective forward to the present day.[2] The first part of the chapter traces the evolution of the English banking system[3] in stylised form. The parallel developments in non-bank financial intermediaries and markets, often a necessary adjunct to banking development, will on the whole be taken as known. In subsequent sections it will be argued that bank behaviour has evolved to a stage sufficiently different from the stage to which Keynes's theory pertained to require alterations to the received theory of investment, saving and interest. Specific changes are proposed and their implications for macroeconomics are drawn.

## STAGES OF BANKING DEVELOPMENT

The banking system has developed continuously; there are no sharp breaks between the 'stages' outlined below. Thus the difficulty for economic theory is always one of judgement: to decide what characterisation captures the salient features of a complex system in continuous change, and when a change in characterisation has significance for theory.

More often than not, perhaps, developments in institutions and their practices are not made explicit in theoretical work. The theorist may be inhibited by the general presumption that economic theory ought to be independent of its time. Those who accept this presumption and yet construct 'relevant' theories must process institutional data intuitively.[4]

Even when the processing is conscious, the ambiguities involved make the task difficult and contribute to the considerable lag of theory behind events.[5] The qualitative nature of the evaluation and the time lapse make it unwise to attempt to date the stages of banking development with any precision.

Having issued those caveats, let us begin with the two stages already referred to in the Introduction: those summarising the 'Keynesian transition' to investment-led growth.

*Stage 1* Banks are numerous and small, and geographically semi-isolated. Bank liabilities are not widely used as means of payment. Banks were thus chiefly repositories for savings; transactions balances did not circulate through them to any great extent. These features implied that an expansion of lending would entail a substantial loss of reserves even to the system as a whole. Banks are thus dependent on deposits for reserves and on reserves for lending capacity.

Letting $R$ = reserves, $L$ = loans (or advances), $D$ = deposits, we have the following causal chain:

$$\Delta D \rightarrow \Delta R \rightarrow \Delta L.$$

Deposits in this stage are savings, on the whole. Their supply to the banks may be regarded as exogenous to the banks, stemming from an increased supply of high-powered money not wanted to be held in cash or from a change in the public's cash/deposit preferences as confidence in the banks grew. If the former were the only important source the existence of banks would not much disturb the quantity theory.

While banks remained at this stage of their development they were exactly as the bankers themselves claimed, 'conduits' between saving and the employment of those savings for investment; they functioned in much the same way as direct-lending institutions, such as the new-issue market, where one has to have saved money before one lends it. In such a circumstance, saving determines the volume of investment.

*Stage 2* The banking system has demonstrated its viability and won the public's confidence. The number of banks is fewer and the average size of banks is larger. Branching is developed, contributing to risk-spreading, reducing the loss of deposits after loan expansion, and contributing to the convenience of deposits as means of payment. The consolidation of clearing arrangements further encourages the shift to deposits as means of payment.

The means-of-payment function is crucial. It means that deposits now represent not just saving but also transactions balances financing the consumption circuit, moving from one bank to another but not leaving the system as a whole to any significant extent. It is this that ensures that deposits arising from loans are not much lost to the banking system. Individual banks with excess reserves are now emboldened to lend 'money they haven't got', setting off the multiple expansion for the system as a whole which we now take for granted.

The causal chain pertaining to this stage is

$$\Delta R \rightarrow \Delta L \rightarrow \Delta D.$$

The 'bank deposit multiplier' is the relevant theory: the banking system can now lend to a multiple of reserves, subject to a conventional or imposed reserve requirement; deposits are a consequence:

$$\Delta D = (1/r)\,\Delta R.$$

The banks, whether by habit or some other force, are still passive with respect to seeking additional reserve-creating deposits; reserves come to the banking system as before through changes in the public's preferences away from cash towards deposits or, increasingly importantly as time progresses, from the central bank via open-market operations.

It must be emphasised that in characterising reserves as the autonomous variable we do not deny that in Stage 2 banks also make use of well-developed financial markets and lender-of-last-resort facilities to make good reserve needs in the event of miscalculation. This action does not undermine the above characterisation of their behaviour under normal circumstances. The experience paves the way for later stages.

The significance of deposits becoming means of payment goes beyond reducing the loss of deposits created by increased lending. Because deposits are now means of payment they represent all income whether destined for consumption or saving. It becomes appropriate to argue that investment can precede saving, because bank loans, based as much on consumption flows as on savings lodged with them, play a significant role in the finance of investment.

The deposits which result from the use of those loans to construct plant and equipment are in the first case held willy-nilly as receipts of new income (*ex post* saving equals *ex post* investment) and later, when the rise in income is perceived, to a great extent they remain willingly held, in order to circulate the new larger volume and value of goods and services.

*Stage 3* Interbank lending mechanisms develop, supplementing the call-money mechanism and contributing to the efficient use of such reserves as are available. The possibilities open to individual banks even more closely approach those of the system as a whole. The causal mechanism of Stage 2 still applies; the 'bank deposit multiplier' acts even more rapidly.

*Stage 4* This stage may have been approached simultaneously with Stage 3. The lender-of-last-resort principle is now firmly established in situations far short of the crises in which Bagehot (1873) recommended its use. To put it another way, the central bank has fully accepted responsibility for the stability of the financial system.

With the expectation that this policy will continue, banks are further emboldened: lending may now expand beyond the reserve capacity of the system.[6] The central bank can be virtually counted upon to make good the shortfall in reserves. When reserves are provided 'at a price', that is, at a penalty rate and/or via open-market operations resulting in higher market interest rates, banks' profits will be affected. The threat of this may constrain their lending.

If a policy of stable interest rates is in place, however, reserves virtually disappear as a constraint on bank behaviour. Banks are now able to meet any reasonable rise in the demand for loans. Deposits will rise as a result and the shortfall of reserves is met by the system. This mechanism has been used often enough in Britain for the Bank of England to be referred to as 'lender of first resort'.

Even if reserves are being supplied only at higher interest rates, banks may still expand beyond the reserve capacity of the system, but they will only do it deliberately if they expect the expansion to be profitable. This depends on the relative elasticities of the demand for credit and the supply of reserves. Most commentators have agreed that in the 1970s, when Stage 4 was becoming fully-developed, the demand for loans was quite inelastic and the supply of reserves was very elastic, which approximates the fixed-interest case.

The causal sequence appropriate for this stage is therefore

$$\Delta L^d = \Delta L \rightarrow \Delta D \rightarrow \Delta R,$$

where $L^d$ refers to the loan demand and $L$ is the actual volume of new loans. The theory of deposit creation appropriate to this stage, with exogenous loans driving the system, has been proposed by Coghlan (1978).

In Stage 4 the banking system is working towards the point where reserves are irrelevant except for over-the-counter transactions. As Tobin (1963) pointed out many years ago, it is when the banks are reserve-constrained that they exhibit the properties described by the deposit multiplier. The arrival at Stage 4 required the adoption of new theory of banking based on the marginal profitability of loan expansion given the marginal costs of obtaining additional reserves. The literature of the 1970s reflects this change at least in microeconomic theories of bank behaviour. (For an exposition see Sinclair, 1983, ch. 6.)

On the macroeconomic side, although there have been allusions to the move to a 'pure credit economy' (e.g., Hicks, 1965, ch. 23), the debate centres around two polarised views: that the authorities control the reserve base and hence the money supply – a view last appropriate in Stage 3 at the latest – and that the money supply is completely elastic, e.g., Moore (1979). If one has to choose between extremes the latter is preferable. However, if the argument is correct that the behaviour of an individual bank has converged on the description appropriate to the system as a whole (a proposition more tenable in the UK and Europe than in the USA perhaps), the results of microeconomic banking theory can be generalised for macroeconomic purposes.

*Stage 5* Banks develop 'liability management'. Until this stage all adjustment, regardless of causal structure, took place on the asset side of banks' balance sheets. Deposits, after Stage 1, were largely the passive consequence of bank lending policy subject to the availability of reserves. In Stage 5, banks have actively sought to attract or retain as deposits savings which might have been held in other financial institutions or as government or corporate financial instruments.

Liability management developed as part of the general increase in financial competition officially encouraged under the 1971 policy of 'Competition and Credit Control', which extended reserve requirements to a wider range of bank-type institutions. The banks were no longer penalised by controls levied only on them, but in return they agreed to abandon their cartelised lending and deposit rates. Banks were thrown into open competition amongst themselves and with other financial institutions. They responded with a policy of aggressive expansion, arguably (though this cannot be proved) expanding beyond the point of profit maximisation, as in a 'sales-maximisation' model. This entailed at least from time to time actively seeking lending outlets rather than merely filling all reasonable loan requests, and 'funding' the asset side by offering higher deposit rates to attract deposits. (See Llewellyn, 1985.)

Insofar as bank deposits came to be held in preference to cash or gilts, the shift to deposits will provide reserves as well as 'funding' the asset expansion. The cost is a higher average interest on deposits.

In 1981 the formal reserve requirement was abolished, so one might be tempted to think that cash and bankers' deposits were no longer important. Banks must still be ready to honour claims on cash, however, and the Bank of England has made it clear that it expects banks to consult about 'appropriate' levels of bankers' deposits. This understanding is presumably designed to avoid a sudden expansion on the basis of existing reserves. Over the longer term reserves may be reduced, relatively to deposits.

The causal nexus for this stage of aggressive expansion is:

$$\Delta L^s = \Delta L \rightarrow \Delta D \rightarrow \Delta R.$$

Stage 5 differs from Stage 4 by the absence of passivity regarding any part of the banks' balance sheets.

One interpretation (Pigato, 1985) is that this stage is merely a transition to some bounded competitive equilibrium. Alternatively, this stage represents a sales-maximisation strategy in a struggle for a dominant market share. This expansion may also be bounded but if the banks are 'winners' in the struggle, the boundary is 'further out' – a larger equilibrium balance sheet is implied. Still a third interpretation, the one I incline to, accepts the possibility that a well-defined and stable competitive solution may not exist. Financial markets are different from the markets for goods; the demand for loans is finite only in the absence of 'moral hazard', and there is no guarantee of the absence of hazards, especially when dealing with incorporated businesses and governments, with no known finite life. The supply of loans is also a problematic concept, as it depends on the lender's assessment of bad debt risk and this estimate, no matter how carefully made, is subject to many different sources of error (including the estimate of moral hazard). The banks' excursion into sovereign lending in the third world illustrates pretty clearly that the level of bad debt risk acceptable to the banks rose considerably in the 1970s.[7] The rise and fall of the secondary banks on the back of a speculative bubble in property is another case in point.

What these episodes point to is the impossibility of defining the concepts of supply and demand for loans in the absence of a firmly-held exogenous constraint such as rationed reserves. If supply and demand are not well-defined a competitive solution is problematic.

A further implication of the ready availability of the lender-of-last-resort facility (even for some Euromarket loans) is that liquidity is taken for granted. Note that the discussion of bank regulation has shifted from questions of liquidity (and control via liquidity constraints or pressures) to the question of capital adequacy. As the sovereign debt crisis illustrated so well, solvency, not liquidity, is now the issue.

## IMPLICATIONS FOR SAVING AND INVESTMENT

Saving and investment represent potential disturbances to steady-state equilibrium: that is the source of their interest to macroeconomists. In largely non-financial economies or in financial economies dominated by *de facto* direct borrowing and lending (including Stage 1 of banking development), saving had to occur prior to investment; investment would be thwarted by a lack of saving. With the arrival of Stage 2 banking, investment could precede saving; the matching saving in the first instance is the new bank deposits resulting from loan expansion. Subsequent banking developments have not changed that process; they have intensified it.

There is a problem of how to describe that initial saving, for though it is not deliberate, it is quite voluntary. A traditional Keynesian would say that consumption had not adjusted to the new level of income and the discrepancy was held as bank deposits. Milton Friedman would probably say there was an excess supply of money; James Tobin would appeal to portfolio disequilibrium. The new deposits also correspond to Hicks's (1939) 'net acquisition of cash by trading', since the deposits represent payment for whatever it was that the loans were used to buy. There are sympathies, too, with the 'buffer stock' approach.

However one describes these first-round holdings, two features are clear. First, though the deposits are willingly held there is no actual decision to save. The deposits represent a passive (and grateful) acceptance of means of payment by workers and traders. Some of it will doubtless be used for consumption, some of it saved, whether as deposits or in some other form. If used to purchase securities, say, the deposits still remain with the banks, title to them being transferred from the buyers of securities to the sellers. If used for consumption, it still remains with the banks.

Second, while individuals quite happily accepted claims on deposits – acceptability after all is the hallmark of the means of payment – the point on which I wish to insist is that no one actually asks those who subsequently have larger deposits whether the expansion of bank balance sheets, including deposit liabilities, was alright with them. In this macroeconomic sense, though not to the individual, the new saving is involuntary (Keynes, 1936, pp. 81–5). From Stage 2 onwards, 'savers' have no influence over the volume of banking business or the volume of deposits. *Borrowers* may repay bank loans out the newly-generated income, but that is the only offset.[8] For the most part, by the time Stage 2 was reached, most income flows circulated through the banks and did not leave.

Nothing in subsequent stages of banking development challenges the causal priority of investment over saving, The difference made by liability management is largely a matter of timing: the 'accidental' deposit may be persuaded back to the banks with greater speed, or even persuaded to stay. The result is an enhanced lending capacity for the banks.

The absence of any meaningful sanction on bank expansion through the cash–deposit ratio or the reserve ratio means, as remarked before, that we have approached the 'pure credit economy', where money generated by the banking system never leaves the banks thereafter. ('Approached', not 'reached', because portfolio shifts away from deposits to cash or government securities may still affect banks' lending capacity.) Yet received macroeconomic theory works in terms of an exogeneous money supply on the assumption that the authorities can and do exercise sufficient control to dominate banking policy. That assumption may have been relevant in Stage 1 and (more doubtfully) Stage 2. It clearly will not do now: the theory of money supply must be a theory of banking policy with the authorities acting, if they act at all, through interest rates.[9]

While banking developments leave the theory of saving and the priority of investment unaffected, a difference with received theory does arise on the investment side. In Keynesian theory, investment evoked saving through income-creation: the initiative came from entrepreneurs and depended on their expectation of long-run profit potential. If their expectations were correct, the investments undertaken would be sufficiently profitable eventually to pay back any lending which supported the undertakings: that is the essence of investing up to the point where the (expected) marginal efficiency of investment equalled the rate of interest.

Despite Keynes's emphasis on inaccuracies and instabilities of expectations, this story has a comforting aspect: the potential to repay depended on real production and the long-term benefit was increased productive capacity. But not all loans had this effect even in Keynes's time: there have always been consumer loans, which do not add directly to productive potential (though they may stimulate investment subsequently) and loans for financial and property speculation.[10]

In Stage 5 the balance of the initiative to increase lending swung to the banks, at a time (the 1970s) when investment was not buoyant. No one ever knows exactly what bank loans are spent on, but we do know of lending which, if it has a base in tangible production at all, has it at several removes. The ideology (and practice?) of self-liquidating loans has been left far behind.

It is currently fashionable to find good in any removal of restrictions and expansion of competition, but there is no assurance of the social value, or even longer-term economic value, of some of the activities supported by Stage 4 and Stage 5 banking. The proposition that investment evokes the necessary saving feels hopeful and progressive. It is far less attractive to say that speculation in City property (as in 1972) evokes the necessary saving to finance it – but if one counts loan-generated deposits as saving, it did, until the bubble burst.

## LIQUIDITY PREFERENCE

The discussion has begun to impinge on the speculative demand for money, in received theory a separate province from the saving–investment nexus. It is perhaps in the area of liquidity preference that the effects of the move to Stage 5 can be seen most clearly.

The received theory of liquidity preference is confused by the transmutation of Keynes's speculative demand theory into the almost antithetical asset demand theory based on static portfolio choice.[11] While initially the asset demand theory arose out of a misunderstanding of Keynes's theory, ironically the competitive posture of the banks may have given it a relevance it did not have at the time of its development.

Keynes's speculative demand theory explains the holding of 'money' (short assets, including bank deposits) on speculative account as a flight from long-term assets when rates on those assets fall so low that the holder believes the risk of capital loss outweighs the superior returns on long assets. In aggregate, at very low interest rates even those who do not normally speculate would join the 'bears'. This theory presupposes the normality of a rising yield curve based on 'normal backwardation'; indeed in the 1930s the curve rose quite steeply, as the banks offered very low rates indeed on deposits. As 'Stage 2' banks they accepted deposits passively and did not compete for them. Thus deposits would be acceptable to security-holders only when they were seeking a capital-safe refuge from potential capital losses on their securities and only for such time as elapsed between forming the expectation of loss and the actual fall in security prices, after which event the funds would be reinvested.

The influx of funds to the banks would occur when the average level of rates was low – a period of pessimistic expectations with little intended investment. So the inflow of funds to the banks did not provide a basis for credit expansion and did not contribute to the financing of investment directly or indirectly. The loan rate was kept high by the flight from long securities and discouraged the desire to invest. There is a bias toward deflation in this theory.

The breaking of the bank cartel in Stage 3 and *a fortiori* the development of liability management have changed all that. Banks have shown their ability and willingness to compete for deposits across a wide range of interest rates. Thus at least from time to time their interest-bearing liabilities are a serious alternative to securities for long-term investment. Deposits have become attractive not just as a vehicle for avoiding capital losses, but for their yield. There now *is* a legitimate reason to hold money as an asset along portfolio-theoretic lines of risk and return rather than merely as a short-term haven from capital losses.

When deposits are competitive alternatives to securities, at the very least they lower the 'loss coefficient' attached to lending by encouraging a return or preventing the departure of loan-induced deposits. When they supplant government securities, they produce reserves as well as settling the balance sheet. The result is greatly enhanced lending power for the banks.

Keynes's liquidity preference theory was asymmetrical in its effect: holding securities as long-term investments, and even on speculative account, was the norm, for rates on deposit accounts and other short-term assets were simply too low for those assets to be attractive except when the threat of capital losses was paramount. Then, bear speculation could keep interest rates from falling just when more investment was needed to restore employment. If the present argument is correct, this asymmetry should be replaced by a symmetrical concern for the inflationary potential of a banking system on which there appear to be few constraints.

There are symmetries on both the asset and liability sides of banks' balance sheets: liability management can be used to draw funds in boom or slump, and the new aggressive attitude to lending may also manifest itself at any phase of the cycle. In Keynes's analysis the demand for loans dries up in a slump. The banks have shown that if they want to lend, they will find outlets even in a slump. The question, mooted earlier, is what they will lend *for*. Too much new credit in too short a time is bound to be inflationary. So is lending for 'unproductive' expenditure.

The banks' aggressive lending activity may contribute to inflation. It should also be noted that inflation may contribute to banks' lending capacity. Backwardation ceases to be normal in inflation, the more so as nominal rates rise to reflect inflation.[12] In the late 1970s borrowers fled the long-term debt market, lowering rates of return there and encouraging bank lending. Banks responded by competing for deposits against long-term securities in lenders' portfolios – and once bank balance sheets have expanded the banks must continue to compete, whether the general level of rates is 'high' or 'low' (however one assesses that in inflation).

Finally, it should be remarked that the main area of applicability of the speculative-demand model in these days of floating exchange rates is undoubtedly foreign exchange. The Keynesian conclusion that the root of unemployment was a rate of interest which would not fall sufficiently could be replaced by the assertion, easy enough to back up theoretically and well-known from recent experience, that speculation may cause both overvaluation of the exchange rate with a resultant loss of competitiveness and an undervaluation which exacerbates inflation. And the remarkable freedom of the Stage 5 banking system to expand in almost any circumstance is an important element in the explanation of why inflation may then persist even in periods of high unemployment.

## CONCLUSION

This chapter argues for a change in theoretical outlook on two points following from the development of 'sales-maximisation' strategies and liability management on the part of the banks. First, while the changes in bank behaviour outlined above have not altered, but rather intensified, the subordinate position of saving, the autonomous expenditure which dominates saving may comprise less investment than formerly. This increases the probability that an expansion of finance and money may not be supported by any 'real' power to pay these loans back. This is a source of inflationary pressure not included in standard macrotheory.

Second, the deflationary bias predicted in 'standard' macrotheory, arising from a preference for liquidity at low rates of interest, has been altered by liability management. Banks have learned to make their liabilities attractive not only in the slump but also in better times, at any general level of interest rates. This has greatly enhanced their lending power in all phases of economic activity, giving a consistent inflationary bias to the economic system. There are, undoubtedly, 'real' inflationary forces too, but it would seem misguided to ignore the existence of financial causes as well.

**Notes**

1. See Hicks (1967, ch. 9) on the significance for theory of the shift from metallic to credit money.
2. The need to do this was stated in Chick (1984). At the time I could not see a way forward, and this paper is itself only preliminary.
3. Such a narrow perspective deserves apology. (I am cautioned not even to say 'British banking system', as the Scottish banks followed a slightly different path.) My reason is insufficient knowledge of other systems and my excuse is a hunch that the history of banking follows broadly universal patterns, with albeit important variations.
4. The only thing 'wrong' with intuition is the difficulty of sharing it. On the role of intuition see Dow (1984).
5. Witness Irving Fisher's (1930) and Keynes's (1930) reluctance to include bank deposits in the definition of money; and Schumpeter (1959) remarked the tardiness of the first appearance of the bank credit multiplier theory of deposits.
6. This potentiality is not new. It was pointed out by Lord Overstone in 1840 (Gregory 1929; 1964, p. 50). In Stage 4 the potentiality became significant in actual behaviour.
7. The counterargument that the banks thought that these debts were safe because they expected lender-of-last-resort facilities to underwrite them makes the point stronger rather than destroying it; it is not the loan itself which the banks thought was safe, or any 'real' collateral, but the indirect financial backing.
8. Kaldor and Trevithick (1981) argue that a credit-based money supply can never be larger than people want to hold because an excess supply will result in repayment. However, the money might not fall into the hands of those with overdrafts in the first instance. The money may be spent and push up prices,

after which the money may be willingly held; or the expenditure could increase profits and the profits used either to finance expectations or to repay bank debt. The latter is only one possibility.

9. In Wicksell's (1936) theory, the pure credit economy exhibits a cumulative process of expansion (contraction) when the 'money rate of interest' (banks' lending rate) falls below (rises above) the 'natural rate of interest' – the real rate of return on productive capital. It has long been acknowledged that this 'natural rate' is, to put it generously, a difficult concept to pin down; both capital and the output it helps to produce are impossible to measure in aggregate except in money terms, and the meaning of such measures is especially problematic in times of inflation.
10. Stock market loans with very low margins were prevalent in the United States before the Crash of 1929; this lending was subsequently regulated.
11. For the differences between the two theories see Chick, 1983, pp. 202–8 and 213–17.
12. There is often a substantial lag in the adjustment of nominal rates to changes – upwards and downwards – in the rate of inflation.

# References


Archibald, G. C. (1956) 'Multiplier and Velocity Analysis: An Annulment', *Economica,* N.S. 23 (August) pp. 265–9.

Arestis, P. (1988) 'Post Keynesian Theory of Money, Credit and Finance', *Thames Papers in Political Economy.* Reprinted in P. Arestis (ed.), *Post Keynesian Monetary Economics* (Aldershot: Edward Elgar) pp. 41–71.

Arestis, P. and A. Skouras (eds) (1985), *Post-Keynesian Economic Theory: A Challenge to Neo-Classical Economics* (Brighton: Wheatsheaf, and Armonk, NY: M. E. Sharpe).

Aronson, J. D. (1977) *Money and Power: Banks and the World Monetary System* (London: Sage).

Arrow, K. J. (1967) 'Samuelson Collected', *Journal of Political Economy*, vol. 75 (October), pp. 730–7.

Arrow, K. and F. H. Hahn (1972), *General Competitive Analysis* (San Francisco: Holden-Day).

Asimakopulos, A. (1983) 'Kalecki and Keynes on Finance, Investment and Saving', *Cambridge Journal of Economics*, vol. 7 (September-December), pp. 221–34.

Atkinson, A. B. (1975) *The Economics of Inequality* (Oxford: Clarendon Press).

Bach, G. L. and J. Stephenson (1974) 'Inflation and the Redistribution of Wealth', *Review of Economics and Statistics*, vol. 56 (February), pp. 1–13.

Bagehot, W. (1873) *Lombard Street: A Description of the Money Market*, 14th edn (London: J. Murray, 1915).

Bain, A. D. (1981) *The Economics of the Financial System* (Oxford: Martin Robertson).

Bank of England, *Financial Statistics* (London).

Bank of England, *Quarterly Bulletin* (London).

Barro, R. J. and H. I. Grossman (1976) *Money, Employment and Inflation* (Cambridge University Press).

Baumol, W. J. (1957) 'Speculation, Profitability and Stability', *Review of Economics and Statistics*, vol. 39 (August), pp. 263–71.

Baumol, W. J. (1962) 'Stocks, Flows, and Monetary Theory', *Quarterly Journal of Economics*, vol. 76 (February), pp. 46–56.

Benavie, A. (1972) 'Disequilibrium Static Analysis', *Western Economic Journal*, vol. 10.

Blanchard, O. and M. W. Watson (1982) 'Bubbles, Rational Expectations and Financial Markets', in P. Wachtel (ed.), *Crises in the Economic and Financial Structure* (Lexington, Mass.: Heath).

Blinder, A. (1975) 'Distribution Effects and the Aggregate Consumption Function', *Journal of Political Economy*, vol. 83 (June), pp. 447–75.

Bliss, C. J. (1975) 'The Reappraisal of Keynes's Economics: An Appraisal', in J. M. Parkin and A. R. Nobay (eds), *Current Economic Problems*, Proceedings of the 1974 AUTE Conference, Manchester (Cambridge University Press).

Bohm, D. (1980) *Wholeness and the Implicate Order*, (London: Ark Paperbacks, Routledge & Kegan Paul).

Brainard, W. C. and J. Tobin (1968) 'Pitfalls in Financial Model Building', *Ameri-*

*can Economic Review, Papers and Proceedings*, vol. 58 (May), pp. 99–122. Reprinted in Tobin (1971), pp. 352–77.

Bronfenbrenner, M. (1945) 'Some Fundamentals of Liquidity Theory', *Quarterly Journal of Economics*, vol. 59 (May), pp. 405–26.

Brunner, K. (1968) 'The Role of Money and Monetary Policy', *Federal Reserve Bank of St Louis Review* (July) pp. 9–14.

Brunner, K. and A. H. Meltzer (1968) 'Liquidity Traps for Money, Bank, Credit and Interest Rates', *Journal of Political Economy*, vol. 76 (January/February), pp. 1–37.

Brunner, K. and A. H. Meltzer (1971) 'The Uses of Money: Money in the Theory of an Exchange Economy', *American Economic Review*, vol. 61 (December), pp. 784–805.

Brunner, K. and A. H. Meltzer (1972) 'Money, Debt and Economic Activity', *Journal of Political Economy*, vol. 80, pp. 951–77.

Burstein, M. L. (1963) *Money* (Cambridge, Mass.: MIT Press).

Calvo, G. A. (1988) 'Tulipmania', in J. Eatwell, M. Milgate and P. Newman (eds), *The New Palgrave: A Dictionary of Economics* (London: Macmillan) vol. 4, p. 707.

Cencini, A. (1988) *Money, Income and Time: A Quantum-Theoretical Approach* (London: Frances Pinter).

Central Statistical Office, *National Income and Expenditure* (Blue Book), annual (London: HMSO).

Central Statistical Office, *Annual Abstract of Statistics* (London: HMSO).

Chick, V. (1973a) 'Financial Counterparts of Saving and Investment and Inconsistency in Some Macro Models', *Weltwirschaftliches Archiv*, Band 109, Heft 4, pp. 621–43. Reprinted, abridged, in this volume as Chapter 4.

Chick, V. (1973b) *The Theory of Monetary Policy* (London: Gray-Mills). 2nd edn, (Oxford: Basil Blackwell, 1977).

Chick, V. (1978a) 'Keynesians, Monetarists and Keynes: The End of the Debate – or a Beginning?' *Thames Papers in Political Economy*, Spring. Reprinted in this volume as Chapter 6, and in P. Arestis and T. Skouras (1985).

Chick, V. (1978b) 'Unresolved Questions in Monetary Theory: A Critical Review', *De Economist*, vol. 126, no. 1, pp. 37–60. Reprinted in this volume as Chapter 9.

Chick, V. (1978c) 'Keynes's Theory, Keynesian Policy and the Postwar Inflation', *British Review of Economic Issues*, vol. 1 (November), pp. 1–24. Reprinted in this volume as Chapter 2, 'Inflation from a Longer-Run Perspective'.

Chick, V. (1979) 'Transnational Corporations and the Evolution of the International Monetary System', in G. J. Crough (ed.), *Transnational Banking and the World Economy* (Sydney University: Transnational Corporations Research Project).

Chick, V. (1981) 'Reply to Professor Harrison', *Australian Economic Papers*, vol. 20 (December), pp. 405–8.

Chick, V. (1982) 'Une question de pertinence: la *Théorie Générale* du temps de Keynes et aujourd'hui, *L'Actualité économique*, vol. 58 (January–June), pp. 61–86.

Chick, V. (1983) *Macroeconomics After Keynes: A Reconsideration of the* General Theory (Deddington: Philip Allan; Cambridge, Mass.: MIT Press).

Chick, V. (1984) 'Monetary Increases and their Consequences: Streams, Backwaters and Floods', in A. Ingham and A. M. Ulph (eds), *Demand, Equilibrium and Trade: Essays in Honour of Ivor F. Pearce* (London: Macmillan) pp. 237–50.

Reprinted in this volume as Chapter 10.
Chick, V. (1988) 'Sources of Finance, Recent Changes in Bank Behaviour and the Theory of Investment and Interest', in P. Arestis (ed.), *Contemporary Issues in Money and Banking: Essays in Honour of Stephen Frowen* (London: Macmillan) pp. 30–48.
Chick, V. (forthcoming) 'The Evolution of the Banking System and the Theory of Monetary Policy', in S. F. Frowen (ed.), *Monetary Theory and Monetary Policy: New Tracks for the 1990s* (London: Macmillan).
Chick, V. and S. C. Dow (1988) 'A Post-Keynesian Perspective on the Relation between Banking and Regional Development', *Thames Papers in Political Economy,* Spring, pp. 1–22. Reprinted in P. Arestis (ed.) (1988) *Post-Keynesian Monetary Economics: New Approaches to Financial Modelling* (Aldershot: Edward Elgar), pp. 219–50.
Christ, C. F. (1967) 'A Short-Run Aggregate-Demand Model of the Inter-Dependence and Effects of Monetary and Fiscal Policies with Keynesian and Classical Interest Elasticities', *American Economic Review, Papers and Proceedings*, vol. 57 (May), pp. 434–43.
Christ, C. F. (1968) 'A Simple Macroeconomic Model with a Government Budget Restraint', *Journal of Political Economy*, vol. 76 (January/February), pp. 53–67.
Clayton, G., J. C. Gilbert and R. Sedgwick (eds) (1971) *Monetary Theory and Monetary Policy in the 1970s* (London: Oxford University Press).
Clower, R. W. (1960) 'Keynes and the Classics: A Dynamical Perspective', *Quarterly Journal of Economics*, vol. 74 (May), pp. 318–23.
Clower, R. W. (1965) 'The Keynesian Counter-revolution: A Theoretical Appraisal', in F. H. Hahn and F. P. R. Brechling (eds), *The Theory of Interest Rates* (London: Macmillan). Reprinted in Clower (1969), pp. 270–97.
Clower, R. W. (1967) 'A Reconsideration of the Microfoundations of Monetary Theory', *Western Economic Journal*, vol. 6, pp. 1–9. Reprinted in Clower (1969), pp. 202–11.
Clower, R. W. (ed.) (1969) *Monetary Theory: Selected Readings* (Harmondsworth: Penguin Books).
Clower, R. W. (1970) 'Is There an Optimal Money Supply?' *Journal of Finance*, vol. 25 (May), pp. 425–34.
Clower, R. W. (1975) 'Reflections on the Keynesian Perplex', *Zeitschrift für Nationalökonomie*, vol. 35 (July), pp. 449–66.
Clower, R. W. and D. W. Bushaw (1954) 'Price Determination in a Stock-Flow Economy', *Econometrica*, vol. 22 (July), pp. 328–43.
Coghlan, R. (1978) 'A New View of Money', *Lloyds Bank Review*, vol. 129 (July), pp. 12–27.
Cohen, B. J. (1981) *Banks and the Balance of Payments* (Montclair, NJ: Allanheld, Osmun).
Council of Economic Advisors (1977) *Economic Report of the President* (Washington, DC).
Crump, S. T. (1981) *The Phenomenon of Money* (London: Routledge & Kegan Paul).
Davidson, P. (1965) 'Keynes's Finance Motive', *Oxford Economic Papers*, vol. 17 (March), pp. 47–65.
Davidson, P. (1968a) 'Money, Portfolio Balance, Capital Accumulation, and Economic Growth', *Econometrica* , vol. 36 (April), pp. 291–321.

Davidson, P. (1968b) 'The Demand and Supply of Securities and Economic Growth and its Implications for the Kaldor–Pasinetti versus Samuelson-Modigliani Controversy', *American Economic Review*, vol. 58 (May), pp. 252–69.

Davidson, P. (1982–3) 'A Fallacious Foundation for Studying Crucial Decision-Making', *Journal of Post Keynesian Economics*, vol. 5 (Winter), pp. 182–98.

Debreu, G. (1959) *The Theory of Value* (New York: Wiley).

Dennis, G. E. J. (1981) *Monetary Economics* (London: Longman).

Dow, S. C. (1984) 'Methodology and the Analysis of a Monetary Economy', *Économies et Sociétés*, cahiers de l'ISMEA, 18, série Monnaie et Production, 1, pp. 7–35.

Drakopoulos, S. (1987) 'Modern Physics and Mainstream Economic Methodology' (Stirling University, mimeo).

Duesenberry, J. L. (1959) *Income, Saving and the Theory of Consumer Behavior* (Cambridge, Mass.: MIT Press).

Eastman, H. C. and S. Stykolt (1956) 'Exchange Stabilisation in Canada, 1950–54', *Canadian Journal of Economics and Political Science*, vol. 22 (May), pp. 221–33.

Einaudi, L. (1936) 'The Theory of Imaginary Money from Charlemagne to the French Revolution'. Translation from the original Italian in F. C. Lane and J. C. Riemersma (eds), *Enterprise and Secular Change* (London: Allen & Unwin, 1953).

Einzig, P. (1948) *Primitive Money* (Oxford University Press).

Ellis, H. S. (1934) *German Monetary Theory* (Cambridge, Mass.: Harvard University Press).

Faxen, K.-O. (1957) *Monetary and Fiscal Policy under Uncertainty* (Stockholm: Almqvist & Wiksell).

Feinstein, C. H. (1972) *Statistical Tables of National Income, Expenditure and Output of the UK, 1855–1965* (Cambridge University Press).

Fisher, I. (1930) *The Theory of Interest* (London: Macmillan).

Fisher, I. (1931) *The Purchasing Power of Money*, 2nd edn (New York: Macmillan).

Fleming, M. (1964) 'The Timing of Payments and the Demand for Money', *Economica*, vol. 31 (May), pp. 132–57.

Foley, D. (1975) 'On Two Sepcifications of Asset Equilibrium in Macroeconomic Models', *Journal of Political Economy*, vol. 88, pp. 303–24.

Foster, J. (1978) 'The Demand for Money: A Critique of the Theory and a Reinterpretation of the Evidence' (University of Glasgow, mimeo).

Frankel, S. H. (1977), *Money: Two Philosophies* (Oxford: Basil Blackwell).

Friedman, M. (1953) 'The Case for Flexible Exchange Rates', in *Essays in Positive Economics* (University of Chicago Press).

Friedman, M. (1956), 'The Quantity Theory of Money: A Restatement', *Studies in the Quantity Theory of Money* (University of Chicago Press) pp. 3–21. Reprinted in Friedman (1969) pp. 51–67.

Friedman, M. (1957) *A Theory of the Consumption Function* (Princeton University Press, for the National Bureau of Economic Research).

Friedman, M. (1958) 'The Supply of Money and Changes in Prices and Output', in Joint Economic Committee, *The Relationship of Prices to Economic Stability and Growth* (Washington, DC: US Government Printing Office). Reprinted in Friedman (1969), pp. 171–87.

Friedman, M. (1959) 'The Demand for Money: Some Theoretical and Empirical

Results', *Journal of Political Economy*, vol. 67 (August), pp. 327–51.
Friedman, M. (1966) 'Interest Rates and the Demand for Money', *Journal of Law and Economics,* vol. 9 (October). Reprinted in Friedman (1969), pp. 141–55.
Friedman, M. (1968) 'The Role of Monetary Policy', *American Economic Review*, vol. 58 (March), pp. 1–17. Reprinted in Friedman (1969), pp. 95–110.
Friedman, M. (1969) *The Optimum Quantity of Money, and Other Essays* (London: Macmillan).
Friedman, M. (1971) 'Government Revenue from Inflation', *Journal of Political Economy*, vol. 79 (July/August), pp. 846–56.
Friedman, M. (1972) 'Comments on the Critics', *Journal of Political Economy*, vol. 80 (September/October), pp. 906–50.
Friedman, M. (1975) 'Unemployment versus Inflation: An Evaluation of the Phillips Curve', *Occasional Paper* no. 44 (London: IEA).
Friedman, M. and D. Meiselman (1963) 'The Relative Stability of Monetary Velocity and the Investment Multiplier in the United States', in Commission on Money and Credit, *Stabilization Policies* (Englewood Cliffs, NJ: Prentice-Hall) pp. 165–268.
Friedman, M. and A. J. Schwartz (1963a) 'Money and Business Cycles', *Review of Economics and Statistics*, vol. 45 (Supplement), pp. 32–64. Reprinted in Friedman (1969), pp. 189–235.
Friedman, M. and Schwartz, A. J. (1963b) *A Monetary History of the United States, 1867–1960* (Princeton University Press).
Friedman, M. and A. J. Schwartz (1982) *Monetary Trends in the United States and the United Kingdom* (University of Chicago Press).
Frydman, R. (1982) 'Towards an Understanding of Market Processes: Individual Expectations, Learning, and Convergence to Rational Expectations Equilibrium', *American Economic Review*, vol. 72 (September), pp. 652–68.
Godley, W. A. H. and F. Cripps (1983) *Macroeconomics* (London: Fontana and Oxford University Press).
Goodhart, C. A. E. (1975) *Money, Information and Uncertainty* (London: Macmillan).
Grant, A. T. K. (1972) *The Strategy of Financial Pressure* (London: Macmillan).
Graziani, A. (1984) 'The Debate on Keynes' Finance Motive', *Economic Notes* (Monte dei Paschi di Siena), vol. 13, no. 1, pp. 5–32.
Gregory, T. E. (1929) *Statutes, Documents and Reports Relating to British Banking.* Reprinted by Frank Cass & Co., London, 1964.
Grossman, S. J. and J. Stiglitz (1980) 'On the Impossibility of Informationally Efficient Markets', *American Economic Review*, vol. 70 (June), pp. 393–408.
Gurley, J. G. and E. S. Shaw (1960) *Money in a Theory of Finance* (Washington, DC: Brookings).
Hahn, F. H. (1980) 'Monetarism and Economic Theory', *Economica*, vol. 80 (February), pp. 1–17.
Hansen, A. H. (1953) *A Guide to Keynes* (New York: McGraw-Hill).
Harcourt, G. C. (ed.) (1977) *The Microeconomic Foundations of Macroeconomics* (London: Macmillan).
Harris, L. (1981) *Monetary Theory* (London: McGraw-Hill).
Harrison, G. W. (1981) 'The Nature of the Keynesian Revolution – Comment', *Australian Economic Papers*, vol. 20 (December), pp. 398–404.
Healey, D. (1975) May Day Speech at Corby, Northants, reported in *The Sunday Times*, 11 May.

Heathfield, D. F. and I. F. Pearce (1982) 'A Tract on Sound Money: Why and How', in C. Hawkins and G. McKenzie (eds), *The British Economy – What Will Our Children Think?* (London: Macmillan) pp. 153–64.
Hicks, J. R. (1939) *Value and Capital*, 2nd edn (Oxford University Press).
Hicks, J. R. (1965) *Capital and Growth* (Oxford University Press).
Hicks, J. R. (1967) *Critical Essays in Monetary Theory* (Oxford: Clarendon Press).
Hicks, J. R. (1975) *The Crisis in Keynesian Economics* (Oxford: Basil Blackwell).
Hicks, J. R. (1980–1) '*IS–LM*: An Explanation', *Journal of Post Keynesian Economics*, vol. 3 (Winter), pp. 139–54.
Hicks, J. R. and R. G. D. Allan (1934) 'A Reconsideration of the Theory of Value', *Economica* N.S., vol. 1 (February), pp. 52–76.
Hines, A. G. (1971) *On the Reappraisal of Keynesian Economics* (London: Martin Robertson).
Horwich, G. (1964) *Money, Capital and Prices* (Homewood, Ill.: Irwin).
Howson, S. (1975) 'Domestic Monetary Management in Britain, 1919–1938', University of Cambridge, Department of Applied Economics, Occasional Paper 48, (Cambridge University Press).
Hume, D. (1752) 'Of Money', in E. Rotwein (ed.), *David Hume: Writings on Economics* (London: Nelson, 1955) pp. 33–46.
International Labour Office, *Yearbook of Labour Statistics* (Montreal).
Johnson, H. G. (1962) 'Monetary Theory and Policy', *American Economic Review*, vol. 52 (June), pp. 335-84.
Johnson, H. G. (1969) 'Seignorage and the Social Saving from Substituting Credit for Commodity Money', in R. A. Mundell and A. K. Swoboda (eds), *Monetary Problems of the International Economy* (Chicago University Press).
Johnson, H. G. (1970) 'Recent Developments in Monetary Theory – A Commentary', in D. R. Croome and H. G. Johnson (eds), *Money in Britain, 1959–1969* (Oxford University Press).
Johnson, H. G. (1975) 'Keynes and British Economics', in M. Keynes (ed.), *Essays on John Maynard Keynes* (Cambridge University Press) pp. 108–22.
Kahn, R. F. (1931) 'The Relation of Home Investment to Employment', *Economic Journal*, vol. 41 (June), pp. 173–98.
Kahn, R. F. (1956) 'Lord Keynes and Contemporary Problems', *The Listener*, 3 and 10 May 1956. Reprinted in *Selected Essays in Employment and Growth* (Cambridge University Press, 1972).
Kaldor, N. (1980) 'Memorandum', House of Commons Treasury and Civil Service Committee, *Memoranda on Monetary Policy*, Session 1979–80, HC720, 17 July.
Kaldor, N. and J. A. Trevithick (1981) 'A Keynesian Perspective on Money', *Lloyds Bank Review*, vol. 139 (January), pp. 1–19.
Keynes, J. M. (1911) 'Review' of I. Fisher, *The Purchasing Power of Money*, *Economic Journal*, vol. 21 (September), pp. 393–8.
Keynes, J. M. (1930) *A Treatise on Money* (London: Macmillan).
Keynes, J. M. (1936) *The General Theory of Employment, Interest and Money* (London: Macmillan).
Keynes, J. M. (1937a) 'The General Theory of Employment', *Quarterly Journal of Economics*, vol. 51, pp. 209–23. Reprinted in Keynes (1973b), pp. 108–23.
Keynes, J. M. (1937b) 'Alternative Theories of the Rate of Interest', *Economic Journal*, vol. 47 (June), pp. 241–52. Reprinted in Keynes (1973b), pp. 201–15.
Keynes, J. M. (1937c) 'The "Ex Ante" Theory of the Rate of Interest', *Economic*

*Journal*, vol. 47 (December), pp. 663–9. Reprinted in Keynes (1973b), pp. 215–23.

Keynes, J. M. (1939) 'The Process of Capital Formation', *Economic Journal*, vol. 49 (September), pp. 569–74. Reprinted in Keynes (1973b), pp. 278–85.

Keynes, J. M. (1973a) *The General Theory and After, Part I: Preparation; The Collected Writings of John Maynard Keynes*, Vol. XIII (London: Macmillan for the Royal Economic Society).

Keynes, J. M. (1973b) *The General Theory and After, Part II: Defence and Development; The Collected Writings of John Maynard Keynes*, Vol. XIV (London: Macmillan for the Royal Economic Society).

Kindleberger, C. P. (1988) 'Bubbles', in J. Eatwell, M. Milgate and P. Newman (eds), *The New Palgrave: A Dictionary of Economics*, (London: Macmillan) vol. 1, pp. 281–2.

Kregel, J. A. (1976) 'Economic Methodology in the Face of Uncertainty: The Modelling Methods of Keynes and the Post-Keynesians', *Economic Journal*, vol. 86 (June), pp. 209–25.

Kuska, E. (1978) 'On the Almost Total Inadequacy of Keynesian Balance-of-Payments Theory', *American Economic Review*, vol. 68 (September), pp. 659–70.

Kuznets, S. (1946) *National Product since 1869* (Washington, DC: National Bureau of Economic Research).

Laidler, D. E. W. (1968) 'The Permanent Income Concept in a Macro-economic Model', *Oxford Economic Papers*, vol. 20 (March), pp. 11–23.

Laidler, D. E. W. (1969) *The Demand for Money: Theories and Evidence* (Scranton: International Textbook Co.).

Laidler, D. E. W. (1974) 'Information, Money and the Macro-Economics of Inflation', *Swedish Journal of Economics*, vol. 76 (January), pp. 26–41.

Laidler, D. E. W. (1978) 'Money and Money-Income: An Essay on the Transmission Mechanism', *Journal of Monetary Economics*, vol. 4 (April), pp. 151–91.

Leijonhufvud, A. (1968) *On Keynesian Economics and the Economics of Keynes* (London: Oxford University Press).

Leijonhufvud, A. (1973) 'Effective Demand Failures', *Swedish Journal of Economics*, vol. 75 (March), pp. 27–48.

Leijonhufvud, A. (1981) 'The Wicksell Connection: Variations on a Theme', in *Information and Co-ordination: Essays in Macroeconomic Theory* (Oxford University Press).

Lerner, A. (1952) 'The Essential Properties of Interest and Money', *Quarterly Journal of Economics*, vol. 66 (May), pp. 172–92.

Lewis, W. A. (1949) *Economic Survey, 1919–39* (London: Allen & Unwin).

Llewellyn, D. T. (1985) *The Evolution of the British Financial System*, Gilbart Lectures on Banking (London: The Institute of Bankers).

Lloyd, C. L. (1960) 'The Equivalence of the Liquidity Preference and Loanable Funds Theories and the New Stock-Flow Analysis', *Review of Economic Studies*, vol. 27 (June), pp. 206–9.

London and Cambridge Economic Service, *Key Statistics of the British Economy 1900–1962*.

Lucas, R. E. and E. G. Prescott (1971) 'Investment under Uncertainty', *Econometrica*, vol. 39 (September), pp. 659–82.

Lutz, V. (1955) 'Multiplier and Velocity Analysis: A Marriage', *Economica*, N.S.,

vol. 22 (February), pp. 29–44.
Mackay, R. J. and W. E. Weber (1976) 'Consumer Behaviour and Quantity Constraints: Some Implications for Monetary Theory', *Federal Reserve Board Special Studies Paper*, vol. 73 (7 June).
Marget, A. W. (1935) 'The Monetary Aspects of the Walrasian System', *Journal of Political Economy*, vol. 43 (April), pp. 145–86.
Marget, A. W. (1938) *The Theory of Prices*, Vol. I (New York: Augustus M. Kelley).
Marget, A. W. (1942) *The Theory of Prices*, Vol. II (New York: Augustus M. Kelley).
Marshall, A. (1923) *Money, Credit and Commerce* (London: Macmillan).
Matthews, R. C. O. (1968) 'Why has Britain had Full Employment Since the War?', *Economic Journal*, vol. 78 (September), pp. 555–69.
Mayer, T. (1978) *The Structure of Monetarism* (London: Norton).
Menger, K. (1892) 'On the Origin of Money', translated by C. A. Foley, *Economic Journal*, vol. 2 (June), pp. 239–55.
Miller, H. L., Jr (1965) 'On Liquidity and Transactions Costs', *Southern Economic Journal*, vol. 32 (July), pp. 43–8.
Minsky, H. P. (1957a) 'Central Banking and Money Market Changes', *Quarterly Journal of Economics*, vol. 71 (May), pp. 171–87.
Minsky, H. P. (1957b) 'Monetary Systems and Accelerator Models', *American Economic Review*, vol. 47 (December), pp. 859–83.
Minsky, H. P. (1982) *Inflation, Recession and Economic Policy* (Brighton: Wheatsheaf). Published in the US as *Can 'It' Happen Again?* (Armonk, NY: M. E. Sharpe).
Mitchell, B. R. and P. Deane (1962) *Abstract of British Historical Statistics* (Cambridge University Press).
Modigliani, F. (1977) 'The Monetarist Controversy, or, Should We Forsake Stabilization Policies', *American Economic Review*, vol. 67 (March), pp. 1–19.
Modigliani, F. and A. Ando (1960) 'The "Permanent Income" and the "Life Cycle" Hypotheses of Saving Behavior: Comparison and Tests', in *Proceedings of the Conference on Consumption and Saving*, vol. 2, (Philadelphia: University of Pennsylvania Press).
Moggridge, D. E. (1969) *The Return to Gold, 1925: The Formulation of Economic Policy and its Critics* (London: Cambridge University Press).
Moore, B. J. (1978) 'Monetary Factors', in A. S. Eichner (ed.), *A Guide to Post Keynesian Economics* (Armonk, NY: M. E. Sharpe).
Moore, B. J. (1979) 'The Endogenous Money Stock', *Journal of Post Keynesian Economics*, vol. 2 (Fall), pp. 49–70.
Morrison, G. (1966) *Liquidity Preferences of Commercial Banks* (University of Chicago Press).
Myrdal, G. (1939) *Monetary Equilibrium* (London: Hodge).
Niehans, J. (1969) 'Money in a Static Theory of Optimal Payments Arrangements', *Journal of Money, Credit and Banking*, vol. 1 (November), pp. 706–26.
Nurkse, R. (1944) *International Currency Experience*, (New York: Columbia University Press, for the League of Nations).
Ostroy, J. M. (1973) 'The Informational Efficiency of Monetary Exchange', *American Economic Review*, vol. 73 (September), pp. 597–610.
Ott, D. J. and A. F. Ott (1965) 'Budget Balance and Equilibrium Income', *Journal*

*of Finance*, vol. 20 (March), pp. 71–7.
Park, Y. C. (1972) 'Some Current Issues in the Transmission Process of Monetary Policy', *International Monetary Fund Staff Papers*, vol. 19 (March), pp. 1–45.
Patinkin, D. (1956) *Money, Interest and Prices: An Integration of Monetary and Value Theory* (New York: Harper & Row), 2nd edition published 1965.
Patinkin, D. (1972) 'Friedman on the Quantity Theory and Keynesian Economics', *Journal of Political Economy*, vol. 80 (September/October), pp. 864-82.
Pearce, I. F. (1982) 'The Time is Not Yet Ripe', University of Southampton Lecture on Economic Policy.
Pesaran, M. H. (1984) 'Expectations Formation and Macroeconomic Modelling', in P. Malgrange and P.-A. Muet (eds), *Contemporary Macroeconomic Modelling*, (Oxford: Basil Blackwell).
Phelps, E. S. *et al.* (1970) *Microeconomic Foundations of Employment and Inflation Theory* (New York: Norton).
Pigato, M. A. (1985) 'Monetary Policy in the Context of Banks Practising Liability Management', PhD Thesis, University of London.
Pollard, S. (ed.) (1970) *The Gold Standard and Employment Policies between the Wars* (London: Methuen).
Radcliffe Report (1959) Committee on the Working of the Monetary System, *Report*, Cmnd 827 (London: HMSO).
Radcliffe Report (1960) Committee on the Working of the Monetary System, *Principle Memoranda of Evidence Submitted to the Committee*, vol. 3 (London: HMSO).
Radford, R. A. (1945) 'The Economic Organisation of a Prisoner of War Camp', *Economica*, N.S., vol. 12 (November), pp. 189–201.
Robertson, D. H. (1922) *Money* (Cambridge University Press).
Robertson, D. H. (1926) *Banking Policy and the Price Level* (London: P. S. King & Son).
Robertson, D. H. (1936) 'Some Notes on Mr Keynes's General Theory of Employment', *Quarterly Journal of Economics*, vol. 51 (November), pp. 168–91. Reprinted under the title 'Effective Demand and the Multiplier', in *Essays in Monetary Theory* (London: P. S. King & Son, 1940), pp. 114–21.
Robertson, D. H. (1940) 'Mr Keynes and the Rate of Interest' *Essays in Monetary Theory*, ch. 1 (London: P. S. King & Son).
Robinson, J. (1960) 'Saving without Investment', *Collected Economic Papers*, Vol. II, (Oxford: Basil Blackwell) pp. 191–6.
Robinson, J. (1972) 'The Second Crisis of Economic Theory', *American Economic Review, Papers and Proceedings*, vol. 62 (May), pp. 1–10.
Robinson, J. (1978) 'A Lecture Delivered at Oxford by a Cambridge Economist', in *Contributions to Modern Economics* (Oxford: Basil Blackwell) pp. 137–45.
Rogers, C. (1985) 'A Critique of Clower's Dual Decision Hypothesis', *South African Journal of Economics*, vol. 53, pp. 111–23.
Rose, H. (1959) 'The Rate of Interest and Walras' Law', *Economica*, N.S., vol. 26 (August), pp. 252–3.
Rosenstein-Rodan, P. N. (1936) 'The Co-ordination of the General Theories of Money and Price', *Economica*, N.S., vol. 3 (August), pp. 257–80.
Rousseas, S. (1986) *Post Keynesian Monetary Economics* (Armonk, NY: M. E. Sharpe, and London: Macmillan).
Runde, J. and Torr, C. (1985) 'Divergent Expectations and Rational Expectations',

*South African Journal of Economics*, vol. 53, pp. 217–25.
Samuelson, P. A. (1958) 'An Exact Consumption-Loan Model of Interest, with or without the Social Contrivance of Money', *Journal of Political Economy*, vol. 66 (December), pp. 467–82.
Samuelson, P. A. (1972) 'Proof that Properly Anticipated Prices Fluctuate Randomly', in R. C. Merton (ed.), *Collected Scientific Papers of Paul A. Samuelson*, vol. 3 (Cambridge, Mass.: MIT Press), pp. 782–90.
Sargent, T. J. and N. Wallace (1973) 'Rational Expectations and the Dynamics of Hyperinflation', *International Economic Review*, vol. 14 (June), pp. 328–50.
Sayers, R. S. (1960) 'Monetary Thought and Monetary Policy in England', *Economic Journal*, vol. 70 (December), pp. 710–24.
Schmitt, B. (1982) 'Time as Quantum', in M. Baranzini (ed.), *Advances in Economic Theory* (Oxford: Basil Blackwell) pp. 115–25.
Schott, K. (1976) Investment in Private Industrial Research and Development in Britain, *Journal of Industrial Economics*, vol. 25 (December), pp. 81–99.
Schott, K. (1981) *Industrial Innovation in the United Kingdom, Canada and the United States* (London: British-North American Committee).
Schott, K. (1984) *Policy, Power, and Order* (New Haven: Yale University Press).
Schumpeter, J. A. (1959) *History of Economic Analysis*, edited by E. B. Schumpeter (Oxford University Press).
Shackle, G. L. S. (1968) *Expectations, Investment and Income*, 2nd edn (Oxford University Press).
Shackle, G. L. S. (1974) *Keynesian Kaleidics* (Edinburgh University Press).
Shiller, R. J. (1978) 'Rational Expectations and the Dynamic Structure of Macroeconomic Models: A Critical Review', *Journal of Monetary Economics*, vol. 4 (January), pp. 1–44.
Sinclair, P. J. N. (1983) *The Foundations of Macroeconomic and Monetary Theory* (Oxford University Press).
Stein, J. (1976) *Monetarism* (Amsterdam: North-Holland).
Stoppard, T. (1988) *Hapgood* (London: Faber & Faber).
Tanner, J. E. (1969) 'Lags in the Effect of Monetary Policy: A Statistical Investigation', *American Economic Review*, vol. 59 (December), pp. 794–805.
Telser, L. G. (1959) 'A Theory of Speculation Relating Profitability and Stability', *Review of Economics and Statistics*, vol. 41 (August), pp. 295–302.
Termini, V. (1978) 'Keynes on Finance' (University of Trieste, mimeo).
Tirole, J. (1982) 'On the Possibility of Speculation under Rational Expectations', *Econometrica*, vol. 50 (September), pp. 1163–81.
Tobin, J. (1958) 'Liquidity Preference as Behavior towards Risk', *Review of Economic Studies*, vol. 25 (February), pp. 65–86. Reprinted in Tobin (1971), pp. 242–71.
Tobin, J. (1961) 'Money, Capital and Other Stores of Value', *American Economic Review, Papers and Proceedings*, vol. 51 (May), pp. 26–37. Reprinted in Tobin (1971), pp. 217–28.
Tobin, J. (1963) 'Commercial Banks as Creators of Money', in D. Carson (ed.), *Banking and Monetary Studies* (Homewood, Ill: Unwin) pp. 408–19.
Tobin, J. (1965) 'Money and Economic Growth', *Econometrica* , vol. 33 (October), pp. 671–84.

Tobin, J. (1969) 'A General Equilibrium Approach to Monetary Theory', *Journal of Money, Credit and Banking*, vol. 1 (February), pp. 15–29. Reprinted in Tobin (1971), pp. 322–38.

Tobin, J. (1971) *Essays in Economics, Vol. 1: Macroeconomics* (Chicago: Markham).

Tobin, J. (1972) 'Friedman's Theoretical Framework', *Journal of Political Economy*, vol. 80 (September/October), pp. 852–63.

Tobin, J. (1975) 'Keynesian Models of Recession and Depression', *American Economic Review*, vol. 65 (May), pp. 195–202.

Tobin, J. and W. C. Brainard (1963) 'Financial Intermediaries and the Effectiveness of Monetary Controls', *American Economic Review, Papers and Proceedings*, vol. 53 (May), pp. 383–400. Reprinted in Tobin (1971), pp. 283–321.

Torr, C. S. W. (1984) 'Expectations and the New Classical Economics', *Australian Economic Papers*, vol. 74 (December), pp. 197–205.

Torr, C. S. W. (1988) *Equilibrium, Expectations and Information: A Study of the* General Theory *and Modern Classical Economics* (Cambridge: Polity Press).

Tower, E. and T. D. Willett (1975) 'The Theory of Optimum Currency Areas and Exchange Rate Flexibility: A More General Framework', *US Department of the Treasury Discussion Paper* (Washington, DC).

Townsend, M. I. (1968), 'The Quantity Theory of Money' (University of Southampton, mimeo).

Townsend, R. M. (1983) 'Forecasting the Forecasts of Others' *Journal of Political Economy*, vol. 91 (August), pp. 546–88.

Tsiang, S. C. (1966) 'Walras' Law, Say's Law and Liquidity Preference in General Equilibrium Analysis', *International Economic Review*, vol. 7 (September), pp. 329–45.

Tucker, D. (1966) 'Dynamic Income Adjustment to Money Supply Changes', *American Economic Review*, vol. 56 (June), pp. 433–49.

United States, Office of Business Economics, *National Income and Product Accounts of the United States, 1929–1965* (Washington, DC).

United States, Bureau of the Census, *Statistical Abstract of the United States*, annual (Washington, DC).

United States, Department of Commerce, *Survey of Current Business*, monthly (Washington DC).

United States, *Economic Report of the President*, January 1980.

Walras, L. (1926) *Elements of Pure Economics*, translated by W. Jaffe (London: Allen & Unwin, 1954).

Wells, P. (1971) 'Liquidity Preference and the Flow of Finance', *Journal of Money, Credit and Banking*, vol. 3 (February), pp. 123–36.

Wicksell, K. (1936) *Interest and Prices*, translated by R. F. Kahn (London: Macmillan). First published in 1898.

Yeager, L. B. (1968) 'Essential Properties of the Medium of Exchange', *Kyklos*, vol. 21, no. 1, pp. 45–68.

Zeeman, E. C. (1974) 'On the Unstable Behaviour of Stock Exchanges', *Journal of Mathematical Economics*, vol. 1, pp. 39–49. Reprinted in *Catastrophe Theory* (Reading, Mass.: Addison-Wesley, 1977) pp. 361–72.

# Name Index

# Subject Index